UNLEASHING THE POWER OF PRAYER

With Appreciation

Ben Jennings

Psalm 65:2

UNLEASHING THE POWER OF PRAYER

Messages from the
International Prayer Assembly

General Editors and Compilers
Vonette Bright & Ben A. Jennings

Dave and Neta Jackson
Contributing Editors

MOODY PRESS
CHICAGO

ISBN: 0-8024-7851-4

1 2 3 4 5 6 Printing/LC/Year 93 92 91 90 89

Printed in the United States of America

Contents

Part Three:
PRAYER FOR THE REVIVAL OF THE CHURCH

Part Four:
PRAYER AND REGIONAL EVANGELIZATION

Part Five:
PRAYER STRATEGY FOR WORLD EVANGELIZATION

Acknowledgments

Deep appreciation is expressed to all those who participated in and financed the IPAWE, such that it became a reality.

Co-chairmen
    Mrs. Bill Bright (Vonette)
    Dr. Cho Choon Park

Directors
    Dr. Joon Gon Kim–Executive Director and Director of the International Prayer and Fasting Rally
    Dr. Ben Jennings–International Coordinator
    Rev. Thomas Wang–Program Director

The Administrative Staff
    Ms. Debbie Jones–Administrator
    Ms. Debbie Brink–Program Personnel
    Ms. Sue McDaniels–Registrar
    Mr. William R. Randall–Treasurer

Special thanks are due to the plenary and seminar speakers:

Dr. Peter Beyerhaus	Dr. William R. Bright
Dr. Kyung Chik Han	Pastor Akira Izuta
Dr. Joon Gon Kim	Dr. J. Edwin Orr
Dr. Cho Choon Park	Rev. Stephen Tong
Rev. Koji Honda	Mr. Kook Il Choi
Mr. Thomas Abraham	Pastor Satoshi Moriyama
Pastor Jun Myung Yoo	Mr. Delbert L. Hosteller
Dr. Bong Ho Son	Dr. Byong Un Min

Pastor Jang Hwan Kim
Pastor Man Shin Lee
Ms. Kee Hyun Song
Mrs. Evelyn Christenson
Mr. David Bryant
Dr. Jong Nam Cho
Dr. Juan Gili
Sung Soo Hwang
Dr. Soo Jii Kim
Pastor Jin Kyung Jeong
Pastor Young Jae Lim
Pastor Sun Do Kim
Dr. Young Kil Kim
Pastor Doo Sub Em
Rev. Norval Hadley
Pastor Jun Man Lee
Pastor Jin Hwan Kim
Pastor Bok Kyu Choi
Dr. Chul Ha Han
Pastor Satoshi Moriyama
Mr. Young Ki Kim
Mr. David E. Ross
Rev. Jack R. Taylor
Dr. Richard Lovelace
Pastor Kyung Sik Park
Rev. Armin Gesswein
Mr. William Converse Jones
Dr. Carl H. Lundquist
Mrs. Vonette Bright
Rev. Kundan Massey
Dr. Sang Hoon Lee
Rev. D. John Richard
Pastor Jae Hyuk Jang
Dr. Byung Sea Oh
Dr. Il Chul Park
Pastor Il Lee
Pastor Noboru Hara
Col. In Soo Lee
Ms. Betty Barnett

Rev. John W. McCracken
Mrs. Joy Dawson
Pastor Han Kyu Byun
Mrs. Iqbal Massey
Pastor Hoon Choi
Pastor Hyun Kyun Shin
Pastor Chang In Kim
Dr. Yoon Sun Park
Dr. David L. Burnham
Rev. Archer Torrey
Dr. Glenn L. Sheppard
Mr. Yeon Hee Jung
Dr. Harold Lindsell
Pastor Ke Man Han
Pastor Duk Chi
Dr. Paul Cedar
Pastor Jong Jin Pi
Dr. Sung Jong Shin
Mr. Hara Noboru
Chaplain Chan Won Choi
Ms. Eun Ah Ko
Pastor Kwan Suk Oh
Pastor Chun Suk Lee
Dr. Ben Jennings
Mr. Jeen Woo Lee
Pastor Dong Jin Choi
Rev. Thomas Wang
Dr. Myung Hyuk Kim
Ms. Kwan Ok Hong
Mr. Dick Eastman
Dr. Je Ok Chun
Pastor Un Sang Jeong
Miss Jeannette Hawkinson
Dr. Kyu Nam Jung
Pastor Ho Moon Lee
Dr. Ronald Jenson
Mrs. Nancy DeMoss
Rev. Gottfried Osei-Mensah
Rev. Han Heum Ok

The Coordinators
  Mr. Dick Eastman–Prayer Sessions
  Mr. D. John Richard–International Representatives
  Mrs. Evelyn Christenson-Women's Ministries
  Mr. William C. Jones–Men's Organizations
  Dr. David Burnham–Pastors
  Rev. John McCracken–Blind Ministries
  Rev. Delbert Hosteller–Deaf Ministries
  Mr. David Bryant–International Mobilization
  Mr. John Jones–Publicity
  Ms. Dian Ginter–Travel Arrangements
  Mr. Pat Pierce–Video
  Ms. Laverne Hintz–Communications

The Lausanne Committee for World Evangelism
The Korean Evangelical Fellowship
The Korean Executive Committee
The Young Nak Church for making their facilities available

Many thanks are due to those who helped in the preparation of the manuscript.

To Susan Sorensen, Joi Hinkson, and Holly Stroud for their help in tracking and researching the influence of the IPAWE and presenting this information.

Foreword

The International Prayer Assembly for World Evangelization (IPAWE) took place in Seoul, Korea, June 5-11, 1984, and was sponsored by the Lausanne Committee for World Evangelization and the Korean Evangelical Fellowship. There were participants representing seventy-one countries attending the IPAWE and an additional one hundred thousand people involved in the prayer rally held at Dook Seom Park. During the Assembly, many internationally known speakers whose hearts are committed to prayer held seminars that taught God's purpose and means for prayer. These seminars deeply enriched the lives of those who attended the Assembly.

The idea for this book originated in the desire to make available to the public the wealth of information that was presented at the Assembly. Although all of the lectures were valuable and were recorded, we were not able to include all of them in the manuscript. We feel that the ones that were chosen represent the emphasis of the Assembly and will be extremely challenging to the reader. Most books of this type, containing messages from conferences, are released shortly after the event. Not so with this book. Four years have passed and we have had that many years to see the resulting impact.

The contents of these messages are as timely as they were the day they were delivered. They will bless your life, enhance your walk with God, broaden your spiritual vision, and help you in a ministry of prayer. It is our hope that the material in this book be used to develop a vision for prayer among pastors and lay people, as well as to provide clear guidance in how to pray specifically and strategically.

As we look back over world events of the last four years and the acceleration of prayer during that time, it is easy to speculate how praying people united together in cities, countries, continents, and from all over the world have been used by God to help shape events. Among many events that could be shared I would like to share two.

In the Philippines, the bloodless revolution that took place in March of 1986 was largely a result of the coordinated prayers of the people. FEBC, a local Christian radio station, kept prayer as an emphasis by providing constant broadcasts, linking prayer groups throughout the city, and giving common direction for prayer. The following report was provided by a Lausanne Associate for Radio Church Planting:

> The spiritual aspects of this revolution are not being reported in the foreign news media. Here in Manila praying people power has had so much to do with the success of the revolution, and this is borne out by the many amazing stories which are being told. Praying priests and nuns, children, and masses of weeping people turned back heavy tanks. There were no weapons being used, no fists being shaken, no beer bottles or violent speech. Everything was peaceful and orderly. Churches were praying around the clock, and those prayers were being answered as God intervened in unusual ways.

A worldwide call to prayer for the Soviet Union, in preparation for the celebration of the millennial of the church in the Soviet Union, resulted in setting aside the month of January in 1987 to pray specifically for the needs of the country. Through the endorsement of the Lausanne Committee and several Christian ministries and broadcasters, this event united many people in prayer around the world. Firsthand reports from Soviet believers attribute both a political relaxation and a spiritual awakening to the concerted prayer during January. Papers authorizing the release of political and religious prisoners were signed on February 2, the first working day after January 31. Soviet believers all around the country also prayed: throughout Russia, the Ukraine, the Baltic States, Siberia, in Vladivostok and Sakalin, and in Central Asia. Many reports came in of spiritual renewal and an increased dependence on the Holy Spirit on the part of the often timid believers.

Incidents of this kind demonstrate to us the profound effect of prayer. We heartily desire for you to catch this spirit of prayer and to trust God to intervene in events of worldwide consequence.

The book is organized into an introduction and five sections, each focusing on a different aspect of prayer.

The introduction attempts to present to the reader both the goals of the IPAWE and a report of what has come about around the world as a result of the Assembly. This report is taken from letters received from IPAWE participants responding to the request for "actual incidents that have grown out of IPAWE."

The topics covered in the following chapters focus on the role of prayer as it relates to revival and world evangelization. The first part focuses on prayer for personal revival. Part two deals practically with learning how to pray. Part three emphasizes prayer for the revival of the church. Parts four and five present material relating to the focus of the IPAWE, evangelization. Part four deals primarily with establishing regional and national prayer strategies. The fifth part relates prayer to the task of world evangelization and demonstrates how we may be a part of this.

VONETTE BRIGHT
Co-Chairman of Intercessory Group
Lausanne Committee for
World Evangelization

The International Call to Prayer

The International Prayer Assembly for World Evangelization in its closing sessions issued a world call to prayer. The draft, which is printed on the next two pages, was hammered out by a special international Prayer Call Committee, and adopted by the full Assembly.

Chairman for the Committee was Sherman Williams, Minister at large from Castro Valley, California, and long associated with the National Association of Evangelicals and the National Sunday School Association of North America. He was ably assisted by David Bryant, Armin Gesswein, and Harold Lindsell.

The passing of five years has heightened the validity and urgency of the Prayer Call. Dr. Lindsell's comment in the final chapter expresses it well, "We need men and women, young and old, from all the nations of the earth to join together in a covenant of prayer that we will pray for worldwide revival and awakening. And that we will pray that the gospel will go to the ends of the earth in this generation."

The approach of the year 2000, and accelerating world evangelization, underscore the unprecedented opportunities in prayer that lie before us.

BEN A. JENNINGS,
International Coordinator
International Prayer Assembly for
World Evangelization

"A Call to Prayer" for Spiritual Awakening and World Evangelization

God, in his calling and Providence has brought us together in Seoul, Korea, from 69 nations. We have sought his face and his guidance. He impressed on us an urgency to call for an international prayer movement to accomplish spiritual awakening and world evangelization.

World evangelization is a sovereign work of the triune God through the ministry of Christ's church. The forces of darkness which block the spread of truth and the growth of the church cannot be displaced by human plans and efforts. Only the omnipotent and omniscient Holy Spirit, applying the fruits of the furnished work of christ through a church constantly awakened through prayer, can deliver the lost from the power of Satan (Acts 26:27-18), as the Lord adds daily those who are being saved (Acts 2:47).

The awakening of the church is thus essential to the completion of world evangelization. The renewed church in Acts 2:42-27 was strengthened by apostolic teaching, the Lord's Supper and sharing fellowship. But these means of grace can only be empowered for us today through fervent and persistent prayer to the Father in the name of the crucified and risen Christ. Evan after Pentecost, the apostles repeatedly turned to prayer for the church to be filled afresh with the Spirit and empowered to proclaim the gospel with boldness, despite Satanic resistance (Acts 4:23-31).

Prayer is God's appointed means whereby the Spirit's power is released in evangelism. By prayer, the Spirit both empowers our witness and opens Satan-blinded unbelievers to seek and desire the Lord Jesus Christ as Saviour. The Lord's promise that his Father will answer us if we ask according to his will and in his name is our strong encouragement in believing prayer.

Before the Lord's return to judge all Satanic rebellion and to consummate his Kingdom in power and glory, the gospel must and will be preached, and disciples made, among every people on earth (Matt. 24:14, 28:19-20, Mark 13'10). Explicit agreement and visible union of God's people in extraordinary prayer for the renewal of the church and world evangelization is essential to the extension of the Kingdon of Christ through the preaching of the gospel.

We rejoice that in the last few years in many parts of the world, though the work of the Holy Spirit, there has been a growing dependence on God which has led to increased unity in prayer in the Body of Christ transcending denominational, national, ethnic and cultural divisions.

We confess that too often prayer is offered only for personal, physical and financial needs rather than for spiritual needs in the church, neighborhood and world.

We confess that frequently there is a lack of meaningful prayer by the congregation in services of the local church as well as a general lack of personal and family prayer.

We confess that there is not enough emphasis on, training for, and dependence upon prayer from the pulpits and in Christian training institutions.

We confess that too often dependence in the Holy Spirit's role in prayer has been minimized and mobilization of prayer has been without reliance upon Him.

We are constrained to call the body of Christ worldwide to mobilize intercession for spiritual awakening in the church and world evangelization. We call specifically for:

1. The fornation of interdenominational prayer committees whenever possible through existing structures on city, national, regional, continental, and international levels.
2. The convening of national, regional, continental and international prayer assemblies as soon as it can be adequately imlemented and thereafter at regular intervals.
3. The establishing of information networks through personal visitation, literature, audiovisual means, etc., for prayer needs, emergencies, methods, reports of prayer movements worldwide, and prayer ministry resources.
4. The promotion, nurture, and teaching on prayer life through seminars, workshops, literature and audio visuals.
5. All churches and theological seminaries, Christian institutions, para-church organizations, Christian leaders and pastors to give priority and emphasis to prayer in life and ministries.

6. The church worldwide to co-operate and participate in the observance of specifically designated days of prayer.

We, therefore, call all believers to a specific and personal commitment to become prayer warriors for spiritual awakening and world evangelization.

Introduction

The International Prayer Assembly for World Evangelization was, as far as we know, the first international gathering focusing on prayer for spiritual awakening and the fulfillment of the Great Commission given in Matthew 28:18-20. For generations, the church has focused on evangelism, but to our knowledge, none of these efforts has ever developed a worldwide prayer strategy for evangelism and spiritual awakening.

From the inception of the idea of an International Prayer gathering several years ago, the purpose was to bring together deeply committed and well-informed people with a special concern for intercession to pray and to explore how to make intercession for world evangelism more effective. The objectives were:

- To highlight prayer as the key strategy for mobilization toward world evangelization
- To pray for world evangelization
- To mobilize a united worldwide prayer support for evangelization
- To encourage believers around the world to pray for worldwide revival, leading to world evangelization
- To assist intercessors by teaching them how to pray specifically and strategically, including the theology of prayer and dealing with spiritual warfare
- To be a catalyst in promoting built-in, meaningful times of prayer in the schedules of Christian conferences and strategy meetings
- To encourage the convening of prayer assemblies in each country
- To encourage Christian leaders and strategists to give greater priority to prayer
- To present examples of prayer, answers, and results

We were trusting God that the International Prayer Assembly for World Evangelization (IPAWE) would build confidence in the power of prayer to affect world situations. The Assembly was held in hopes that it would enable international Christian prayer leaders to spur worldwide prayer movements for spiritual awakening, leading to world evangelization.

With this motivation, the International Prayer Assembly took place in Seoul, Korea, June 5-11, 1984, during the week of Pentecost—the same week in which the Holy Spirit was poured out on the first Christians. Every great movement of the Spirit of God has been borne out of the fervent prayer of God's people, individually, collectively and nationally. We believe that the Holy Spirit was indeed present at the assembly, and that His work in many nations over the last five years may be traced back to the influence that He had in peoples' lives during the assembly.

The IPAWE instilled in its conferees a new vision of the power of prayer in the world. As they returned to their home countries they carried with them the seeds of spiritual change. For some it was an emphasis on personal renewal and holiness grounded in prayer. For others it was the vision to help build regional and national prayer movements. In all cases we believe that God has greatly used the IPAWE to call His people to prayer.

Letters that we have received from IPA delegates demonstrate how God has used the IPAWE in a variety of ways around the world. We are encouraged to be able to report the thrilling growth of prayer ministries, and other results that have occurred throughout the world.

• National Prayer Ministries or organizations have been formed in twenty-four countries.
• There have been National Prayer Assemblies or Congresses in at least twenty-five countries.

In seventeen countries, one or more nationwide Days of Prayer have been held.

• Delegates returning from twenty-two countries held either National or Regional Prayer Seminars to pass on to their countrymen the things they had learned at the IPAWE.

- In many countries there are many obstacles which hinder the ability to coordinate nationwide prayer chains. Yet, in at least thirty-seven of these countries there are effective prayer chains that involve thousands who are devoted to prayer for the express purpose of world evangelization.

- As a result of the emphasis of the IPAWE, in four countries prayer bulletins have been established which channel prayer concerns to groups throughout those countries.

The statistics which we have been able to gather are, no doubt, limited. Although we have received many letters which speak of evangelistic crusades, dramatic church growth and planting, and thousands of converts from all walks of life, it is extremely difficult to reflect with numbers, the work of the Holy Spirit. We feel there is much more that is occurring about which we have not heard, and there is much more that will come to fruition in the future. Yet the reader cannot fail to give glory to God when he reads of some of the specific situations in which God has been at work. For this reason we would like to give a few examples of these prayers, answers, and results borne out of the IPAWE. We have not been able to visit specific areas to verify these reports. However, we have no reason to believe that the information reported to us through correspondence is in any way inaccurate.

A Realization of Prayer for the Revival of Believers

The personal renewal that comes from a focus on prayer renders Christians as open vessels for the Holy Spirit. In many regions, the prayer encouraged by the IPA brought revival to churches. As a result additional churches were planted.

In *Ghana,* prayer retreats, prayer seminars, all night prayer meetings, and Wednesday and Friday prayer and fasting meetings were intensified and resulted in revivals in the churches. This in turn resulted in an increase in evangelism. After the members were filled with the Holy Spirit, one congregation began to grow and see many converts. As a result, three new churches were planted.

In *India,* the establishment of prayer and fasting on Friday mornings at the New India Bible College affected the spiritual and academic life of the college. This in turn affected their evangelistic outreaches in the villages, and the many churches which they have planted devote themselves to prayer and fasting on Fridays.

In the *Philippines,* the two hundred missionaries of the Philippine Missionary Fellowship each organized prayer groups as a result of the IPA in Korea. These two hundred prayer groups pray daily at 7:00 P.M. The outgrowth of these prayer groups has been the establishment of 110 new churches with buildings, and a further two hundred congregations which meet without a building.

CULTIVATING COMMITMENT TO PRAYER

Teaching believers how and why to pray is essential in order to engage them in prayer. The prayer seminars held in twenty-two countries have directly addressed this need. In addition, one of the most significant impacts that the IPA could have is to spark a vision for prayer among believers, who in turn pass on the burden and vision to others.

An excellent example of this is one delegate from the Philippines who, after her return from the IPA, was able to influence the whole region where she lives. Her letter shows the rapid spread of a devotion to prayer:

> The things that I've learned during the seminar and workshop at the IPAWE equipped me to accelerate the prayer movement at Western Visayas region particularly in Iloilo City.
>
> I was able to share what I've learned at IPAWE with the Western Visayas Campus Crusade for Christ staff team where I was assigned as Senior woman and prayer coordinator. . . .
>
> Greater priority on prayer was given. We started the day (Monday-Friday) praying together as a team (6 staff) for one hour. Thus, staff prayer life was strengthened. As a result, giving greater priority to prayer was emphasized to the involved campus leaders and students in the [Campus Crusade for Christ] movement.
>
> Thus, weekly prayer meetings in the campuses, noon-time prayer meetings, prayer partnership, and a citywide prayer rally were the prayer activities we had. Then to develop more pray-ers, we held a prayer seminar and workshop among the involved student leaders.
>
> We had seen the need for prayer and unity among believers in our country in the Visayas region. That is why in August, 1985, an All Christian Overnight Prayer Meeting was born. The first meeting was

. . . attended by 50 people and composed of students, professionals, pastors and staff of Navigators, [Inter-Varsity Christian Fellowship], PSALM and Campus Crusade for Christ.

This overnight prayer meeting was held one Friday night of each month and continued until 1987. Then, it was changed to a Half Night Prayer Meeting every Friday night. . . . Through the years there has been an increase in number of men and women who were involved in the meeting.

Having caught the joy of prayer and seeing that prayer changes many lives, evangelical churches in Western Visayas in 1986 started their own overnight prayer meetings and they've given greater emphasis on prayer.

More prayer groups started as well.

STRATEGIES FOR PRAYER FOR REGIONAL AND NATIONAL EVANGELIZATION

Seeing National Prayer Movements established in at least twenty-four countries and on all continents is an incredible realization of the hopes and prayers of the IPAWE Committee.

In *Canada,* the IPA was the catalyst for the formation of a National Prayer Committee. The foremost achievement of the Committee has been the formation of smaller committees in major cities coast to coast of Christian leaders who see their role primarily as stimulating prayer in their cities. This is done through constant prayer and prayer programs, such as

- a national Prayer Conference,
- Concerts of Prayer,
- a National Intercessors bimonthly newsletter,
- city prayer campaigns,
- various prayer programs and ministries.

In the *Dominican Republic,* a National Prayer council, with participation from most denominational leaders and Christian ministries, was established and helped to bring about the proclamation of a National Bible Day.

In *Madagascar,* a National Prayer Movement was built in which the prayer partners observe two National Days of Prayer each year. A monthly prayer newsletter is sent to over three thousand addresses and prayer seminars are being run across the island.

In the *Middle East* in nine countries, National Prayer Ministries have been started. The first Friday of each month is set aside as a day of prayer and fasting for the whole Middle East. The challenge for intercessory prayer given at the IPAWE resulted in the establishment of two thousand prayer groups through seminars and conferences. In addition to this, a program called "New Life Watchmen of Today" was begun, and hundreds of people pray daily for their country, community, church, children, family, and Christian outreach.

In *Singapore,* in 1986 a group met to intercede for the nation. In 1987 this fellowship grew to organize and call together all who felt called to pray for the nation. The fellowship was named "Intercessors' Fellowship," and the group applied to have the prayer movement legalized. After a wait of seven months, it was legalized.

In *Switzerland,* a committee called "Prayer for Switzerland" was established. It was initiated by the cooperation of seven prayer organizations, and involves three hundred prayer groups totalling 2,300 pray-ers, who intercede for their nation by praying specifically for the population in their postal code. Monthly regional prayer meetings are held in the form of prayer concerts.

In *Nepal,* the first Friday of August is declared the National Day of Prayer. National, as well as regional and city-wide Prayer Conferences have been organized, including two National Women's Conferences, held in 1986 and 1988.

In *Sierra Leone,* the IPAWE sparked the introduction of a Universal Week of Prayer and Fasting. Together with other groups, the United Christian Council encourages groups and individuals on the importance of prayer and makes them aware of national and international prayer needs.

A CALL TO CORPORATE PRAYER FOR EVERY NATION

Using the IPA as a model, National Prayer Assemblies have been held around the world.

In *Bangladesh,* two National Prayer Assemblies, one in 1985, and a second in 1986, were held. In response to these, 150 pastors pledged to pray at least one hour daily before sunrise. Early morning church prayer meetings were established, and watchnight prayer services and prayer chains have become regular activities. Monthly Prayer

Bulletins are being circulated, and prayer is being preached from the pulpits. The slogan "DUI DAPHA" (two points demand), was introduced to encourage each Christian in Bangladesh to two hours of prayer and tithing their income.

In *Finland,* a National Prayer Congress was held in 1984 with six thousand people attending. A second Prayer Congress was held this past November. Several smaller prayer events have been held, as well as the formation of several prayer chains. They are also witnessing a growing interest in prayer retreats, and prayer schools are held in many churches.

WORLD EVANGELIZATION AND THE ADVANCEMENT OF THE GOSPEL

Since the purpose of the IPAWE was to see how an acceleration of the evangelization of every nation might be caused, it is fitting to give some reports on the fruit that has come from prayer. Many letters related how God has opened many closed doors to the gospel. People from Hinduism, Islam, and unreached tribal groups are hearing the message of the good news of Jesus Christ, and coming to know Him as their Savior. In addition to this, many evangelistic crusades have borne tremendous fruit.

The following letter received from the Prayer Fellowship of All India Believer's Association in India is a testimony to the incredible result of trusting God to change peoples' lives.

As a result of the International Prayer Assembly for World Evangelization held in Korea in 1984, and as a result of continued prayer, the following results have been seen. The places where the Gospel has not reached so far, i.e., Vypen Island, now as a result of the work being done by AIBA, thousands from the fishermen caste have come to the Lord. Bamboo and clay workers who have been ignored before, have been contacted and now thousands of them have come to saving grace of Jesus Christ. The name of Jesus Christ was not even heard amongst the Scheduled caste and tribes and now thousands of them have come to Christ.

In Gujarat State, there were hundreds of villages where the name of Jesus had never reached, but today the situation has completely changed, and thousands of tribals have come to Christ.

In the district of Trichur, there is a place called Muringpoor which was ignored by all as it was a leper colony. As a result of continuous prayers, our ministry reached Muringpoor—preached the Word of God to the lepers, and now, we have a leper congregation over there. Praise the Lord. It has proved that nothing is impossible to our heavenly Father.

The hand of God works mightily when His people bring themselves to prayer.

Part One

Prayer for Personal Renewal

1

Confession and Revival

J. Edwin Orr

The late Dr. J. Edwin Orr was part-time professor of history of awakenings and dynamic of missions at Fuller Theological Seminary School of World Mission from 1966 to 1987. He was an ordained Baptist minister, noted author, and a traveling lecturer in 150 of the world's 160 countries. He died in May of 1987.

Before he died at the age of ninety-three, I had the opportunity to speak to William Newton Blair, a great missionary to Korea, about the Korean revival early in this century. It began in Wong San in 1903, spread all over Korea in 1905, and then there was a great outpouring of the Holy Spirit in Kyung Yan in 1905. Blair said it began with confession.

One church leader stood up and confessed hatred in his heart for another church leader. Another man offered prayer. He was going to say, "Heavenly Father, bless our dear brother who has spoken his heart." But he never got any further than "Heavenly Father." The Holy Spirit fell upon all those men—eighteen hundred strong—and the confession lasted until two o'clock in the morning.

It surely must be noticed by everyone who has heard or read of a reviving of the people of God that the confession of sins has played a significant part in the movement. This has been true of contemporary movements as at Asbury College or in the Solomons in the 1970s, or historic works of grace of the magnitude of the Welsh or Korean Revivals, or in the earlier great awakenings. Thus, in forming his first societies of converts in Bristol, John Wesley started class meetings that "they might confess their faults one to another, and pray for one another that they might be delivered." This was also a feature of the ongoing East African Revival two centuries later.

THE ROLE OF CONFESSION IN REVIVAL

Why is such confession by Christians so important in the work of God and operation of the Spirit? It is related to the forgiveness of sins: "If we confess our sins, he is faithful and just and will forgive us our sins and purify us from all unrighteousness" (1 John 1:9). This is the forgiveness of believers, not the ungodly, though there is a relationship between the two.

FORGIVENESS AND THE SINNER

There are two principles of forgiveness. The first is that *someone must pay.* In natural law, civil law, and criminal law, a person who commits wrongdoing has to pay a penalty. In family discipline, school discipline, and military discipline—even in the laws of health—there is a penalty to be paid for disregard of the law. It is in the very nature of things. This is likewise true in moral law: guilt is determined by a higher authority, as well as is the punishment to fit the crime.

A lawyer once objected: "I don't understand it. If God made the rules, why can't God just break the rules and forgive whomever He wishes?" During the Watergate scandal, President Gerald Ford issued a pardon to President Nixon. He was trying to do the right thing. He thought the country couldn't stand trying its own president. But one of the other conspirators went to jail. People said, "That's not right. Why should one man be punished and another man go free?" No, God cannot be unrighteous in demonstrating His love. Someone must pay the penalty.

I remember lending some money to a friend of mine in Ireland—100 pounds. He had been gambling and thus had endangered his job. He agreed to pay back one pound per week for one hundred weeks, but he never paid a penny. After feeling some annoyance for a couple of years, I decided to forgive him. But who suffered? The sinner or the sinned against? I could have taken him to court, in which case he would have suffered. Just how much would he have suffered? To the extent of the amount that he owed me. Instead I forgave him and I suffered the loss of what he owed. Thus I learned the second principle of forgiveness: *the one who forgives is the one who suffers.*

Atonement for sin is a nightmare in most of the world's religions. In the gospel of Christ, however, it is a bright awakening to a new day. "In him we have redemption through his blood, the forgiveness of our sins, in accordance with the riches of God's grace" (Eph. 1:7) How do we have redemption? Someone must pay the penalty! The basis of forgiveness for the unregenerate is the cross of Christ, the atonement. But, asks someone, "Would it be right for Jesus, the son of Mary, to suffer for me or for any other?"

Many years ago, I heard the police had captured a burglar who was caught red-handed. His younger brother went to the police and said, "My brother has a wife and two children. I'm not married; let me take his place." But the authorities would not consider it, saying: "You did not commit the crime; you cannot pay the penalty."

Moses could not die for us, nor Joshua, nor Peter, nor Paul. Why could Jesus? "God was reconciling the world to himself in Christ" (2 Cor. 5:19). Only God can forgive, hence only God in Christ could suffer. This thought illuminates both the meaning of atonement and incarnation.

How much does a sinner pay to be forgiven? There is a hymn that says, "Nothing in my hand I bring, simply to Thy cross I cling." God forgives us freely. The guilty cannot buy forgiveness, nor earn it, nor bargain for it—nor does he deserve it. *But is there any condition prescribed for forgiveness which the sinner must meet?* Yes, indeed. He is told to repent and be converted. *What is his real objective in seeking forgiveness?* It is clearly and specifically salvation.

FORGIVENESS AND THE CHRISTIAN

What about forgiveness of the sins of the converted believer? There is much misunderstanding about this. A university student, a member of an evangelical church, once protested to me: "Why should I confess that I cheated last week? I was converted ten years ago, and all my sins past, present, and future, are already forgiven."

I asked her quietly: "Are you going to cheat on the examination next term?"

"I hope that it won't be necessary." She was quite prepared to cheat again, if necessary.

"Do you think that you have a license to sin?"

That upset her. She retorted: "Are my sins forgiven or are they not?"

"What do you make of the verse, 'If we confess our sins, God is faithful and just to forgive our sins'?" I asked.

"That's the unconverted, of course," she said.

"Certainly not. The first epistle of John was written to believers. Look at the salutation: 'My little children, my beloved, see what love the Father has bestowed on us that we should be called the children of God.' "

"Are you trying to tell me my salvation depends on confessing again and again?"

I told her simply that she was confusing forgiveness of sins for salvation with forgiveness of sins against fellowship. God forgives our sins against fellowship with a different condition than conversion required; otherwise we would live in a confusion of conversion and unconversion.

Corrie ten Boom, an associate of ours in evangelism for several years, found her heart filled with bitterness against the Nazis after she was released from a concentration camp. She had told the Lord, "I'll go anywhere in the world you want me to go." But when God said, "I want you to go back to Germany," she said, "No, I can't go back there. They killed my sister; they ill-treated my father and he died. Anywhere but Germany."

Then she found she could not pray. She tried the Lord's Prayer, but when she came to the petition, "Forgive us our trespasses as we forgive those who trespass against us," that frightened her. "Oh, God, help me; give me grace," she cried. She went back to Germany, and turned an empty concentration camp into a home for refugees.

Knowing her Dutch theological upbringing, I asked her, "If you had continued to hold bitterness in your heart toward Germans, would your soul's salvation have been in danger?"

She said, "My theology would tell me, no, I would not be lost, but my heart was confused." So I showed her the secret: the Lord's Prayer was not given to unbelievers on how to become a Christian; it was given to believers on how to maintain fellowship with God. If we do not forgive others' trespasses, God will not forgive us, and we will be out of fellowship with God. "If we claim to have fellowship with him yet walk in darkness, we lie and do not live by the truth" (1 John 1:6).

I remember once sending my son to the bedroom during dinner for being rude to his mother. He came back very quickly and announced to everyone, "I'm sorry."

I said, "Tell your mama." Well, he wouldn't.

"You're not sorry," I said, "just hungry." And I sent him back to the bedroom.

But it doesn't take a four-year-old long to repent. So he came back again and went straight to his mother. "Mama, I'm sorry I was rude to you." Then, instead of going back to his own place at the table, he climbed on her lap. And his mother brought his plate over beside her plate, and they ate "turnabout" the way mothers and children sometimes do: one bite for mama, one bite for child. Fellowship was restored.

Now while he was in the bedroom, he was still my son, still in my house, and still in my care, but he was out of fellowship.

On what basis does God forgive the sins of His children? When a believer does something he knows to be wrong, he is out of fellowship with God. But "if we walk in the light, as He is in the light, we have fellowship with one another, and the blood of Jesus Christ His Son cleanses [continues to cleanse] us from all sin" (1 John 1:7, NKJV*). Every time we say: "Lord, forgive me, for Jesus' sake," we plead the the blood of the cross.

How much does a believer pay to be forgiven? God forgives us freely. His wayward child cannot buy forgiveness, nor earn it, nor bargain for it—nor does he deserve it. *Is a condition prescribed for a believer's forgiveness and restoration to fellowship?* Yes. We are told to repent and make confession. *What is our objective in seeking forgiveness?* It is clearly fellowship with God, which of course results in better fellowship with other believers.

Conversion is essential for salvation, and confession is necessary for fellowship. Conversion is the climax of evangelism, but not its end. Billy Graham tries to get people converted—then he tells them they must be disciples and follow the Lord. In the same way, confession is the climax of revival, but not its end. Confession leads

New King James Version.

to restitution and reconciliation. God becomes very precious to the person who is willing to confess.

APPROPRIATE AND AUTHENTIC CONFESSION

There has always been confession in revival movements. And yet certain movements have suffered shipwreck through abuse or a misuse of confession. To avoid inappropriate confession we need to ask: What does confession mean? To whom do we confess? How much should we confess? What happens after confession? What are the rules of private confession? Are there any limits to confession? Let us look at each of these questions.

WHAT DOES CONFESSION MEAN?

What does the word *confess* really mean? There are two words in the Greek: *exomologeo*, "to speak out the same," and *homologeo*, "to speak the same thing." The Greek terms have three roots: *ek* means "all"; *ho* means "same"; *logos* meand "word," or literally "all of the same word."

The Lord Jesus asked His disciples, " 'Who do people say the Son of Man is?' They replied, "Some say John the Baptist; others say Elijah; and still others, Jeremiah or one of the prophets.'. . . Simon Peter answered, 'You are the Christ, the Son of the living God' " (Matt. 16:13-16).

This is called the confession of Peter. Jesus commended him and then said, "This was not revealed to you by man, but by my Father in heaven" (v. 17). In other words, Peter expressed outwardly what the Holy Spirit showed him inwardly about the deity of Christ. What the Holy Spirit spoke and what Peter spoke were the same thing.

When an unbeliever becomes a Christian, he confesses his new faith through baptism. It is an outward confession of an inward reality.

To confess our sin as believers, then, is to declare outwardly what the Holy Spirit shows us inwardly about our sin—to speak the same thing.

I had a very bad temper as a young boy. One day I took two pennies out of my mother's purse, bought a box of matches, and tried to set fire to two other boys. My mother found out and thrashed me. I thought, "No one can treat me like that!" So I threw myself in the river. I was going to commit suicide at age eleven— but the water was too cold.

But I never admitted I had a bad temper. When I was in business, I'd lose my temper. The girls in the office would say, "Oh, look at the Christian now. Temper, temper."

I told myself, "I don't have a temper; it's righteous indigna- tion." But it was a bad temper, and I was finally able to say, "Yes, Lord, I have a bad temper." In confession, we express outwardly what God shows us inwardly about our sin.

TO WHOM DO WE CONFESS?

When we sin against God alone, we must confess to God. But if we have sinned against someone else, we must make it right with the person we have wronged. The Lord Jesus taught the necessity of putting things right with an offended brother (Matt. 5:23-24). If I asked you, "Is it more important to be right with God, or with man?" you would say, "With God, obviously." But then with whom shall we put things right first, with God or with man? The Lord Jesus implied, with man. Why is this? God knows whether or not we have sinned, but our brother does not know until we tell him. God knows whether or not we have repented, but our brother does not know until we say so.

The maxim, "Let the circle of sin committed be the circle of sin confessed," has great merit. Private sins should be privately con- fessed, and public sins, publicly. Private sin should be confessed openly, however, when the sin has hindered the work of God, as with Achan and the armies of Israel (Josh. 7).

HOW MUCH SHOULD WE CONFESS?

James the apostle urged believers: "Confess your sins to each other and pray for each other so that you may be healed" (James 5:16). The object in confession is deliverance from a sin; the means of deliverance is prayer. How much, therefore, should be confessed? Just enough to secure effective intercession. This warrant for open confession does not imply indiscriminate confession. To confess a carelessness in paying taxes may enlist effective prayer and chal- lenge others; to describe a method of cheating the tax collector presents a temptation instead of a prayer request. Even more, the indiscreet confession of sexual sin provokes temptation and gossip.

The nineteenth-century evangelist Charles G. Finney noted that a revival of religion may be expected when Christians begin to confess their sins to one another. "At other times," he stated, "they confess in a general manner, as if they are only half in earnest." The Scriptures teach the necessity of specific confession, a principle enunciated in Levitical law: "When anyone is guilty in any of these ways, he must confess in what way he has sinned." (Lev. 5:5).

I was in Brazil during the revival there in 1952, and lots of people asked for prayer. One woman stood up and said, "Please pray for me; I need to love people more."

I said to her gently, "Sister, that's not a confession. Everyone needs to love people more."

She took her seat, but twenty minutes later she got up again and said, "Please pray for me. My tongue has caused a lot of trouble in this church."

Her pastor was sitting beside me, and he said out of the side of his mouth, "Now she's talking."

It costs nothing for a church member to admit: "I am not what I ought to be," or "I ought to be a better Christian." It does cost something to confess: "I have been a trouble-maker in this church," or "I have nurtured bitterness of heart," following it up with apologies in person. While to sin is general, acts of sin are particular and should be specifically confessed.

WHAT HAPPENS AFTER CONFESSION?

Confession should not only be specific, but thorough. Proverbs 28:13 says: "He who conceals his sins does not prosper, but whoever confesses *and renounces them* finds mercy" (emphasis added).

I was once foreman in an engineering shop in Ireland. Two men in our workshop came to blows, then wouldn't speak to each other for days. The other men in the shop finally protested: "You've had your fight. Now shake hands and apologize, for you're spoiling the whole atmosphere here." Reluctantly, the two men apologized and shook hands, but one muttered afterward: "If he ever says anything like that to me again, I'll punch him right in the nose." There was confession, but no forsaking of sin.

There's also the story of an Irishman who went to his priest and confessed that he had stolen two sacks of potatoes. The priest said, "Who did you steal them from—Mr. Murphy?"

"How did you know, Father?"

"I was talking to Mr. Murphy this morning and he said someone had broken into his store. But he's only missing one bag of potatoes."

"That's right, Father," the man said, "I only stole one. But it was so easy I was going to steal the other one this evening." The man "confessed," but his confession did not include repentance, reconciliation, or restitution.

Scripture teaches the necessity of making restitution for wrongs done. The Levitical law specified the full restitution of anything gained by theft or deceit, or even the loss of an item committed to one's trust. The New Testament illustrated this principle when Zacchaeus told the Lord that, if he had taken anything from anyone by false accusation, he would repay it fourfold. In times of revival, the Spirit has constrained believers to make restitution. In fact, there were so many persons offering to make restitution in Korea during 1903 that those receiving restitution pooled their recovered resources and used the funds to support a full-time Bible colporteur in the district.

WHAT ARE THE RULES FOR PRIVATE CONFESSION?

The principle of private confession has been established from the Lord's advice, "If you . . . remember that your brother has something against you, . . . First go and be reconciled to your brother" (Matt. 5:23-24). This injunction follows a warning regarding bad temper and insulting language.

But our Lord is equally plain in another exhortation: "If your brother sins against *you*, go and show him his fault, just between the two of you" (Matt. 18:15*a*; emphasis added). Who here is the innocent party? You are. And who is to take the initiative in reconciliation? You are. Why? Any strife between believers is a wound in the Body of Christ. The goal is to be reconciled, not point fingers at who is right or wrong. "If he listens to you, you have gained your brother" (Matt. 18:15*b*). By going alone, you have been sensitive to your brother and not turned injury into revenge.

But, Jesus said, "If he will not listen, take one or two others along" (Matt. 18:16a). Why are witnesses needed? Sometimes a third person is needed to mediate between two persons. There may be misunderstandings or counter accusations. Sometimes a bitter man will twist words of reconciliation. The truth may need to "be established by the testimony of two or three witnesses" (Matt. 18:16b).

Then there is a third step: "If he refuses to listen to them, tell it to the church" (Matt. 18:17a). This does not mean that you stand up in church on Sunday morning and announce it to everyone. The word *church* here is the Greek word *ekklesia*—any gathering of believers where there is enough spirituality to settle the difficulty. "If he refuses to listen to the church, treat him as an unbeliever and a tax collector" (Matt. 18:17b). This does not mean to be uncivil, or to retaliate, but to refuse to confide in him again. Don't treat him as a brother if he won't act like a brother.

WHAT ARE THE LIMITS OF CONFESSION?

The words of James—"confess your sins to each other and pray for each other so that you may be healed" (James 5:16)— authorize the open confession so often experienced in times of revival. Opportunity for such confession may be given without opportunity for accusing others or promoting scandal. It is certain that after extraordinary prayer and conviction of sin, the expression of revival comes in confession. But, as the purpose of the confession is to obtain a deliverance through the atoning sacrifice of Calvary, it is not necessary to keep on re-confessing the sin, as is the custom of some. If God has forgiven and forgotten, it is not necessary to keep it in continuing remembrance. Confession should become a ladder to a higher plane of living, not a temporary lodging. As John wrote: "If we confess our sins, he is faithful and just and will forgive us our sins *and purify us from all unrighteousness*" (1 John 1:9; emphasis added).

But in times of repentance and revival, there is another kind of confession: vicarious confession. Daniel the prophet received illumination while "confessing my sin and the sin of my people." An intercessor should confess his shortcomings and the sins of any society with which he identifies himself. Revival may affect a family, a congregation, a city, or a nation; so confession should be made for "the people."

These are some of the rules of confession. If there is real revival, there will be confession of sin by believers; we won't be able to stop it. But we can be wise in encouraging authentic and appropriate confession that identifies specific sins, not general unworthiness; aids deliverance, not gossip; leads to repentance and restitution, not license to sin again; and results in reconciliation, not retaliation.

2

Our Source of Revival

Bill Bright

Dr. William R. Bright is the founder and president of Campus Crusade for Christ International. This worldwide ministry and movement of evangelism and discipleship, with a staff of more than fifteen thousand ministers to many millions of students and laymen in more than 150 countries and protectorates of the world.

The Holy Spirit is the author of revival! Apart from the person and ministry of the Holy Spirit there can be no revival, no power to live a holy life, no power to be a fruitful witness for God. If there were only one truth I could share with the Christian world, it would be this truth: how to be filled and controlled with the Holy Spirit as a means of experiencing daily revival. There is no single truth that is more important to the believer. The Holy Spirit enables the believer to live a more joyful, exciting, and adventuresome life. As a Christian leader, there is nothing more important that I could share with you to help you to be more fruitful in your witness for the Savior than an understanding of the person and ministry of the Holy Spirit.

Let me begin by asking you a question. Are you filled with the Holy Spirit right now? Are you experiencing personal revival? Do you know for sure that your life is directed and controlled by the third person of the Trinity? A good test is found in Ephesians where we are admonished to be filled with the Spirit: "Do not get drunk on wine which leads to debauchery. Instead, be filled with the Spirit" (Eph. 5:18). "Be *being filled* with the Spirit" is what it means in the original Greek.

The apostle Paul continues to describe what is involved when one is "filled with the Spirit": We will talk with each other much about the Lord. We will meditate on the Word of God. We will sing songs and make melody in our hearts to the Lord. And we will have a thankful spirit and give thanks to God in all things. We will honor Christ by submitting to each other. Husbands will love their wives as Christ loved the church. Wives will love their husbands and fit in with their plans. Children will honor their fathers and mothers, and parents will rear and discipline their children in wisdom and love. Evidence of being filled with the Holy Spirit is that the fruit of the Spirit is increasingly becoming a reality in our lives. This is revival! When you and I are experiencing this kind of revolutionary walk with God, we are living in a spirit of revival.

In the second chapter of the book of Revelation we read about the great church at Ephesus. It was there that the apostle Paul touched a wicked city through the enabling of God's Holy Spirit. But as time passed, the Spirit of God withdrew His blessing because something tragic happened, something that is characteristic of the church of Jesus Christ today in many parts of the world. Paraphrased, God's message to the church of Ephesus was this: "There are many commendable qualities about you. You work hard for me. You sacrifice for me. You are willing to suffer for me." But, He added, "There is one thing wrong. You have forsaken your first love." He warned them that He would remove them from their place of prominence among the churches unless they returned to their first love.

NOT IN OUR STRENGTH

Some time ago I was visiting a famous university in the United States. A young man came to me who said, "I spend three hours every day serving God. I read my Bible for an hour each day, I pray for an hour each day, and I witness for Christ for the third hour each day. Every day I go knocking on the doors in the dormitories and the various living groups. People laugh at me and they ridicule me," he said. "It's tough. I have never led anyone to Christ in my life, and I don't know what to do about it. Will you help me?"

I asked him if he had ever heard about the Holy Spirit. "Of course, I know about the Holy spirit," he replied.

Then I aked, "Have you ever experienced the fullness of the Holy Spirit in your life?"

"Well," he said, "I don't know anything about that."

So I explained to him some of the truths which I will be sharing with you. Then we prayed together. By faith he claimed the fullness of God's Spirit. There was no great dramatic experience; I don't even remember anything special happening. But he went away from our time of prayer with an expectant heart. God impressed him to believe that he was going to be used to introduce others to our Lord.

That afternoon as he walked across the college campus, he told me later, he asked, "Lord, who is the first person you want me to talk to?" And the Lord led him to a student studying in the library with whom he had shared Christ before without any results. "Look," he explained, "I want to talk to you about something very important." They came out and sat on the library steps. They talked and prayed together and he led this student to Christ.

What a difference! He had spent months trying to lead others to Christ in his own power without any success; now, when he was filled with the Holy Spirit, revived, and empowered, the first person with whom he shared the gospel received Christ. He was so excited he could hardly sleep that night. The next morning when he awakened he asked, "Lord, who is next?" And the Lord led him to another whose heart He had prepared, and the next day another. Each day for several days he led someone to Christ. His life was so transformed by the Holy Spirit that he changed his business major at the university and went to seminary. Today he is the pastor of a model church and through the years has led many to Christ.

I was in Kenya a few years ago for a pastors' conference on evangelism. Pastors, bishops, priests, and a couple of archbishops came for training. We spent a week together and it was a joyful experience. But most of them, by their own admission, were desperately in need of revival; they did not understand the role of the Holy Spirit in their lives.

The head of a mission station came to the conference for counsel. He was greatly discouraged and defeated. "I've been out here on the mission field all these years," he said, "but I have never led anyone to Christ. I'm the head of the mission station, and my missionaries out in the villages are leading people to Christ regularly, but I have never been fruitful. I've read many books on prayer and the Bible and the Holy Spirit, but nothing works for me. Help me," he pleaded, "because unless God does something for me at this conference, I'm going to resign from my position as director of this mission and return to the secular world of business from which I came."

I explained to him some of the truths which I will be sharing here, and by faith he claimed the fullness of the Spirit. Again there was no great emotion but he was revived and his spirit was quickened within him. Later that afternoon, he joined with the other delegates who went into the city of Nairobi to witness, as part of their training. As a group they talked to several hundred people and literally hundreds received Christ that afternoon. My missionary friend led three people to Christ! Remember, he had never led anyone to Christ during all the years that he had served Him in his own power. Now, filled with the Holy Spirit, he led three people to Christ within hours after he had by faith appropriated the fullness and power of the Holy Spirit. This is true revival.

A dear personal friend of mine was a layman who grew up in the church where his father was a minister. This man was a deacon and Sunday school superintendent. He became the president of all the leaders of his denomination in an entire state in America. He had great means and gave generously to the cause of Christ. On one occasion, he and his wife attended one of our training seminars for laymen. When he came for counsel, he said, "I've never led anyone to Christ before, and now I realize that all the long years of dedication, Sunday school work, being a deacon, and the money that I've given are all wasted—'wood, hay, and stubble'—because I've done it without any understanding of the ministry of the Holy Spirit." Because, you see, the only thing that really pleases God is that which is done by the enabling and empowering of the Spirit. This man understood, for the first time in his life, the role of the Holy Spirit in his life.

As we prayed, he was filled with the Spirit by faith. The first person to whom he talked was a prominent businessman and he received Christ. My friend came back for additional training and began to lead other people to Christ until finally he said, "I would like to lead a seminar like this myself." So he and his wife began to lead seminars attended by hundreds of people. On one occasion the pastor of a large church called me to report that at a seminar of twelve hundred people this businessman and his wife had been used of God to "touch all of us by the power of the Holy Spirit. We'll never be the same." They were not only experiencing revival but communicating revival to others. God has since used that couple to influence and train tens of thousands of Christians who in turn have reached many thousands more for Christ.

Do you know that kind of relationship with the Holy Spirit? Are you experiencing daily revival? Maybe you work with many laymen you want to train in the area of discipleship and evangelism. One of the first and most important things that you will want to teach your disciples is how to experience personal, continual revival through yielding to the person and ministry of the Holy Spirit by faith.

BUT BY THE HOLY SPIRIT

There are five questions I want to ask and offer answers to: First, who is the Holy Spirit? Second, why did He come? Third, what does it mean to be filled with the Holy Spirit? Fourth, why is it that the average Christian is not filled with the Holy Spirit? And finally, how can one be filled with the Holy Spirit?

WHO IS THE HOLY SPIRIT?

The Holy Spirit is not a vague, ethereal being or an impersonal force. The Bible tells us He is a person. He has infinite intellect (1 Cor. 2:11), will (1 Cor. 12:11), and emotion (Rom. 15:30). The Holy Spirit is the third person of the Trinity. He possesses all the divine attributes of God. He is equal in every way with God the Father and God the Son, Jesus Christ.

I cannot define the Trinity. No one can. One of my seminary professors once said, "The man who tries to understand the Trinity will lose his mind; the man who denies the Trinity will lose his soul." We who are finite do not comprehend God, who is infinite. However, there are some human illustrations which have helped me. I could describe water as ice, liquid, or steam—three separate forms—yet all are water. Another illustration: though I am one man, I am a son to my parents, a husband to my wife, a father to my sons. But no human illustration is adequate. At best it can only suggest what the

Trinity is like: There is one God who has revealed Himself to many as God the Father, God the Son, and God the Holy Spirit.

The Holy Spirit inspired the writers of Scripture, He intercedes for us in prayer, He draws people into a saving relationship with God, He produces in believers a new life, and He gives power to our witnessing.

WHY DID THE HOLY SPIRIT COME?

On the eve of His crucifixion, a few hours before Jesus went to the Garden of Gethsemane, He said to his disciples in the upper room, "I am going away, and sorrow fills your hearts. But it is expedient for you that I go because unless I go, the Comforter will not come. And when He comes He will lead you into all truth. He will not speak for Himself, but will glorify Me" (John 16:5-15; paraphrased). That is the purpose of the Holy Spirit's coming—to glorify Christ. That is the result of individual and corporate revival—to glorify Christ.

Acts 1 is a record of our Lord's final meeting with the disciples before He ascended into heaven. He admonished them to wait in Jerusalem until they were anointed with power from on high. And he said, "You will receive power when the Holy Spirit comes on you; and you will be my witnesses in Jerusalem, and in all Judea and Samaria, and to the ends of the earth" (Acts 1:8).

Long before their meeting in the upper room, Jesus knew that Judas would betray Him, that Peter would deny Him three times, and that the rest of the disciples were going to desert Him. Can you imagine Jesus pouring His life into those twelve men, day and night for more than three years, and then see them desert Him? Picture yourself under similar circumstances. How would you feel if your disciples deserted you? Our Lord knew that they were going to desert Him and that is the reason He sent the Holy Spirit.

Many Christians today are like the disciples before Pentecost—carnal, unfulfilled, weak, impotent, fruitless. I do not say that to be critical, for I was a carnal Christian for many years. I fasted, prayed, begged, and pleaded with God for His power. I longed to be a man of God more than anything in the world. But I was always failing because I did not understand the ministry of the Holy Spirit.

Why did the Holy Spirit come? The Holy Spirit came to glorify

Christ. He came to lead us into all truth. He came to empower us for holy living and for fruitful service. The fruit of the Spirit is love, joy, peace, long-suffering, gentleness, goodness, faith, meekness, temperance. I cannot live the Christian life apart from the Holy Spirit. Even our new birth is the result of the Spirit. Jesus said to Nicodemus, "I tell you the truth, no one can enter the kingdom of God unless he is born of water and the spirit. . . . 'You must be born again' " (John 3:5-7).

A minister friend said to me one day, "I don't like all this talk about the Holy Spirit. I just like to talk about Jesus."

I said, "That's wonderful. So does the Holy Spirit. That is the reason He came, in fact—to talk about Jesus."

"But," he said, "why don't you just talk about Jesus and forget the Holy Spirit? You confuse people when you talk about the Holy Spirit."

To which I replied, "I talk about the Holy Spirit because Jesus and the disciples talked about the Holy Spirit. I stand on biblical and historical tradition. I talk about the Holy Spirit because I've discovered, not only in my own life but in the lives of literally millions of people with whom Campus Crusade staff have worked all over the world, that when men and women really understand who the Holy Spirit is, how they can appropriate His fullness, and how they can walk day after day in the fullness and power and joy and the excitement of the resurrection, their lives are revolutionized and they become fruitful for God as a result." This is true revival!

WHAT DOES IT MEAN TO BE FILLED WITH THE HOLY SPIRIT?

Very simply, to be filled with the Holy Spirit means to be *filled with Jesus*. When I'm filled with the Holy Spirit, the risen Christ in all of His mighty power walks around in my body, thinks with my mind, loves with my heart, and speaks with my lips. And since He came to seek and save the lost, He walks around in my body, seeking and saving the lost. That is what it means to be filled with the Spirit and that is what it means to live in a state of revival.

Being filled with the Spirit means to *abide in Christ*, and that is revival. "If you remain [abide] in me and my words remain in you, ask whatever you wish and it will be given you" (John 15:7).

It means to *walk in the light* as God is in the light. "God is light; in him there is no darkness at all. If we claim to have fellowship with him yet walk in the darkness, we lie and do not live by the truth. But if we walk in the light, as he is in the light, we have fellowship with one another, and the blood of Jesus, his Son, purifies us from all sin" (1 John 1:5-7). That is what the Christian life is all about—walking day by day, moment by moment, in the fullness and joy and power and adventure of the third person of the Trinity, God the Holy Spirit.

Some persons talk about the Holy Spirit to the exclusion of the Son, or talk about the gifts instead of the giver. The Body of Christ is divided over the emphasis on gifts. Dear brothers and sisters, gifts are not the issue when we talk about being filled with the Spirit. We are called to be witnesses for the Savior, not to emphasize peripheral things like tongues. Jesus Christ must be central. God, the Holy Spirit, came to glorify *Him*. I have never spoken in tongues, but whether or not you speak in tongues, I love you. I do not go around criticizing those who do or beating the drum for those who do not. We need to love one another. God has commanded us to love one another!

What does it mean to be filled with the Spirit? The Christian life is both critical and progressive. There is a moment when, as an act of the will by faith, we receive Christ. Also as an act of the will by faith, we appropriate the fullness of the Spirit. As time passes, the fruit of the Spirit develops in us—love, joy, peace, patience, kindness, gentleness, self-control. As we walk in the Spirit we mature through the stages of babyhood, childhood, young adolescence. young adult, and mature adult. We do not become spiritual giants overnight. In fact, there are few spiritual giants! But all of us have the mighty power of God available to us from the moment we believe.

Your body is the temple of God: Father, Son, and Holy Spirit. Revival in the Christian life is simply a matter of His lordship in your life, yielding to His direction, and relying on His power to work in and through your life. You cannot live the Christian life in your own power through self-discipline and determination. Jesus Christ, while He was on earth, was the only one who could perfectly live up to God's standards for a holy life. And Jesus Christ is the one who must live the Christian life in and through you, in the person of the Holy Spirit. Even in your ministry, you cannot lead people to Christ by your own efforts. It must be the Holy Spirit in you who draws people to Christ. In fact, successful witnessing can be defined as simply taking the initiative to share Christ in the power of the Holy Spirit and leaving the results to God. When we rely on His power and not our own, we experience the joy, the fruitfulness, and the excitement of the Christian life.

WHY IS IT THAT THE AVERAGE CHRISTIAN
IS NOT FILLED WITH THE HOLY SPIRIT?

Why is the average Christian not experiencing revival? I believe it is for two reasons: a lack of knowledge and a lack of faith.

A lack of knowledge. For many years I longed to be a man of God, but I didn't understand the ministry of the Holy Spirit. I often experienced defeat and frustration, trying to please God, and failing in my own efforts. I did not realize that the Holy Spirit could help me. I did not know I could rest in His power to free me from my sin for which Christ died and shed His blood (though we will not experience a sinless life until we go to be with Him). I did not know I could rely on the Holy Spirit's power to love through me, or that His power would draw people to Christ through me. It was not until God opened my eyes through His Word and showed me the truth that I am sharing with you that this all became clear to me.

Let me give you an illustration. There was a man who was taking a cruise on a ship from the United States to East Asia. He had money enough for only the ticket. It was a long trip, yet all he had to eat were some biscuits. For many days that was all he ate. Then one day he was talking to another man on the ship, and the second man was describing all the good food he had been enjoying on the cruise. The man with the biscuits explained that he had only enough money for the cruise ticket and was becoming very tired of his biscuits. Upon hearing this, the other man exclaimed, "Didn't you know that when you paid for your ticket, the ticket included all your meals on this trip?" Here was this man eating biscuits, and yet he had every right to join the other passengers in the dining room and enjoy all those delicious meals.

Some years ago I visited a famous oil area in the United States. In that area there was a man by the name of Yates who owned a large sheep ranch. Years earlier, Mr. Yates had been unable to pay the mortgage on his ranch and was in danger of losing it. He had very little money and did everything he could to try to provide food and clothing for his children, while trying to pay the mortgage. This poverty stricken rancher was actually one of the most wealthy men in the world, though he did not know it. One day, representatives from an oil company came to visit him. "We believe that there is oil on your property." they said, "and we'd like to drill a test well." They began to drill and at 1,115 feet they discovered a great ocean of oil. The first well came in at 80,000 barrels a day; the second came in at 180,000 barrels. And after more than forty years of production, one of the wells still has the capacity to produce 125,000 barrels per day. Mr. Yates owned it all. The day he purchased the land, he received all the oil and mineral rights. He was a man of great wealth from day one, but he did not know it. For years he lived in great poverty because of his lack of knowledge.

I do not know a better illustration of the Christian life. The moment we receive Christ, all the mighty power of God is available to us. But the average Christian does not understand who he is and who Christ is. As a result, the average Christian lives in self-imposed spiritual poverty instead of continual revival because of a lack of knowledge. And a lack of knowledge results in a lack of faith.

A lack of faith. The most important thing we can teach new Christians is the attributes of God. The Bible says, "The just shall live by faith" (Rom 1:16; Gal. 3:11; both KJV*) and "without faith it is impossible to please God" (Heb. 11:6). The object of our faith, of course, is God Himself. God is sovereign and holy, righteous and loving, all-wise and powerful. Once we understand who God is we have no trouble trusting Him. God, our holy, loving Father, loves us unconditionally, not if or when or because we are good, but because of who *He* is. As we learn who He is, and who we are through Scripture, we learn that we can trust Him with our lives totally and completely.

If you are afraid of God and are not willing to say to Him, "I want to surrender my life totally to You," let me share an illustration that has been helpful to me. My wife and I have two grown sons. Suppose that when they were little lads they had come to greet me when I returned home from a trip and said, "We love you. We missed you. We are so excited about your being home. We have been

* King James Version.

talking together and we have decided that we will do anything you want us to do. From now on, you issue the command and we will obey without any questions. We just want to please you."

Now, what do you think my attitude would have been in response to their expressions of love for me? If I had responded the way many people think God will respond if they say to Him, "Lord, I love you; I'll do anything You want me to do; I'll go anywhere You want me to go," I would have taken my children by the shoulders, looked at them with an evil eye, and said, "I have just been waiting for you to say that. Now I'm going to make you regret your decision to trust me. I am going to take all the fun out of your lives. I will make you miserable as long as you live."

No, I wouldn't have said that! I would have put my arms around them, given them a big hug, and said, "Zac, Brad, I love you, too, and I want to justify your faith in me. I want to do everything I can to help you find full and meaningful lives." Do you think God would do anything less for us—this God who loves us so much that while we were still sinners, He sent His only begotten Son to die for us? No, He wants to bless us. He wants us to experience ongoing revival. He wants to fill our lives with joy and love and meaning and purpose! But He cannot bless us unless we trust and obey Him. He is waiting for us to trust Him.

Why didn't the Israelites enter into the Promised Land? The author of the book of Hebrews in the New Testament wrote that they failed to mix the promises of God with faith (Heb. 3:7-19). They did not obey God and He could not bless them. So they wandered in the wilderness for forty years. And that is where many Christians are today, wandering in the wilderness, not experiencing their rights as children of God, but living in a foreign land because they have not learned to trust God. I assure you, you can trust God with every detail of your life.

HOW CAN ONE BE FILLED WITH THE SPIRIT?

How can one know continual revival as a way of life? It is so simple. And yet, I, like most other Christians, spent many years looking for God's power. We are filled with the Spirit and experience revival *by faith*, just as we received Christ by faith. And we are filled as an act of our wills by faith, not as a once-and-for-all experience, but moment by moment, experiencing spiritual revival day by day, for the rest of our lives.

I like the expression, "spiritual-breathing." Whenever any attitude or action in one's life that hinders or grieves the Spirit, we should exhale by confessing, "Lord, I was proud, I was jealous, I was critical, I was lustful, I did this, I did that. Lord, forgive me, I confess it." The word *confession* means to agree with God that whatever we do that grieves the Spirit is sin. Confession means that we repent, that we cease doing whatever grieves or quenches the Spirit, because repentance means a change of attitude. A change in attitude toward that sin results in a change of action toward that sin. And when you exhale, the blood of Jesus Christ washes away all those things that hinder the working of the Spirit.

Then we inhale and are filled with the Spirit by faith. We do not need to live another five seconds outside the will of God, grieving or quenching the Spirit. The Holy Spirit comes to dwell within us at the moment of spiritual birth; He never leaves us. Though there is only one indwelling of the Holy Spirit, there are many fillings. *And we are filled with the Holy Spirit by faith.* We do not have to plead with or persuade the Holy Spirit to fill us. Just as it is God's desire that all men come into a saving relationship with Jesus Christ, so it is a command recorded in Ephesians 5:18: "Be filled with the Spirit," or literally, "be *being filled* with the Spirit." If we find ourselves back in control of our own lives or relying on our own self-effort, we need to surrender our lives afresh to God and ask Him to fill us again with His Holy Spirit. And if we ask Him to fill us, we can be assured, according to His promise recorded in 1 John 5:14-15, that He will fill us: "If we ask anything according to his will, he hears us. And if we know that he hears us—whatever we ask— we know that we have what we asked of him."

REVIVAL AS A WAY OF LIFE

Right now, on the authority of the Word of God, you can be filled with the Holy Spirit by faith and begin to experience revival as a way of life. All day long you can walk in the fullness of the Spirit, relying on His power in you to produce revival. Whether you walk with the Lord twenty, fifty, or perhaps for some you, seventy-five years or more, you can walk in the joy of the resurrection. That is our heritage.

There are four factors that are important to consider before you pray and claim revival by faith.

YOU MUST WANT REVIVAL IN YOUR LIFE

Scripture promises, "Blessed are those who hunger and thirst for righteousness, for they will be filled" (Matt. 5:6). If you do not want to be filled and experience revival, you cannot be filled and experience revival. If you do not hunger and thirst after righteousness and revival, you can pray all kinds of prayers or submit to all kinds of religious disciplines and nothing will happen to you or in your life.

YOU MUST BE WILLING TO SURRENDER YOUR LIFE TO CHRIST

You cannot be filled with the Holy Spirit unless you surrender your life fully to Christ, totally, completely, irrevocably, laying everything on the altar, saying, "Holy Savior, I surrender my life to you, my home, my ministry, my husband, my wife, my children, my parents, my present, my past, my future—I surrender it all to You. I surrender all my frustrations, my feelings of insecurity and inadequacy, my poor self-image, my psychological problems, my fruitless witnessing, my sometimes cold heart and unbelieving spirit." Lay it all on the altar and say, "Oh, Holy Spirit, fill me as I surrender everything to the lordship of Christ. Enable me to know and experience true heaven-sent revival."

YOU MUST TURN FROM ALL KNOWN SIN

Consider for a moment if there are any known sins which the Holy Spirit is revealing to you. For most people it is helpful to jot any known sins down on a sheet of paper. It is not necessary to become introspective. Simply ask the Holy Spirit to bring to your remembrance anything He wants you to confess before Him. Then confess your sin, remembering that confession means to agree with God concerning your sin. Then thank Him for His forgiveness which is promised in 1 John 1:9: "If we confess our sins, he is faithful and

just and will forgive us our sins and purify us from all unrighteousness."

CLAIM YOUR INHERITANCE

And now by faith, and faith alone, claim the fullness of the
Holy Spirit. It is all a gift, just as salvation is a gift. We receive His
fullness and experience revival by faith. You do not even have to
pray, if you want to be technical about it; you are filled by faith. But
I like to think of prayer as an expression of faith.

A doctor who was also the lay leader of a large church once
came to me for counsel. "I don't care what it costs me," he said,
"I'm ready to leave a very lucrative medical practice to go to the
mission field, if that's what it takes. But I don't want to live another
day without the Holy Spirit's power."

I asked, "Do you believe it is God's will that you be filled with
the Holy Spirit?"

He said, "Of course, because it is His command."

Then I asked, "Do you believe He would fill you if we bowed
together and prayed?"

He didn't answer. He just slipped from his chair onto his knees
and began to pray. Nothing dramatic happened. He did not get
excited and jump up and down for joy (frankly, there's nothing
wrong with that if that is the way you respond to the fullness of the
Spirit). But six months later he wrote to say, "Every day since I
prayed with you, I have been more fruitful for God through my life
than all the rest of the many years I have served Him combined."

It is not important that we "feel" we are filled with the Spirit.
Emotions can be very deceptive. We are commanded by God to be
filled, and He promised He would fill us if we asked Him, and if we
meet the above conditions. You do not need to live another moment
of your life outside the fullness of the Holy Spirit and continual
revival. And as you grow to rely on the power of the Holy Spirit
more and more, you will grow to love our Lord more and more, and
spiritual revival will become a way of life.

3

Understanding the Baptism of the Holy Spirit

Joon Gon Kim

Dr. Joon Gon Kim, national director of Korea Campus Crusade for Christ and director of affairs for Campus Crusade's East Asia area, graduated from Chosun University, and took graduate work at Fuller Theological Seminary. He has received honorary doctoral degrees from Chun Buk University, King Sejong University, and Southwest Baptist University. Dr. Kim is an ordained Presbyterian minister and has served as chaplain and principal of the Soongsil High School in Kwangu. Dr. Kim served as the executive chairman for both EXPLO '74 and '80 World Evangelization Crusade. He was the general director for the International Prayer Assembly.

In Acts 1:4-8, after Jesus rose from the dead but before He ascended to be with the Father, He gave the following important instruction to His disciples:

> And gathering them together, He commanded them not to leave Jerusalem, but to wait for what the Father had promised, "Which," He said, "you heard of from Me; for John baptized with water, but you shall be baptized with the Holy Spirit not many days from now." And so when they had come together, they were asking Him saying, "Lord, is it at this time You are restoring the kingdom to Israel?" He said to them, "It is not for you to know times or epochs which the Father has fixed by His own authority; but you shall receive power when the Holy

Spirit has come upon you; and you shall by My witnesses both in Jerusalem, and in all Judea and Samaria, and even to the remotest part of the earth." (NASB*)

So they waited as Jesus instructed, and not long thereafter four explosions happened among these believers: (1) the explosion of prayer, (2) the explosion of the Holy Spirit, (3) the explosion of evangelism, and (4) the explosion of love.

The believers in the book of Acts were fervent, like a ball of fire. It seemed as though it wasn't just Peter himself walking around, but that Jesus, through the Holy Spirit, drove him around. Jesus worked through the Holy Spirit within people continuously, and in that way the human beings who are mentioned in the book of Acts were not the main figures in that work.

I would like to discuss several aspects of the effect that the baptism of the Holy Spirit had on these believers and the implications for us.

THE NATURE OF BAPTISM IN THE HOLY SPIRIT

WE DO NOT HAVE TO WAIT FOR IT

You and I do not have to wait for some kind of personal Pentecost. It's true that in speaking to the disciples Jesus commanded them "not [to] leave Jerusalem, but [to] wait for the gift [His] Father [had] promised," the Holy Spirit (Acts 1:4). But for us, the Holy Spirit has already come. If it were not for the Holy Spirit, we could not call God our Father or Jesus our Lord. The moment we are born again by receiving Jesus, the Holy Spirit comes to live within us. We are the temple of the Holy Spirit. The fact that the Holy Spirit comes and dwells in us means we have received our Pentecost.

Many believers think that in order to be able to witness to the gospel, they must receive the power of the Spirit in some new way, and that otherwise they are not qualified to go witnessing until they have some kind of dramatic experiences of being filled with the Holy Spirit. So, they dare not go to Jerusalem, but seek special churches, special conventions, or special ways or people for the fullness of the

---

* *New American Standard Bible.*

Holy Spirit. And they await the coming of the Spirit.

But God's Spirit has already come. We do not have to wait for His coming. The Holy Spirit has come and has been dwelling in whoever believes in Jesus. The Holy Spirit of the Pentecost and the Spirit who indwells us today is the same One. God's Spirit who came upon John Wesley and who comes upon us is the same One.

IT IS JESUS' REASONABLE EXPECTATION

To be filled with the Spirit is the command of Jesus, and He does not command us to undertake impossible missions. The Spirit-filled life is a normal style for all Christians. We may not be able to accomplish a holy life or a clean Christian life by our own efforts, for everyone has sinned, as the Scripture says. But we are to be filled with the Spirit.

The definition of a Christian life is that Jesus lives within us through His Spirit. We love by His love through the Holy Spirit. We witness from God's Word in the power given by the Spirit.

Christians often do not understand their responsibility to witness. Because they assume that they are to "make converts," the task seems too great—a mission impossible—and so they do nothing. But we are not able to make people believe in Jesus, nor produce Christians by ourselves. We are but instruments of the Holy Spirit who works through us. We spread the good news, and He is in charge of the consequences of our ministry.

Our task is modest—just witness—but critical. Because many of us do not understand this responsibility, we do not recognize and repent of the sin of not witnessing of Jesus. Even in secular law, one can be charged with a crime if he or she could have saved a drowning person, for instance, but made no attempt to do so. Knowing that people are dying spiritually, and yet abandoning them to perish by not witnessing to them of Jesus, is just as much a crime. Among all the sins that Christians commit, I believe the most serious and the most frequent is to abandon people to perish by not telling them of Jesus.

The sin of not praying for the unbelievers is yet another grave one. Now, consider for what we usually repent. We repent of sins of stealing or adultery, but that is not enough. We must repent of our sin of not spreading God's Word to individuals, churches, and throughout the world. We must repent with open hearts, tears of sorrow, and with prayers of repentance over many nights and days, for we have been disobeying God's command.

IT PROVIDES ALL WE NEED

Having been filled with the Holy Spirit, we are well equipped, and must go forth to be witnesses of Jesus in Jerusalem and in Judea and in Samaria and to the ends of the earth. I would compare the condition of being filled with the Spirit with the electric power for an appliance, whether it be an electric shaver or a giant computer. When the device is connected, the power is available; it is only a matter of turning on the switch to begin the operation.

We can apply this image to the Holy Spirit. The believer has been "connected up" as a result of Pentecost and his or her personal faith in Jesus (and the consequent inclusion in the church). All that is necessary is to draw on the power by turning on the switch. All the power that is needed has already been provided.

The important thing to remenber is that by faith we are already filled with the Holy Spirit. What we need to do is to obey God's Word to switch "on" for evangelism, "on" for love. Love grows by itself when we decide to love through the power of the Spirit.

I had an old bicycle from the time of the Japanese colonial rule in Korea. It was not as well built as the ones nowadays. But its light was operated by a generator rather than a battery. It only came on when I was riding the bike. If I stopped, the light went out. It is the same for the Spirit-filled life. We have to move before the Spirit can empower *or* guide us.

Once I thought that I could not witness of God's Word unless I was filled with the Holy Spirit, nor love until I was filled with the Spirit, and I didn't do anything but wait. But then I realized that the Spirit already had come into my life at the moment I received Jesus, that I am filled with the Spirit by faith, since I confessed my sins and asked Him according to His will. With that faith and trust in the power of the Holy Spirit, I witnessed freely for Him, and found that it worked and worked well.

IT IS SUSTAINED BY FAITH

Many have misconceptions on the fullness of God's Spirit. For instance, there is the concept of enlightenment, particularly among

Eastern religions. It is supposedly achieved by self-discipline, and by cleansing the mind and body through ultimate penance and asceticism—celibacy, begging one's bread, feeding oneself with coarse and miserable foods, and secluding oneself on a remote mountain for not one or two years, but for a lifetime.

This concept has been accepted by some Christians. And many who are invited to trust Jesus say that they will believe in Him later, when they become "cleaner." When told of the need to be filled with the Spirit, some others say that they shall be full of the Spirit automatically at the point when they have become just as impeccable as God Himself, as crystal-clear as the High above, and as sinless in their thoughts and speech. But the whole idea is a complete deception.

The fact is, at the moment we receive Jesus into our lives we are filled by the Spirit. Regardless of where we are, or even whether we are thieves or communists, we become the children of God, being called the righteous, cleansed from all sin. We are as righteous as we will ever be, not by works, but by Jesus' shed blood. Not one soul can add to his or her righteousness through abiding by the law. We are saved by faith; we receive eternal life by faith; we are declared righteous by faith. "The righteous shall live by faith," was, and is, the theme of the Reformation. Believers are to participate in the resurrection. People of faith do not come into judgment. People of faith are said in the Bible to do the same things that Jesus did and able to do greater things through the power of God's Spirit.

Now, we must reevaluate this faith. Today, we in Protestantism have lost again the meaning of faith and an understanding of its values. When Jesus was crucified on the cross and the veil of the temple was torn in two, He took away the first offering according to the law, the entrance of the high priest once a year into the Holy of Holies, so that from then on all the laymen could communicate with God and confess their sins directly to Him.

However, the Catholic churches prohibited them from doing this for one thousand years through medieval times. The hierarchy took away the right of direct confession to God of sin and hindered the people from personally receiving God's Word by reading and interpreting the Bible themselves. For those functions the people had to go through a priest. And the period is called the Dark Ages because of it.

But for all believers, the way had already been provided to

come easily and directly to God. But we are again losing a grip on this important privilege. With all our theologizing we are in danger of making Christianity too difficult and complicated for the common person. It must become simpler. Christian belief is really much simpler than we tend to make it. Jesus taught and spoke about God to people in quite a different way than others did. He called on God the Father. Not an ordinary father, but "Abba, Father." That's what children of the day called their father; it's comparable to "daddy." Consequently, one definition of Christians, among others, is that they are people who call on God the Father, believing in Him, and loving Him as their good Daddy. What a simple faith it is!

Marxism has power and persuasion to draw the poor, but Christianity seems to be placed in the lofty sky far from the ground and the people. Too many people think that only the special ones are to be filled with the Holy Spirit. It is not true. We all are to live eating and drinking Jesus, breathing the Spirit, loving others, and spreading the good news through His power. God's Spirit is more like a Father, who has come to me on behalf of the Trinity, more like a Groom, a Teacher, a Helper, my Guide, and my Light and Power, my Love, my Joy, and the One who satisfies all my needs. I am His child. It must be this simple.

When a criminal crucified alongside Jesus asked Him, "Jesus, remember me when you come into your kingdom," Jesus said to him, "Today you will be with me in paradise" (Luke 23:42-43). Whoever calls on the name of Jesus Christ shall be saved. The blood of Jesus is that precious!

Unlike what Buddhism offers for personal salvation—which is harder and more difficult to enter than to pass the highest civil service examination—the Christian faith is so simple that whoever wants to be, can be saved. All are only to receive what is given. All we have to do is to say "yes" and open the door.

Jesus told the parable of a man who goes to a friend at midnight and asks him to lend him three loaves of bread for a friend, and He said, "Yet because of his persistence, he will get up and give him as much as he needs" (Luke 11:8). Further, He said, "Now suppose one of you fathers is asked by his son for a fish; he will not give him a snake instead of a fish, will he? Or if he is asked for an egg, he will not give him a scorpion, will he? If you then, being evil, know how to give good gifts to your children, how much more shall your heavenly Father give the Holy Spirit to those who ask Him?" (Luke 11:11-13; NASB).

The best gift God wants to give us is the Holy Spirit. He gives us the Spirit just as He gives Himself and His Son. By giving the Spirit to us, He gives us His heart, His mind, His soul, and Himself as a whole. He wants to give this Spirit to everyone.

Therefore, by faith you can be given the fullness of the Spirit. Jesus said that anything we ask according to His will, we will receive it. It is the word of Jesus. Being filled with the Spirit is as simple as breathing. We breathe out our sins and breathe in the Spirit, all the time, moment by moment. We confess our sins to God as we breathe out, and appropriate the fullness of the Spirit as we breathe in, allowing Him to work within us as our Master. Being filled with God's Spirit is a continuing process of faith, like breathing.

THE RESULTS OF BAPTISM IN THE HOLY SPIRIT

IT MAKES US ONE WITH CHRIST

There is the phrase in the first chapter of Acts which says, "In a few days you will be baptized with the Holy Spirit" (Acts 1:5). Of course there are different theological opinions, interpretations, and thoughts about being baptized by God's Spirit. But one thing is clear: baptism itself means to become one. Thus it means that Jesus and I become one, that the death of Jesus becomes my own death, and that the resurrection of Jesus Christ becomes my resurrection. Jesus speaks what He wants to say through me. Jesus and I have one heart. Believers are people who resemble Jesus.

Jesus and I have but one fate. Jesus takes away all my sin. His glory and His righteousness and His power are bestowed upon me. I would compare this to marriage. When she marries, a woman accepts her husband's family name so that the couple has the same legal identity. They share the same sociological fate. The woman calls her husband's parents hers and regard his brothers as her own.

Moreover, many psychological changes evolve in marriage. The couple's likes and dislikes often become similar. The wife's religious faith often follows her husband's belief. Two people become one psychologically. Oftentimes, after many years, even their faces begin to resemble one another's. It is strange but natural, in some sense, for couples to begin to resemble one another, for they have shared a harmonious daily life for a long time.

Likewise, I become a member of the Body of Christ when I am baptized through the Holy Spirit by faith, resembling Christ's personality. I become one with Jesus, receiving Christ's Spirit. I can recognize His compassion as mine. I endeavor to become in tune with Christ's feelings. Being baptized and united with Jesus, we are to resemble His personality and have His Spirit and His heart so that we are able to see the world dying around us like He sees it, for we see the world through His eyes.

We also are able to see sin with the same sensitivity as Christ. That is the baptism of the Holy Spirit. It signifies the union of our personality and our spirit with Christ's rather than some mystical experience and feeling, or mere formality or exotic ritual. Baptism fundamentally means that the Spirit of Jesus is incorporated into my spirit, thus becoming one.

IT CREATES UNITY AMONG BELIEVERS

We are living in the earth village on the brink of the last days for mankind. In this tiny earth village, there are more than six hundred Protestant denominations. Korean churches also have wasted their energy in fighting among themselves. It is time to reconcile and evangelize with one accord.

Note how Japan revived its economy after the war. The Japanese came together and agreed among themselves to make their country a gigantic company, "Japan Incorporated," and concentrate their economic power into one great force. Even the communists often set up a united front in cooperation among themselves for the purpose of spreading world communism.

But the Christian churches do not behave as one. All advocate their own churches, their own denominations. There are differences, of course, in biblical interpretations, styles, theology, and denominational principles. From this time on, however, Christians in the earth village must gather together on the national basis as a starting point. Billy Graham emphasized at Amsterdam '83 that Christians who receive Jesus as personal Lord and are born again through the Holy Spirit are brothers and sisters in Christ.

All who embrace the Apostle's Creed are brothers and sisters, not because that creed unites, but because it testifies of Jesus. And all must become one through each one's personal relationship with God. All must work together with concerted energy for the evangelization of the world. Nobody should be left out in this. All must be embraced by love.

Jesus prayed for us to be one and love each other, and we must all repent for our part in hindering the fulfillment of Jesus' prayer. We are fighting a holy war. All the Christian resources, both financial and human, should be fully mobilized, strategies shared, experiences in the ministry exchanged. I suggest that each church appropriate half of its finances for its own programs and the other half for evangelism. Some churches have already mobilized 80 percent of their finances for evangelism. Yet other churches put 90 percent, or even 100 percent, of their finances into evangelism. The more energy and resources that are put together, the stronger our united forces will become.

Mormons serve in their worldwide mission for two years while they are nineteen and twenty years old. It is a stipulated duty, similar to that of the armed services. They minister at their own expense. As Thailanders serve for two years in Buddhist temples before they become monks, young Christians should go to other countries around the world for two years, equipped with love in one hand, and the good news in the other, working for world evangelization.

I think the time is ripe for hundreds of thousands of young Christians to spread Jesus throughout the world. Then, by the year 2000, there should be no one left out from hearing God's message. On the last day of the Duksum Fasting Prayer Rally, as in the WEC '80 Crusade on Yoido Plaza, we pledged ourselves to four devotions:

- To devote ourselves to intercessory prayer for world evangelization
- To contribute financially for world evangelization
- To bring up our children to be involved in evangelism
- To devote ourselves to missionary service

Many Christian meetings and gatherings around the world today emphasize world evangelization, unity, love and prayer for the fullness of the Holy Spirit. We know the Holy Spirit cannot work in

His fullness where people fight against each other. There are so many churches and people who are suffering in the communist countries of China, U.S.S.R., North Korea, and many others. For the sake of those suffering people, we must be one in uniting our prayers, our financial and human resources, and our hearts and love so that we may achieve world evangelization.

We are the forerunners in this last revival as powerful as earthquakes, volcanic eruptions, floods, and tempests, to see the fullness of the Holy Spirit working through us. Let us all join hands and participate in this revival movement.

IT RESULTS IN EVANGELISM

According to Acts 1:8, Jesus said, "But you will receive power when the Holy Spirit comes on you." The phrase "comes on you" means the same as being filled with the Holy Spirit. The power of the Spirit is like dynamite. What did the apostles do when the Holy Spirit came upon them? They were able to witness for Christ in foreign languages, in fifteen different tongues, so that each one in the crowd could hear the apostles speaking in his or her native tongue. Of all the meanings of speaking in tongues, this is the important and basic one. Jesus said, "But you will receive power when the Holy Spirit comes on you; and you will be my witnesses in Jerusalem, and in all Judea and Samaria, and to the ends of the earth" (Acts 1:8).

The phrase "being filled with the Holy Spirit" appears nine times in Acts.

1. Initially 120 believers were filled with the Holy Spirit in the upper room, then came out fearlessly to witness for Jesus Christ. The fullness of the Spirit enabled them to overcome various barriers of culture, race, country, ideology, and philosophy in their ministry (Acts 2:1-13).
2. Peter was filled with the Holy Spirit. And he appeared before scores of priests and freely spoke to them that Jesus Christ is the only Savior (4:5-22).
3. All the apostles were filled with the Holy Spirit and fearlessly witnessed of God's message (2:1-13).
4. The church chose seven deacons full of the Holy Spirit and of wisdom (6:1-7).

5. A leading deacon, Stephen, a man full of the Spirit and of faith, was martyred during the ministry of God's Word (6:1–7:60). Though deacons were chosen to serve tables, they were full of the Holy Spirit and some were martyred because of their fervent witnessing of Jesus. Stephen, in the fullness of God's Spirit, saw the glory of Jesus in heaven when he was stoned to death.

6. The apostle Paul met Jesus on the road to Damascus. He recovered his sight through Ananias. Then he, in the fullness of the Spirit, went into Damascus and preached Jesus Christ, the Son of God (9:1-30).

7. Barnabas was a man full of the Holy Spirit and of faith. According to the Scripture, when he preached the gospel, a considerable number were added to the Lord Jesus. What did Barnabas achieve in the fullness of God's Spirit? He witnessed of Jesus and many people were added to the Lord (4:36; 9:27; 11:22-24).

8. Paul, filled with the Holy Spirit, spoke from God's Word and the proconsul Sergius Paulus believed in Jesus Christ (13:6-12).

9. The last verses of chapter 13 in Acts say that the disciples went into Iconium in the fullness of joy and of the Holy Spirit (vv. 51-52) and spoke in the name of Jesus so that a large group both of Jews and of Greeks believed in Him (14:1).

Therefore, what will people filled with the Spirit do? They will always produce the fruit of evangelism through the power of the Holy Spirit. They will fervently witness of Jesus.

There are two kinds of fruit; one is the fruit of souls and the other is the fruit of the Spirit. The fruit of the Spirit is itemized in Galatians 5:22-23. It becomes increasingly evident in our daily lives. It is the product of the love of Jesus residing in one's inner self. People who exhibit the fruits of the Spirit always produce the fruit of souls automatically through evangelism.

By observing the nine fruits of the Spirit—which are the product of the fullness of the Spirit—and seeing these followed by the fruit of souls, we can verify whether one is truly filled with the Spirit and His power. We know a tree by its fruit. God's Spirit is the Spirit of ministry, which came to bear witness to the name of Jesus Christ, to glorify Him, to stir men's hearts, to make them believe in Him so that they may be born again. Therefore, sharing Christ in the power of the Holy Spirit is the proof of being filled with the Spirit.

4

Prayer and the Cleansed Life

Evelyn Christenson

Evelyn Christenson is the author of What Happens When Women Pray *and has conducted seminars all over the United States and in several countries on the subject of prayer. She is organizer and chairman of the Board of United Prayer Ministries, a non-profit corporation based in Minnesota. Evelyn has helped organize citywide prayer chains in many cities throughout the United States.*

In John 15:7, Jesus promised His followers power in their prayer: "Ask whatever you wish, and it will be given you." That is an utterly amazing promise. However, Jesus preceded it with His conditions concerning that kind of prayer power. He said: "If you remain in me and my words remain in you," then—and only then—can this promise be claimed and these powerful results be expected.

What did Jesus mean when He spoke of remaining in Him and allowing His words to remain in us? What Jesus taught His disciples included the very words that the Father gave to Him to give to us (John 17:8); these are the words we are to remain in or by which we are to live. They were the truths that He said the Holy Spirit would later bring to the disciples' remembrance and teach them more deeply about (John 14:25-26). Also, He Himself opened the Old Testament to them after His resurrection and before His ascension (Luke 24:27, 45), so that they could understand how the prophecies foretold of Him.

But among His words, Jesus taught the importance of the cleansed life, particularly as it relates to the life of the praying person.

THE STATE OF SIN

When Jesus taught us to pray in His model prayer (the Lord's Prayer) in Matthew 6:9, He told us to pray, "Our Father. . . ." From this we see that the Lord's Prayer was given to Christians, those who could call God, "Father." We know that only Christians can properly call God Father because He also taught us that "No one comes to the Father except through me" (John 14:6). If someone has not acknowledged that Jesus is God's Son and has not accepted Him as his Savior, then he is not a Christian. He has not established that relationship with Him which would allow him the authority to gain access to the Father. so the Lord's Prayer is instruction for Christians in the way they are to pray.

All people are born into a *state* of sinfulness which separates them from God. Jesus said in John 16:7-9, "I will send him [the Comforter, the Holy Spirit] to you. When he comes, he will convict the world of guilt in regard to sin . . . because men do not believe in me." Similarly, Romans 5:12 says, "Therefore, just as sin entered the world through one man, and death through sin, and in this way death came to all men, because all sinned."

"The world," in Jesus' vocabulary, always referred to those outside of Himself, those who did not know Him as Savior and Lord by believing on Him. There is only one way to get out of that state of sin and into a relationship where one has the authority to call God, "Father": That is to repent and believe on Jesus as Savior and Lord. Then all original sin is forgiven by God.

So as long as one is living in that original state of sin, there can be no prayer power because Jesus has said that the Father responds only when we ask in Jesus' name, that is to say, when we approach through Jesus (John 14:13-14).

SINS THAT CHRISTIANS COMMIT

In addition to speaking of our being forgiven for original sin, Jesus taught us in His model prayer to say, "Forgive us our debts," or as it might be translated, "Forgive us our sins" (Matt. 6:12).

Jesus is telling us to ask for forgiveness for the various sins (debts, trespasses) that we as Christians are prone to commit from day to day. We should keep up-to-date on them, else you and I as Christians will not have that John 15:7 power in prayer, where Jesus promised, "Ask whatever you wish, and it will be given you." If there is sin in our lives—because we are not obeying Jesus' words—we short-circuit the power.

The disciples, who personally heard Jesus teach on this subject, not only reported what Jesus said when they wrote the gospels but also incorporated the concept so thoroughly into their understanding that they also taught the same truths themselves and made quite a point in emphasizing them.

For instance, John said in 1 John 1:8-10, "If we claim to be without sin, we deceive ourselves and the truth is not in us. If we confess our sins, he is faithful and just and will forgive us our sins and purify us from all unrighteousness. If we claim we have not sinned, we make him out to be a liar and his word has no place in our lives." Notice that in this context John used the word, "we." He was including himself as someone prone to commit sins. And because the book was written to believers ("My dear children," 1 John 2:1), he was assuming that they, too, had the potential to sin, and indeed did sin from time to time and needed to confess those sins and be forgiven.

Similarly, in 1 Peter 3:12, Peter related the issue of unconfessed and unrepented sins to the effectiveness of our prayer: "For the eyes of the Lord are on the righteous and his ears are attentive to their prayer, but the face of the Lord is against those who do evil." Again, this book was written to the believers ("To God's elect," 1 Pet. 1:1). And they needed to be reminded that unrighteousness in their lives (the sins and trespasses they might commit) had direct bearing on the effectiveness of their prayers.

Revival always comes when Christians see that a cleansed life is essential. And this happens when they apprehend the holiness of God in contrast to their sinfulness and repent in response to that contrast.

A CLEANSING EXERCISE

In James 4:17 we read: "Anyone, then, who knows the good he ought to do and doesn't do it, sins." This passage reminds us that it is important to obey God's Word. When we realize we have sinned, we don't need to be crushed by guilt; we need to follow God's instruction for dealing with it: confess our sin and change our behavior.

The following set of questions provides an exercise for cleansing your life. It may not include all the things that the Spirit would want to speak to you about, but it is a good place to start. Prayerfully read through it. Every "Yes" answer shows a sin that needs confessing.

1. *Unthankfulness.* "Give thanks in all circumstances, for this is God's will for you in Christ Jesus" (1 Thess. 5:18). Do you worry about anything? Have you failed to thank God for *all* things, the seemingly bad as well as the good? Do you neglect to give thanks at mealtimes?

2. *Feelings of inferiority.* "Now to him who is able to do immeasurably more than all we ask or imagine, according to his power *that is at work within us*" (Eph. 3:20; emphasis added). Do you fail to attempt things for God because you are not talented enough? Do feelings of inferiority keep you from trying to serve God? When you accomplish something for Christ, do you fail to give Him all the glory?

3. *Failure to witness.* "But you will receive power when the Holy Spirit comes on you; and you will be my witnesses in Jerusalem, and in all Judea and Samaria, and to the ends of the earth" (Acts 1:8). Have you failed to be a witness with your life for Christ? Have you felt it was enough to live your Christianity and not also to witness with your mouth to the lost?

4. *Pride.* "I say to every one of you: Do not think of yourself more highly than you ought" (Rom. 12:3). Are you proud of *your* accomplishments, *your* talents, *your* family? Do you fail to see others as better than yourself, more important than youself in the Body of Christ? Do you insist on your own rights? Do you think as a Christian you are doing quite well? Do you rebel at God wanting to change you?

5. *Resentment.* "Get rid of all bitterness, rage and anger, brawling and slander, along with every form of malice" (Eph. 4:31). Do you complain, find fault, argue? Do you have a critical spirit? Do you carry a grudge against Christians of another group because they don't see eye-to-eye with you on all things? Do you speak unkindly about people when they are not present? Are you angry with yourself? Others? God?

6. *Failure to take care of your body.* "Do you not know that your body is the temple of the Holy Spirit, who is in you, whom you have received from God? You are not your own; you were bought at a price. Therefore honor God with your body" (1 Cor.

6:19-20). Are you careless with your body? Are you guilty of not caring for it as the temple of the Holy Spirit in eating and exercise habits? Do you defile your body with unholy sex acts?

7. *Unwholesome talk.* "Do not let any unwholesome talk come out of your mouths" (Eph. 4:29). Do you ever use filthy language, tell slightly off-color jokes? Do you condone others' doing so in your presence? In your home?

8. *Giving the devil a foothold.* "Do not give the devil a foothold" (Eph. 4:27). Do you fail to see that you are a "landing strip" for Satan when you open your mind to him through T.M., yoga, seances, psychic predictions, occult literature and movies? Do you get advice for daily living from horoscopes rather than from God? Do you let Satan use you to thwart the cause of Christ in your church through criticism, gossip, nonsupport?

9. *Slothfulness.* "Not slothful in business" (Rom. 12:11, KJV*). Do you fail to pay your debts on time? Avoid paying them altogether? Do you charge more on credit cards than you can pay when due? Do you neglect to keep honest income tax records? Do you engage in any shady business deals whether as an employer or employee?

10. *Taking license.* "Be careful, however, that the exercise of your freedom does not become a stumbling block to the weak" (1 Cor. 8:9).Do you feel you can do anything you want to do because the Bible says you are "free in Christ" ? Even though you were strong enough not to fall, do you fail to take responsibility for the weaker Christian who has fallen because of following your example?

11. *Unfaithful in church attendance.* "Let us not give up meeting together" (Heb. 10:25). Are you irregular or spasmodic in church attendance? Do you attend preaching services in body only, whispering, reading, or planning while God's Word is being preached? Are you skipping prayer meeting? Have you neglected family devotions?

12. *Lying.* "Do not lie to each other" (Col. 3:9). Do you ever lie? Exaggerate? Fail to see "little white lies" as sin? Do you tell things the way you want them to be rather than the way they really are?

13. *Indulging lust.* "Dear friends, I urge you . . . to abstain from

*King James Version.

sinful desires, which war against your soul" (1 Pet. 2:11). Are you guilty of a lustful eye toward the opposite sex? Do you fill your mind with sex-oriented TV programs, movies, books, and magazines? Do you indulge in any lustful activity God's Word condemns—fornication, adultery, perversion?

14. *Divisiveness.* "By this all men will know that you are my disciples, if you love one another" (John 13:35). Are you guilty of being a part of factions and divisions in your church? Would you rather add fuel to a misunderstanding than help to correct it? Have you loved only the ones in your own church, feeling those of other denominations are not of the Body of Christ? Are you secretly pleased over the misfortunes of another? Annoyed by their successes?

15. *Unforgiveness.* "Bear with each other and forgive whatever grievances you may have against one another. Forgive as the Lord forgave you" (Col. 3:13). Have you failed to forgive anybody anything they might have said or done against you? Have you turned certain people off? Are you holding grudges?

16. *Stealing.* "He who has been stealing must steal no longer" (Eph. 4:28). Do you steal from your employer by doing less work, staying on the job less time than you are paid for? Do you underpay?

17. *Wasting time.* "Redeeming the time, because the days are evil" (Eph. 5:16, KJV). Do you waste time? The time of others? Do you spend time watching TV trash, reading cheap books, procrastinating?

18. *Greed.* "No man can serve two masters. . . . You cannot serve both God and Money" (Matt. 6:24). Is your goal in life to make as much money as possible? Accumulate things? Have you withheld God's share of your income from Him? Is money your God?

19. *Hypocrisy.* "On the outside you appear to people as righteous but on the inside you are full of hypocrisy and wickedness" (Matt. 23:28). Do you know in your heart you are a fake, just pretending to be a real Christian? Are you hiding behind church membership to cover a life still full of sin? Are you faking Christianity for social status, or for acceptance in your church, your community? Do you smile piously during the Sunday sermon but live in your sin all week? Are you the same person at

home as you are away from home? Or do you try to impress people by being something you are not?

20. *Gossiping.* "Finally, brothers, whatever is true, whatever is noble, whatever is right, whatever is pure, whatever is lovely, whatever is admirable—if anything is excellent or praiseworthy—think about such things" (Phil. 4:8). Do you enjoy listening to gossip? Passing it on? Do you believe rumors or partial truths, especially about an enemy or your competitor? Do you fail to spend time every day reading the Bible? Do you fail to think on the things of God—only good and true and pure things—always?

James 5:16 tells us to "confess [our] sins to each other and pray for each other." Therefore I recommend that after prayerfully going through the above exercise, you gather with a small group of trustworthy Christian brothers and sisters and confess aloud your sins, using short, one sentence prayers. Be sure to include the words "forgive me." It is appropriate in such a context for each person to assure the others, in the name of Christ, that their sins have been forgiven.

Forgiving Others: A Final Condition

Though there are no conditions for God's forgiving the "state of sin" when people believe on Jesus and accept Him as Savior and Lord, Jesus tell us about a condition that God places on the forgiveness of the sins that we as Christians commit.

In the Lord's Prayer, Jesus continued His words by saying: "Forgive us our debts, as we also have forgiven our debtors" (Matt. 6:12). Jesus required not only a right relationship with God, but also a right relationship with our fellow man. The word, "as," means "just like," "in the same way that," "to the extent that" we forgive others; that is how God will forgive us. Remember now, this is just for the Christian. God cares so much about our relationship with others and so wants us to avoid bitterness and resentment, that there is this condition on the forgiveness we receive.

Following the Lord's Prayer in Matthew 6:14-15, Jesus expanded upon the issue of forgiving others. He said, "For if you forgive men when they sin against you, your heavenly Father will also forgive you. But if you do not forgive men their sins, your Father will not forgive your sins." Then you are back to the place of having no prayer power. According to this, sin in your life, although possibly confessed, is still unforgiven by God.

Elsewhere, Jesus similarly connected our power in prayer and God's forgiveness of our sins to the way we forgive others. In Mark 11:24-25 Jesus said, "Whatever you ask for in prayer, believe that you have received it, and it will be yours. And when you stand praying, if you hold anything against anyone, forgive him, so that your Father in heaven may forgive you your sins." If you don't forgive others, He won't forgive you, and you will lack power in your prayer.

A FORMULA FOR FORGIVING OTHERS

In 2 Corinthians 2:5-11 Paul provides us with instruction on the way we can forgive others.

> If anyone has caused grief, he has not so much grieved me as he has grieved all of you, to some extent—not to put it too severely. The punishment inflicted on him by the majority is sufficient for him. Now instead, you ought to forgive and comfort him, so that he will not be overwhelmed by excessive sorrow. I urge you, therefore, to affirm your love for him. The reason I wrote you was to see if you would stand the test and be obedient in everything. If you forgive anyone, I also forgive him. And what I have forgiven—if there was anything to forgive—I have forgiven in the sight of Christ for your sake, in order that Satan might not outwit us. For we are not unaware of his schemes.

This is a formula for our response to those who have "caused grief" and need to be forgiven by us or the body as a whole. This applies to someone who has sinned against us or against the church. Note that God understands and agrees with us that we are sometimes really grieved. He understands being grieved, because we grieve Him every time we sin, and He knows His grief at having to send His Son to pay for our sins.

Other Christians frequently ostracize those who have caused grief, but Paul says that they have received enough punishment. God doesn't want factions to develop over the one who has been grieved. Rather we must forgive.

Of course, it is not easy to forgive when we have been grieved and hurt. Our natural desire is to want the one who has hurt us to come to us and comfort us. But God has other ideas. He says that should not be our expectation. We can ask God to help us forgive the person. Then we are to go to that person and comfort him, affirming our love for him and lifting him up.

Why does God want us to undertake this extraordinary response, this "going the second mile," this "returning good for evil"? The reason is "so that he will not be overwhelmed by excessive sorrow." God's deep wisdom is evident here. If a person is overwhelmed with excessive sorrow, he is going to feel very bad about himself. When that happens, it will be accompanied by increased insecurity, and before you know it, he will lash out again in defensiveness toward you or someone else in the body. But God wants to stop the cycle. That's why He tells us to comfort and lift the person up.

Paul tells us to confirm our love toward the offender. Of course, we can't confirm something we don't have, so we may need to pray for love for the other person. And then we should wait in silence until we feel God's love come.

This procedure for forgiving others will prevent Satan from outwitting us. Remember, that he is all too eager to convince us of some reason for not forgiving someone, because he knows by that means he will neutralize the power of our prayer.

AN EXERCISE IN FORGIVING OTHERS

Pray through the above formula by following the steps below in a small group with other brothers and sisters in Christ using short, one sentence prayers.

1. Each participant should think of one person he has not completely forgiven.
2. In silence forgive that person (asking God to help if necessary).
3. Aloud (but not mentioning the name of person about whom you are praying), ask God to forgive you for your attitude of unforgiveness.
4. Aloud, ask God for love for that person. (Then wait in silence while He sends this love.)

5. Ask God how you should confirm that new love. Everyone should listen in silence while He puts thoughts in their minds.
6. Promise God aloud that you will confirm your new love every time and in every way God tells you to do it.
7. Pray one sentence aloud for the person you now love—as Jesus taught us in Matthew 5:44, "Pray for those who persecute you, that you may be sons of your Father in heaven."
8. Thank God that now that you have forgiven the one who wronged you, Jesus said the Father would forgive you also. As a Christian, claim forgiveness for the sins you confessed earlier.

5

The Cost of Revival

Stephen Tong

Rev. Stephen Tong, a professor at Southeast Asia Theo-
logical Seminary in Malang, Indonesia, has been a lecturer
in theology, philosophy, and evangelism since 1964. He
has preached to more than one million people in Asia,
Europe, the United States, and Australia during the past
two decades.

What is revival? Surely it is the renewal of the church initiated by the Lord and not by efforts of men. Renewal means God's intervention to bring the church back to His original plan. When the church is slowing down or falling asleep, Christ uses the Holy Spirit to readjust the steps of His church to speed up our walk in accordance to His eternal will.

WHAT IS REVIVAL?

REVIVAL IS THE PROCESS OF A DYNAMIC CHURCH IN THE MAKING

It is the process of transforming the church from weakness and disability into strength and dynamic activity by the power of the Holy Spirit.

REVIVAL IS A REAFFIRMATION OF FAITH AND ACTION

The church should claim the supreme authority and sovereignty of God in the universe and His church.

We should also claim the authority of the Bible as the divine revelation which is inerrantly revealed to His church. The Bible is the only source through which we can come to the true knowledge of God and man. The Bible is the criteria for our faith and conduct; only through the Bible do we know how to worship God and how to be saved by Him; only through the Bible can we see how the problems of mankind can be solved. Neither by secular psychology nor modern science, which are inadequate, can the world have true hope. This can be found by His Word alone.

We should reaffirm the authority, finality, and incomparable uniqueness of Jesus Christ and His salvation. Jesus Christ is the only way, the only truth, and the only life who brings us to God. This is the greatest claim in the history of mankind! Asia has produced the great religions, whereas Europe has produced the great schools of philosophy to discover truth—yet we see that finally all of them turn to relativism and skepticism. Did not the great schools of Greek philosophy and Roman civilization end up in the question of Pontius Pilate when he asked Jesus, "What is truth?" Pilate's question indicated that even the long line of Greek tradition, all the Socratic definitions, Platonic idealism, and Aristotelian logic gave no answer. Even the Hellenistic search ended up in skepticism. Only Jesus gives finality to the answer for truth. That is the reason we must stand up and claim this affirmation of the truth to the world.

REVIVAL IS A NORMALIZATION OF CHRISTIAN PRAYERS

To pray is one of the greatest privileges we have; to pray is to submit ourselves before His sovereignty; to pray is also to declare our finiteness before the infinite God.

Prayer is the key to true revival. Normalization of Christian prayer will produce normalization of the Christian's relationship with God. Let us pray together through the merit of our Lord! God will revive us with power to reconcile ourselves with God, ourselves with ourselves, ourselves with others, others with others, and the world with God. This kind of revival will be seen in the effort of true evangelization.

REVIVAL IS A RENEWAL OF CHRISTIAN MINISTRY

It is not through our talents, efforts, or experiences that we can accomplish God's work and do God's will, but through His own Spirit and His anointing alone. In our ministry, we need the renewal of our calling, lest we go astray and walk in our own ways. We need the renewal of our vision to make us see clearly our task and responsibility. And we need the renewal of our conscience so that we can serve Him with pure hearts.

REVIVAL MEANS RECONSTRUCTION OF THE CHRISTIAN SOCIAL CONSCIENCE

The church of Jesus Christ should pick up once again the deep concern for social problems. Theology is knowing God, in addition to knowing the salvation of God. We should also know about His attributes, His nature of love and righteousness. The church should establish the righteousness of God in the society and also practice the love of God in the world. When revival occurs, society will be changed and the needy will be taken care of. The pulpit of the church will become the conscience of the society, and the world will become our mission field. Nevertheless, this is a secondary need next to the primary need of salvation in Jesus Christ.

REVIVAL IS RE-FIRING THE EVANGELISTIC EFFORTS OF THE CHURCH

In revival we receive fire again from heaven to evangelize. Only through evangelization can the church grow healthily. Some think that evangelization is the cause of continuous revival. In evangelization we experience the reality of the presence of Jesus Christ. This is promised in His Great Commission. A hundred years after the founding of the China Inland Mission (now the Overseas Missionary Fellowship), that organization celebrated its one-hundredth anniversary by singing the song "Let the Fire Burn On." It touched me with tears because I know that all of them have been cast out of Communist China, yet they still prayed to be refired with divine love from Calvary to bring forth the gospel and salvation to mankind until the end of the world.

REVIVAL IS THE REFRESHING OF BODY LIFE

In revival we are re-anointed with the spiritual gifts to serve one another, creating better acceptance within the Body of Christ. We are created differently, and to some extent, unequally; however, we should accept one another. By mutual acceptance, we show forth God's love. In His love we can understand and edify one another. All these tell us what revival is. By the body life being refreshed, the church will be made more perfect, more powerful, and more efficient in testifying to and glorifying Christ in the world.

WHAT KIND OF REVIVAL DO WE NEED?

A DOCTRINAL REVIVAL

So many churches despise or fail to see the importance of doctrinal revival. It is one of the most pitiful things in the church today. If the church does not keep sound doctrine, the church will totally fall into the hands of Satan. Let us always remember the days of the apostles, the church Fathers, the apologists, Augustine, the Reformers, and the days of all great and faithful servants of God in church history, who courageously fought against wrong teachings, cults, and heresies even until their blood was shed, in order to keep the church on the right path of faith. The Reformers did not establish any new doctrines for the church; they only taught the church to go back to the Bible and to the original faith according to the Apostles' Creed. This is the greatness of all faithful teachers of all times, because only by solid teaching of the Bible can we stand and fight against all kinds of wrong ideology, philosophy, and doctrines.

AN ETHICAL REVIVAL

Besides a doctrinal revival to reaffirm our true faith, we also need a manifestation of true life. True faith must be manifested in true living and good work. As we put on our "new man" as created in the image of God, we should manifest holiness, righteousness, and the truth of God in our daily living to prove that we belong to Him and witness of Him in this world. Otherwise, to evangelize non-Christians is impossible. So many people do not want to be Christians simply because many Christians are even more wicked than they. True revival always produces true ethical change immediately.

AN EVANGELIZING REVIVAL

Revival means mobilizing the whole congregation to witness for the Lord. How do you feel when you hear that 90 percent of Communist Party members are working very hard for their ideology, whereas 90 percent of church members are sleeping? How dare we say that we are the children of God and witnesses of Jesus Christ? Let us pray that God will give us the power to mobilize our people so that every reborn Christian will take part and practice the gift of the Holy Spirit in his life in order to share his faith with others.

A REVIVAL OF CHRIST AS LORD

The resurrected Christ must be Lord of the living church. The resurrected Christ has been given all power in heaven and earth, and lives to be Lord not only of the church but King of kings throughout the universe. Jesus Christ must be preeminent in all aspects of culture. We need a revival where all thrones submit before the throne of Christ, and all powers surrender to the power of Christ. Through His victory we will gain key persons in politics, philosophy, education, art, and in all other important fortresses of the culture in order to submit them before the Creator. May human reasons, understandings, and powers of knowing the truth, together with all things created by God, submit before Him, that Jesus Christ will be claimed as the King of mankind!

What Is the Cost of Revival?

Since revival is not achieved by the efforts of men but initiated by God Himself, revival is therefore the grace of God. Yet the grace of God is free but not cheap! It means that we must pay the cost. By His grace we should stand up and fight against false revival, which is not from God and is not scriptural. We must not be satisfied by gimmicks and the superficial, nor by the emotional stimulation of mass psychology. We must not be satisfied nor deceived by dishonest reports of many so-called Christian workers. We must also not be satisfied by shallow and unrooted teachings in the Body of Christ today. Let us pray with total submission to Christ, anticipate true revival from the Holy Spirit, and be prepared to pay the cost.

FULL SURRENDER TO THE WORD OF GOD

First full surrender to the Word of God is the basic cost of revival. There is no other way to establish our faith; we cannot choose what we want to believe; we cannot select only some parts of the Bible to please ourselves. Faith is faithfulness to the truth (fidelity). What is "truth"? Jesus said in John 17:17: "Sanctify them by the truth; your word is truth."

We must pay the cost of submitting our reason before the revelation of God, searching for the truth of the Bible, and diligently studying the Scriptures together with accurate interpretation of the Word. May the content of God's Word in our sermons become richer and richer, so that those who are hungry and thirsty after truth can be filled and the emptiness of their hearts can be satisfied. Unshakable faith can be established through solid and systematic teaching in the church. I hope to see people come for the truth of God rather than for story-telling, experience-sharing, or curiosity of the performance of divine healing. Let us reestablish solid epistemology of God's revelation in His church.

We should base our ministry on biblical principle and establish a kind of circle in our ministry. We should turn our apologetics from a defensive attitude into one which seizes the offensive. If apologetics fail to win people to the Lord, I think there must be something wrong in that kind of apologetics. Apologetics should be the servant of evangelization. We are not only to proclaim the good news of Jesus Christ to the world, but also to present the reasonableness of believing in Him. We must be willing and able to show the unreasonableness of rejecting Christ and to challenge sinners to accept the gospel.

An apologetic that seizes the offensive will make evangelization dynamic. This kind of biblical, theological, and enterprising evangelization will make the church strong. Theology without evangelization is dead, and evangelization without theology is weak. We cannot have flesh without bones or bones without flesh. Man with flesh without bones will fall down. Man with skeleton and bones without flesh will be scary. Praise the Lord! He has given us the most solid teaching in the world, which is unchangeable, unshakable, forever and ever. Our faith cannot be shaken by modern discoveries in science because God is truth and the source of all truth in the world, and all truth is God's truth. Let us be courageous and steadfast before the world and before all of our enemies with confidence.

MASS TRAINING FOR EVANGELIZATION

Second, we should have mass training for evangelization. I see an imbalance happening in theological studies in recent years. So many seminaries are upgrading their academic studies but losing their zeal for souls. Why should we sacrifice our concern for sinners simply because we are getting more and more academic? Why should we move ourselves further away from societies and lose our sensitivity to the cry of unreached souls? They need Christ badly even when they do not feel it. This is the paradox of preaching the gospel. Let the training of evangelization reach more and more people. We must search over and over again to discover what the hindrances and obstacles are to effective evangelism; we must apply again and again those methods of winning people to the Lord that are the most efficient. And let all truly regenerated Christians who have experienced the power of the Holy Spirit share the gospel with others. Let all Christian leaders, church pastors, theological lecturers, and Christian educators or teachers renew their vision and burden for evangelization as part of their task. And let all churches open up their classes for more and more people to be trained in evangelization.

FULL-TIME WORKERS

Third, we should establish the value of being full-time workers. What is the reason that the most intelligent and qualified young people of our churches turn to computers and businesses more willingly than to be used by the Lord? Isn't it most valuable to serve the Lord? Why are people not ready for this? Why are their concepts confused? It is because they do not see the true value of being a minister. The Lord of lords and King of kings deserves the best among the young people to serve Him. The church leaders of this generation must be able to challenge the best of the younger generation to respond to the calling of God for full-time workers. During more than two decades of my ministry, there have been more than twenty thousand people who dedicated themselves to be full-time workers in my meetings. Last year, more than twelve hundred people dedicated themselves to the Lord in one meeting when I preached in Jakarta. Here in Korea, I encourage myself to pray before God, asking Him to call ten million young people to be servants of God for the coming ten years. Do you think that is a big number? Definitely not! It is less than one percent of the total of 1.3 billion Christians in the world. I'm shouting and crying that we would pray together for this.

THE CHALLENGE TO POTENTIAL LEADERS

Fourth, we should challenge the potential leaders of our society to submit themselves before the throne of Jesus Christ. Kenneth Scott Latourette, the great church historian of our day, who once served as a missionary in China, touched me so much when I read of his saying, "If Mao Tse-tung had been in my class in Zian, China would never have been like this." It is pitiful that Darwin, Marx, Hegel, and Nietzsche had all been seminarians before they turned from the church. We must not wait again; with faith and the power of the Holy Spirit, we must challenge the key persons of future society to submit themselves before God even in their campus days now. Let them realize that there is no key to solve the problems of mankind besides Jesus Christ.

Communism can never solve the problems of the world; dialectical materialism fails to see the total aspect of man's need. It cannot even solve the material needs of man. It can only equalize people into poverty, but it cannot equalize them into plenty. The inadequacy of the materialistic world view will leave emptiness in the human heart.

Existentialism is not able to solve the problems of man either. It did destroy some of the strongest fortresses in Western culture and has discovered the existential sphere in human life, but it has failed to answer the questions it has raised. There is no escape from the anxiety of a threatening power of existence. I define this philosophy in two sentences: The existentialists discuss emptiness as if emptiness exists, and they discuss existence as if existence did not exist. They turn existence into emptiness and emptiness into existence.

Likewise, logical positivism or atheistic psychology of the Freudian school and others are all self-defeating. Actually, all human effort since the Renaissance Enlightenment until now have failed to present the perfect ideas, efficient methods, and sufficient power to save mankind.

May God show us and the world more and more clearly that the only hope of the world is Jesus Christ! Our faith in Jesus Christ is supra-cultural; He transcends all the ideologies and all the religions of the world because only God, the One who created man, has the answer for everything.

May the church grow continually through our obedience to

Him. Through the grace of God we must pay the cost in prayer and evangelization, which is not only the *result* of revival but is the secret of *continuous* revival. Let us repent before God for our laziness, ignorance, and unfaithfulness, and rededicate ourselves to be purified servants and vessels in His hands, witnesses of Jesus Christ until His return.

6

The Sin of Judging:
A Hindrance to Revival

Joy Dawson

Joy Dawson serves on the staff of Youth With A Mission. Her Bible teaching ministry takes her to many nations on every continent of the world. Her deep prayer life and intense knowledge of the Scriptures give depth and authority to her messages.

God has laid upon my heart a message for spiritual leaders about judging. You may be wondering, "What in the world has this subject to do with prayer for world evangelization? Our main focus is to pray for revival as it relates to world evangelism."

But one of the greatest hindrances to answered prayer is the sin of God's people. And one of the most prevalent sins in the Body of Christ, worldwide, is the sin of judging. One of the greatest costs of revival is the church of God humbling themselves in relation to specific sin.

Even if we have come to the place where we have ceased to judge others verbally, I believe there is a tremendous amount of sin in judging others in our thought life. And the Word of God says, "As [a man] thinketh in his heart, so is he" (Prov. 23:7, KJV*). We are only as free from the sin of judging others as our thought life is pure.

In the gospel of John we read, "Stop judging by mere appearances, and make a right judgment" (John 7:24).

*King James Version.

Righteous Judgment

What is "right judgment"? In the Bible we are told that prophecy is to be judged and sin is to be judged.

PROPHECY IS TO BE JUDGED

There are judgments we need to make if we are to be wise and not tossed here and there by everything someone says is true. Paul instructed, "Do not put out the Spirit's fire; do not treat prophecies with contempt. Test everything. Hold on to the good. Avoid every kind of evil" (1 Thess. 5:19-22). Paul is here encouraging us to be open to the Holy Spirit's moving or working in new ways; but at the same time, we are supposed to "test"—meaning to make a considered, well-investigated judgment—what is put forth as from God (prophecies).

This is not a Lone Ranger operation but involves the whole Body of Christ. "Two or three prophets should speak, and the others should weigh carefully what is said" (1 Cor. 14:29). Testing in this manner is making right judgments.

SIN IS TO BE JUDGED

As Jesus said, we are not supposed to judge by appearances, but we are supposed to make right judgments. And in his first letter to the Corinthians, Paul makes it very clear that making judgments includes addressing sin in the church:

- 1 Cor. 5:1-5:—Paul chastised the Corinthians for tolerating sexual immorality in their fellowship; instead of being proud of their tolerance, they should have passed judgment and "put out of [their] fellowship the man who did this" (v. 2).
- 1 Cor. 5:11-13:—Paul made it clear that it's the church's business to judge sin among themselves—not passing judgment on those outside the church. "God will judge those outside" (v. 13).
- 1 Cor. 6:1-6:—Paul also made it clear that disputes within the church should be judged within the church—not going to court. He said we have the wisdom and authority to do this: "Do you not know that the saints will judge the world? And if you are to judge the world, are you not competent to judge trivial cases?" (v. 2).

But while judging sin is part of our task within the church, there are some cautions: "Do not entertain an accusation against an elder unless it is brought by two or three witnesses. Those who sin are to be rebuked publicly, so that the others may take warning" (1 Tim. 5:19-20). In other words, right judgment involves careful consideration and thorough investigation—not hasty conclusions based on hearsay.

UNRIGHTEOUS JUDGMENT

What is "wrong judgment"? Wrong judgment is reaching a conclusion without enough knowledge of the facts to make a righteous judgment.

We need to be reminded that only God has 100 percent knowledge of the facts in every situation. No wonder James tells us, "Do not criticize one another, my brothers. Whoever criticizes a Christian brother, or judges him, criticizes the Law and judges it. . . . Who do you think you are, to judge your fellow-man?" (James 4:11-12, TEV*). Paul also warned, "You, therefore, have no excuse, you who pass judgment on someone else, for at whatever point you judge the other, you are condemning yourself, because you who pass judgment do the same things" (Rom. 2:1).

These are black and white truths. Unless we have enough knowledge of the facts and unless we are in a position of spiritual leadership to deal with a brother or sister in error, we have no right to form a conclusion or to make a comment. We are not in a position of authority, according to the Word of God, to judge that situation.

How can we apply this word about judging in a practical way?

JUDGING ANOTHER'S MOTIVES

Another Christian makes a move, marries someone, goes to another job, joins another church, buys another house, goes to another city or country—and we in our ignorance or disobedience to revealed truth immediately form our conclusion and make negative comments to others. But what in actual fact have we done in relation to the sin of judging?

If in thought or word we have said, "I don't think they should

Today's English Version, Third Edition.

have done that," from God's point of view we have actually said, "They have rejected the revealed will of God." Or, second, we are saying, "They haven't sought God at all to know what His will is." Or, third, "They haven't heard or obeyed what He said."

That's pretty heavy judgment. But it's happening all the time all over the world—millions of Christians are sitting in judgment.

There are many times that we do not understand why others in the Body of Christ do what they do. We should say, "I do not understand why they have gone there or haven't gone there. But I believe they are sincere, as I am, to do the will of God. And therefore, I trust them." And if we cannot say that the other Christian is as sincere as we are to do the will the God, we have elevated ourselves in pride. So the sin of pride is underneath the sin of judgment. It is unrighteous judgment.

JUDGING ANOTHER'S SIN

Let's say we know firsthand that someone has definitely sinned; we have all the facts. Five minutes before we have judged them and spoken about their sin to somebody else, they could have repented. And who are we to be judging what the blood of Jesus Christ has cleansed and forgiven?

The classic example of this in the Bible is the woman caught in the act of adultery and brought to Jesus. I do not believe there was a long period of time between her act of adultery and standing in front of Jesus. Why did Jesus speak against the people who had judged her? And why did He say to the woman, "Neither do I condemn you. . . . Go now and leave your life of sin"? (John 8:11)

Does Jesus condone adultery? Of course not. But obviously this woman had repented of her sin between the act and her standing before the sinless Son of God, whereas her accusers had not repented of the sins of immorality in their lives—either in their thought lives or their words or their deeds.

JUDGING ANOTHER'S RESPONSE—OR LACK OF IT

We often judge someone because they didn't speak to us, or didn't take enough time to be with us, or failed to respond in the way we wanted them to. But I'm going to give you six reasons why a person may not always respond as we wish.

1. The person may never have seen me in the first place. That can very easily happen in crowds. Because he was concentrating on a conversation with another person, he may not have seen me even if there were no crowd.
2. The person may not have been well physically and therefore was not able to communicate at that point.
3. The person could have been under some emotional strain or could have been struggling with a problem.
4. The person could have been loaded with heavy responsibilities that required focused attention.
5. The person was in great haste and could not stop to speak.
6. The person was just plain exhausted and couldn't take talking to one more person. He may have been what I call "peopled out."

Rather than judge the person who is in any of these categories by saying that he or she was cold or proud, we need to say, "God show me my pride because I didn't get the attention that I felt was due me under those circumstances."

JUDGING MATERIAL POSSESSIONS

We often judge when we see someone with material possessions—food or clothing or home or furniture or a car—and assume their priorities are in the wrong place. We are not aware of the steps of obedience and faith which God may be rewarding.

How ridiculous to judge people when God may be rewarding them because they have depth of commitment, they believe Him for the impossible, they've been taking enormous steps of obedience and faith, and they have given up all their rights, saying, "Lord, I'll go where You want me to go—to any country, in any climate, under any conditions. I'll do anything You want me to do, regardless of whether I have any money or not." Because that's what He's like! When God sees we will obey Him, not for what we get, but for who He is, then He says, "I'm going to reward you." Not right away because God tests His children, but in His own way and in His time there will be privileges from God, there will be rewards from God, and best of all there will be friendship with God.

Another Christian comes along and says, "What are you doing with that bonus? I'm over here being deprived and you've over there having fun." They are resentful and say God is not judging fairly. To make it worse, God then judges with punishment the one who is judging!

Now this doesn't mean that a person with a lot of possessions always has them because of commitment or obedience or faith or relinquishing of rights. People under the devil's control can also have many possessions.

But this is one area where we are not to judge another Christian. God told Jeremiah, "I the Lord search the heart and examine the mind, to reward a man according to his conduct, according to what his deeds deserve (Jer. 17:10). And in Matthew 25:14-30, Jesus made it clear in the parable about the talents that the man who has deep levels of commitment, obedience, and faith, and who has relinquished his rights, is actually given more by God than the man who maintains a shallow level of those things.

When God gives a ministry to a person, in His way and in His time He also releases the necessary equipment and staff and finances to enable him to fulfill that ministry.

Unfortunately, not many Christians desire money or possessions for stewardship responsibilities. Few have said, "God, I want you to give me great possessions in order to have greater stewardship responsibility and to enable me to give greatly to you." So many Christians say, "I want to make more money for God," because they want to make more money and give some money to God.

But I stress again: it is a sin to judge someone else's steps of obedience and faith. When people heard that my husband and I were taking off again to three more nations around the world, they could well have said, "It's incredible, that couple traveling the world over. There's no way that they could go a week in Korea, a week in Hong Kong, and a week in China without it costing at least $5,000. They are doing it all the time. Who can travel the world like that, as well as pay all the costs of maintaining their house in Los Angeles, without being wealthy?"

The facts are that thirty-six hours before we had to catch the plane to Korea, we were $2,000 short. And not one single person in the world, including our own children, knew anything about it, except God. We had absolutely no idea in the world where the money was going to come from. But we had sought God's face months and months before about going to the International Prayer Assembly in Seoul, and He said *go.* So in faith we had taken the next step to declare that we would be there.

We made our hotel and airplane bookings and told people to please meet us at the airport. Our responsibility was to seek His face, hear His voice, and obey—regardless of money. It was entirely God's responsibility to come through with the money. Our testimony is that there has never been a source that God has used more than once to supply our needs, to tempt us to depend on it. God's source has always been a total surprise every time.

Thirty-six hours before leaving we had a phone call from an individual also attending the prayer assembly. She asked, "Have you got your money for this trip?" I said "No." She said, "I believe that God has told me to phone you and ask how much you are short." Now listen to the timing of God. At that exact moment, my husband, who didn't know what I was doing, was just working out the amount that we still owed. He was still working out the figures when my friend said, "And how much do you owe?" My husband looked up and said, "Around $2,000 for the barest minimum, not even the taxi fares."

The split second timing of God is tremendous. Yes, our ministry takes us around the world—but we don't know in advance where the money will come from.

JUDGING PEOPLE'S PROBLEMS

We look at people in tragedy or who are in the midst of adverse circumstances, and we judge: "Oh, that's because they've sinned." They may have sinned; they may not have sinned.

What if people had looked at Joseph and said, "He must have sinned. That's why he's down in the pit. That's why he's having problems in Potiphar's house. That's why he's in prison." These tragedies had nothing to do with his sin. He was being tested and prepared by God.

Don't judge the person in adverse circumstances. He could be a Joseph in the making.

God Will Judge

GOD WILL VINDICATE THOSE WRONGLY JUDGED

God is going to vindicate the person if we're wrong in our judgment—and, unless we have sufficient knowledge of the facts, we are wrong! " 'No weapon forged against you will prevail, and you will refute every tongue that accuses you. This is the heritage of the servants of the Lord, and this is their vindication from me,' declares the Lord" (Isa. 54:17).

God did just this for some who were falsely accused in Joshua 22. First a little background.

Before Israel went across the Jordan River, the Reubenites, the Gadites, and the half-tribe of Manasseh wanted to settle on the east bank. Joshua said, "All right, but first you must come across the Jordan with the rest of your brothers [the other nine and a half tribes] to conquer the land. You can settle down when we can all settle down." So it was agreed.

When all the battles had been fought and won, and "The Lord gave Israel all the land he had sworn to give their forefathers, and they took possession of it and settled there. . . . Then Joshua summoned the Reubenites, the Gadites and the half-tribe of Manasseh and said to them, 'You have done all that Moses the servant of the Lord commanded, and you have obeyed my voice in everything I commanded. . . . [Now] return to your homes in the land that Moses the servant of the Lord gave you on the other side of the Jordan" (Josh. 21:43; 22:1-2, 4).

Note that Joshua commended these two and a half tribes for faithfulness and obedience. Usually that means you get full marks from God, right? And merit some trust from your brothers and sisters, right? But see what happened.

On their way home, this group set up a large altar to the Lord at the edge of the River Jordan, so that in the days to come their children would see the altar as a sign marking their obedience to God at this stage in their lives and witnessing that they were under the blessings of God. And every time their children would go past the heap of stone it would remind them of obedience and blessing.

But then an incredible thing happened. When the larger group on the west side of the Jordan heard about the new altar, "the whole assembly of Israel gathered at Shiloh to go to war against them" (22:12). To their credit, a delegation of spiritual leaders, headed by Phinehas son of Eleazar the priest, were sent ahead of the war party to accuse them personally. " 'How could you break faith with the God of Israel like this? How could you turn away from the Lord and build yourselves an altar in rebellion against him now?' " (22:16).

They did not inquire *why* they built the altar. They assumed an altar other than the one in the Tabernacle was an act of rebellion against the Lord.

The Reubenites, the Gadites, and the half-tribe of Manasseh hastened to explain that the altar wasn't meant to be a place of worship, but a "replica" of the Lord's altar, a "witness" that they, too, were God's chosen people even though they were living on the east side of the Jordan. The delegation was pleased with their explanation, and the two and a half tribes were vindicated. Scripture says, "And they talked no more about going to war against them" (22:33).

SPIRITUAL LEADERS MUST LEAD IN JUDGING RIGHTLY

It's interesting to note that the same Phinehas who jumped to hasty conclusions in this case, was the same spiritual leader who had been used by God to righteously judge the sin of immorality involving a leader in Israel and a Midianite woman (see Num. 25).

The warning from God to spiritual leaders today is this: We may have been used of God to judge righteously and expose sins, but in all situations we must be seeking God to know God's mind with regard to other people. Without first finding the facts, without inquiring to know that what we have heard is true, we can actually lead the people under our leadership to wrongly judge another in the Body of Christ.

GOD JUDGES US AS WE JUDGE OTHERS

Judging others unrighteously carries with it its own judgment. Jesus made this clear in the Sermon on the Mount when He said, "Do not judge, or you too will be judged. For in the same way you judge others, you will be judged, and with the measure you use, it will be measured to you' " (Matt. 7:1-2). God will judge us by the same criteria with which we judge others.

Instead of pointing fingers at others, we would do well to examine ourselves. Paul warned the Corinthians not to eat the bread and drink the cup of The Lord's Supper "in an unworthy manner," observing that "a man ought to examine himself" first (1 Cor. 11:27-28). He went on to say, " If we judged ourselves, we would not come under judgment. When we are judged by the Lord, we are being disciplined so that we will not be condemned with the world" (1 Cor. 11:31-32). In other words, we need to be judging our own actions in order to avoid a greater judgment from God, and also, we need to accept God's judgment along the way, here and now, as helpful discipline.

All of us face judgment. Paul reminds us, "You, then, why do you judge your brother? Or why do you look down on your brother? For we will all stand before God's judgment seat. . . . So then, each of us will give an account of himself to God" (Rom. 14:10, 12). Our brother or sister will have to give account of himself or herself; we will each have to face our own music.

JUDGING REVEALS OUR TRUE SELVES

When we judge others, we show what we're really like. "For at whatever point you judge the other, you are condemning yourself, because you who pass judgment do the same things" (Rom. 2:1).

My aunt once said, "If you want to know what I'm like, listen to what I say about others." I never once heard her criticize anyone.

Jesus said, "Out of the overflow of the heart the mouth speaks" (Matt. 12:34). When we criticize, when we judge hastily, when we speak against another to someone else, our words expose the jealousy, envy, lack of love, resentment, unforgiving spirit, and a pride which says, "I'd never do that!" When we judge unrighteous-ly, we expose our lack of seeking God, our refusal to give Him a chance to say what He thinks about a person or situation.

IT WILL ALL COME OUT

We do not have to be anxious that sin will triumph, that we have to rush in with judgment. Whereas we cannot know perfectly, God knows the heart—your heart, my heart, this person's heart, that person's heart. Paul realized that "it is the Lord who judges me. Therefore judge nothing before the appointed time; wait till the Lord comes. He will bring to light what is hidden in darkness and will expose the motives of men's hearts. At that time each will receive his praise from God" (1 Cor. 4:4-5).

That God will judge with truth and righteousness should not cause us to fear. He is a God of justice, and also of mercy. "He who conceals his sins does not prosper," said the writer of Proverbs, "*but whoever confesses and renounces them finds mercy*" (Prov. 28:13; emphasis added).

I challenge you, as God challenges me every day, to dare to live by the standard of God's Word—not by the standard of other spiritual leaders. If we live by these words, it will stop a great deal of criticism and unite the Body of Christ so that the world may be evangelized according to Jesus' prayer to the Father: "May they be brought to complete unity to let the world know that you sent me and have loved them even as you have loved me" (John 17:23).

Part 2

Learning How to Pray

7

Prayer: The Why and How

Harold Lindsell

Dr. Harold Lindsell is editor-emeritus of Christianity
Today *and a former professor of church history and missions. He is an author of a number of publications as well.*

I want to start, not by discussing prayer, but by giving attention to the importance of the Bible. The reason I do this is very simple: the only way we know how to pray is by reading the Bible. The only reason we should pray is because the Bible says to. The only way we can know what happens when we pray is to read the Bible. Are you a reader of the Bible?

Of course, it is not enough to read the Bible; you must also understand the Bible. The Bible says that the Holy Spirit is our teacher. If you read the Bible and you want to know what the Bible means, you ask the Holy Spirit to help you. When you do that, you are praying.

Not only must I read the Bible and understand it. I must obey the Bible. That being the case, what are some of the important things the Bible tells me to do?

- The Bible tells me that I must not neglect the assembling of myself together with other Christians. This means that I need to be a church member and go to church regularly if I am to obey the Bible.
- The Bible tells me that I should observe baptism and the Lord's Supper.
- The Bible also commands me to tithe.

- The very same Bible that tells me to do these things also commands me to pray.

WHY WE SHOULD PRAY

We should pray because we are commanded to pray. I should pray because Jesus takes it for granted that His followers everywhere will pray. In Matthew 6:5 Jesus said, "When you pray. . . ." By this He knew that all faithful Jews prayed regularly—at least three times a day.

We should pray because it is our way of communicating with God. God speaks to you through the Bible, if you are not reading the Bible, you won't hear God speak. But through prayer we speak to God. God wants to have a two-way conversation with each of us. We hear Him when we read the Word of God, and He hears us when we pray to Him. Reading the Bible and praying go together.

We should pray because God hears and answers prayer. In John 14:14 Jesus said, "You may ask me for anything in my name, and I will do it." Therefore when we pray we say, "in the name of Jesus," or "in Jesus' name, Amen." That is the name that opens the gates of Heaven. That is the name of the person who *never* told a lie. He gives us the assurance that God hears and answers prayer.

A MODEL FOR PRAYER

Jesus told His disciples that they ought to pray, but they had a problem. Even though prayer was common for them, they realized that they didn't know how to pray properly. Therefore, they said to Jesus "Teach us [how] to pray" (Luke 11:1). Jesus' answer was what we call the Lord's Prayer:

> Our Father in heaven, hallowed be your name, your kingdom come, your will be done on earth as it is in heaven. Give us today our daily bread. Forgive us our debts, as we also have forgiven our debtors. And lead us not into temptation, but deliver us from the evil one. [For yours is the kingdom and the power and the glory forever. Amen.] (Matt. 6:9-13; in the NIV* the portion in brackets is given only in the margin; cf. Luke 11:2-4).

* *New International Version.*

The Bible teaches that there are five components of prayer. If you follow the model of the Lord's Prayer, you will find all five elements for the prayers we are supposed to pray.

1. *Adoration.* The first prayer we are supposed to pray is the prayer of admiration and worship of God. That's why we say, "Our Father in heaven, hallowed be your name."

2. *Thanksgiving.* The second kind of prayer we are supposed to pray is the prayer of thanksgiving. There are many examples of this in Scripture. Although it is not obvious in the Lord's Prayer, the concluding sentence, "For yours is the kingdom and the power and the glory forever," is a thanksgiving and praise for who God is.

3. *Confession.* The third kind of prayer we are supposed to pray is the prayer of confession of sins. Here, of course, the phrase, "Forgive us our debts, as we also have forgiven our debtors" fits quite obviously.

   Let me note that this is one prayer that you can be absolutely certain will be answered. God has promised in His Word that "If we confess our sins, he is faithful and just, and will forgive our sins and purify us from all unrighteousness" (1 John 1:9). When we confess, He buries our sin behind His back to be remembered against us no more. He buries them in the deepest part of the deepest sea. Isn't it wonderful to have the assurance of the forgiveness of sin by prayer?

4. *Petition.* The fourth kind of prayer is the prayer of petition in which we ask for things for ourselves and for our own life. "Give us today our daily bread," and "lead us not into temptation, but deliver us from the evil one" fit here.

5. *Intercession.* The fifth kind of prayer is the prayer of intercession. In the prayer of intercession, I may pray for you, and you may pray for me, but we are also to pray for the spreading of the gospel. That is why in the Lord's Prayer we are instructed to ask: "Your kingdom come, your will be done on earth as it is in heaven."

I want to communicate something very important concerning these five elements of prayer. When you and I get to glory with Jesus, three of these prayers we will never pray again. We will never need to confess sins, because we will commit no sin. We will never ask God to heal our bodies, because our bodies will be perfect. And we will not need to intercede for one another, because everyone will have everything he or she needs.

So our prayers throughout the endless ages will be prayers of adoration to God, whom we adore, and of thanksgiving to Him for what He has done. We will never cease to pray because we will always be grateful to God, and we will be adoring and worshiping Him throughout the ages.

JESUS, OUR EXAMPLE IN PRAYER

You learn to pray by practice. The more you pray, the better you will be able to pray. When it comes to the practice of prayer, we have a perfect example in Jesus. So we ask ourselves, "How did Jesus pray?" If we pray the way Jesus prayed, we will have a great prayer life.

PRAYER WAS IMPORTANT TO HIM

In Luke 6:12, the Scripture says that He "continued all night in prayer to God" (NKJV*). He did this before He appointed the twelve disciples to follow Him. If Jesus had to pray before doing something like that, how much more do you and I need to pray before we go any place or do anything.

EVEN JESUS, THE SON OF GOD, HAD TO ASK

Do you remember that Jesus said, "Ask and it will be given to you; seek and you will find; knock and the door will be opened to you" (Matt. 7:7)? When Jesus said that, He was saying something else as well. He was saying that the way to get answers to prayer is to ask. Conversely, if you don't ask, you won't receive! Don't ask me why God has ordained it that way, but He has. I only read the Bible, I don't change it.

The apostle James picked up this same refrain. He said, "You do not have, because you do not ask God" (James 4:2). This tells us that we are always to ask.

JESUS BELIEVED HIS FATHER HEARD HIM

When Jesus was in the Garden of Gethsemane, He prayed, "My Father, if it is possible, may this cup be taken from me. Yet not as I

* *New King James Version.*

will, but as you will" (Matt. 26:39). He believed His Father would hear Him and help Him. He prayed in faith. As a matter of fact, even later when He had accepted that the cup was God's will, He declared His belief that if He would ask, God would still deliver Him. In Matthew 26:53 He said this: "Do you think I cannot call on my Father, and he will at once put at my disposal more than twelve legions of angels?"

Consider this: if Jesus could call twelve legions of angels to help Him, think of what God can do for us. The angels are ministering spirits sent forth to help us. If we could draw aside the curtain that separates us from the unseen world, we would see angels around us all the time. God can send His angels to help us.

If you are to have an effective prayer life, there is something about which you must make a decision. Do you believe God will hear your prayer? Do you believe God will help you? Can you claim the promise in faith before the answer comes? I think the problem with most of us is that we don't have the faith to believe that God can do even more than we want.

I was speaking in a Baptist church in Boston recently. They sang a chorus which went like this.

> All I have needed, He hath provided.
> All I have needed, He hath provided.

They sang it about five times, and I said to myself, "It's better than that. It's 'More than I needed, He hath provided,' " because He provides exceeding abundantly above all that we can ask or even think. But most of us don't really believe that He provides even all that we need.

When I was a freshman in college, I lost my fountain pen. It was in the days of the Great Depression, and I had no money. I was walking across a field where I thought I might have lost it, and being young I said, "Lord help me find my fountain pen." I walked across that field, and there in front of my face was my fountain pen. God is interested in fountain pens as well as anything else. He wants me to come to Him in everything!

Of course, as with Jesus' example in the Garden of Gethsemane, not all of God's answers are yes. There are three ways that God answers prayer. He may say yes, He may say later, and He may say no.

PAUL IN PRAYER

Another example of prayer may be seen in the life of Paul. In 2 Corinthians 11:23-27 Paul reviews all his sufferings—such things as numerous floggings, a stoning, three shipwrecks, constant danger, hunger, and a lack of adequate clothing. The obvious question is: didn't Paul pray that those circumstances would be changed? I'm sure he did. In Philippians 4:6 he said, "In everything, by prayer and petition, with thanksgiving, present your requests to God." He was a man who took his own advice, so I'm sure that when he faced things as serious as the list of sufferings in 2 Corinthians, he prayed about them. Why didn't God grant his requests? Well, in many cases He did, or Paul would have been dead long before, because many situations he faced were truly life threatening. But there were also some circumstances in which the difficulties brought glory to God or furthered the gospel. For Paul to have insisted that he not have any problems would have been a truly selfish prayer.

As with Jesus, Paul prayed with an openness to accepting God's will in the matter.

WHAT GOD CAN DO WHEN WE PRAY

I want to review for you several situations in which people did pray, and God changed the circumstances. Praying with an openness to God's will does not mean that we view life fatalistically. God wants us to ask.

SENNACHERIB KING OF ASSYRIA

Sennacherib invaded Judah, seized gold and silver, and made King Hezekiah pay tribute money. At first Hezekiah sought the help of Egypt. But Sennacherib sent a messenger to Jerusalem with a threatening message. The letter was insulting. It called upon Hezekiah to surrender before he was killed. Finally, Hezekiah took the letter and laid it before the Lord God Almighty. In 2 Kings 19:15 the Bible says: "Hezekiah prayed to the Lord." He let God know what the problem was and asked for divine help.

Do you remember what happened? God sent an angel—just one angel—but an angel with mighty power. And that angel of God slew 185,000 soldiers of Sennacherib in one night. If one angel can do that, just think what our God who has infinite power can do. Sennacherib fled to Nineveh, where he was killed by his own sons and could no longer harm Judah.

JEHOSHAPHAT

Jehoshaphat also illustrates the power of God through prayer. Let me review his story. He was the king of Judah. Three enemies got together—the Moabites, Ammonites, and Edomites—and they went to war against Jehoshaphat. The people knew they would be defeated unless they had help. So they turned to God.

The Bible says: "The people of Judah came together to seek help from the Lord; indeed, they came from every town in Judah to seek him" (2 Chron. 20:4). And King Jehoshaphat called upon the Lord before all the people.

Jehoshaphat's prayer in 2 Chronicles 20:6 begins with his praising God and telling Him what the problem is. In verse 12 he says: "O our God, will you not judge them? For we have no power to face this vast army that is attacking us. We do not know what to do, but our eyes are upon you." Jehoshaphat may have been powerless and may not have known what to do in practical terms, but he had good sense. He turned to God for help.

God sent the Prophet Jahaziel, son of Zechariah. He brought a message from God. It was a strange message. God told Judah to do nothing. All He wanted them to do was to sit by and watch God work. What happened?

The enemies began fighting among themselves. They killed each other off until no one was left to fight against Judah. Then the king and his people went out and picked up the spoils from the battle they never fought. God delivered them by His mighty power. God answered prayer.

PENTECOST

At Pentecost the disciples waited for the Holy Spirit, and they prayed as they waited. Acts 1:14 says, "They all joined together constantly in prayer." As a result of their prayers, God gave them signs and wonders. There were tongues of fire. There were sounds of a rushing mighty wind. They spoke in tongues. They were filled with the Spirit. They had a power they had never had before.

PETER

Peter was a coward. He deserted Jesus. But when he was filled with the Spirit and preached the first sermon after Pentecost, three thousand people were saved. That's a large number of people to be saved through one sermon.

PETER AND JOHN

Peter and John healed the man who was born lame. When he was healed, the two apostles were seized by the police and brought before the Sanhedrin. They were told never to preach in the name of Jesus. They went back to the brethren and told them what had happened. In Acts 4:24 the Bible says: "They raised their voices together in prayer to God." Later it says: "After they prayed, the place where they were meeting was shaken" (Acts 4:31). Moreover they were filled with the Holy Spirit, and they spoke the Word of God with boldness. That's what happens when the people of God pray. Prayer indeed has power.

How Shall We Pray?

WE MUST PRAY EVERY DAY

We can do it sitting, standing, flat on our faces, with uplifted hands, walking in the street, driving an automobile, while we are in bed—wherever we are, we can pray.

WE MUST PRAY IN THE SPIRIT

This means we are under the control of the Holy Spirit; He teaches us how to pray and what to pray for. He empowers us so that our prayers are effective. He guides us each step of our journey. He will speak to us and through us. We must pray in the Spirit. *We are to persevere in prayer.* We must keep on praying until we get the answer from God.

Elijah teaches us the need for persevering in prayer. He challenged the gods of Baal to a contest. He took them to the top of Mount Carmel. Fire came from heaven and consumed his sacrifice. But the gods of Baal had no power. The false prophets were slain. Before that happened, Elijah had prayed and, because of his prayer, there had been no rain for three and a half years.

But after defeating the false prophets, Elijah wrapped himself in his robe and began to pray for rain. You will find the account in 1 Kings 18. In the Book of James we are told that "Elijah was a man just like us. He prayed earnestly that it would not rain, and it did not rain on the land for three and a half years. Again he prayed, and the heavens gave rain, and the earth produced crops" (James 5:17-18).

While he was praying, he sent his servant to look for a cloud in the sky. There was none. He had him look seven times. That was perseverance. He did not stop once, or twice, or three times. He sent the servant seven times. He did not stop praying until the answer came. The seventh time the servant saw a small cloud in the sky. Elijah arose and went away because his prayer was about to be answered. The rains came. God had heard and answered the prayer.

For What Should You Pray?

You should pray

- for your church
- for your pastor or your people
- for your missionaries
- for your family
- for your own needs
- for the needs of others
- for your country—and also ask God to keep you from its enemies
- for worldwide revival
- for the hastening of the coming of the Lord Jesus

We are commanded to pray. We must pray. We will pray. God will answer our prayers.

8

Hindrances to Prayer

Norval Hadley

Norval Hadley serves as the director of ministry services for World Vision. As coordinator of many World Vision services to churches and Christian leaders, he and his associates seek to strengthen the American church for its mission in the world today. He directs World Vision's International Intercessors, and manages seminar and retreat ministries.

Why do you suppose Jesus taught us to pray with persistence when God knows what we want before we ask and is more willing to give to us than we are to give good gifts to our children? Perhaps it is because through the process of persistence, He is able to lead us to deal with the factors in our lives and relationships that hinder prayer. The Bible lists several such factors.

LACK OF FAITH (MATTHEW 21:22; MARK 11:24; AND JAMES 1:5-7)

The Scriptures teach that prayer must be with faith. In fact, James 1:7 says that the one who prays without faith should not expect to receive anything from the Lord. One reason it is so important to pray with praise and thanksgiving is that before the "glorious majesty of our Lord and the wonders of His love and grace, unbelief and doubt will vanish away as mists before the rising sun" (*The Kneeling Christian*, p. 119).

There may be some prayer projects that are too difficult for your faith. Some projects should be committed to others. The disciples were not able to handle the demon-possessed son (Matt. 17:14-21). Some prayer projects are better handled where two or three are gathered in Christ's name (Matt. 18:19).

Faith and obedience cannot be separated (1 John 3:22-23). Faith is possible only while abiding in Him and while His Word is abiding in you (John 15:7). The prayer God answers must be according to His will, and we know His will by abiding, by obeying God's Word. Romans 10:17 says, "Faith cometh by hearing, and hearing by the word of God."

Faith is also given by the Spirit (1 Cor. 12:9). It's the prayer that God the Holy Spirit inspires that God the Father loves to answer.

Unconfessed Sin (Isaiah 59:1-2)

Faith is impossible when there is the knowledge that sin has separated one from God. People think God doesn't answer prayer as He did in the old days or that the thing they pray for is not in the will of God. No. It is sin that hinders answers. Earnest prayer must include searching the heart and confession.

"If I regard iniquity in my heart, the Lord will not hear me" (Ps. 66:18). There is no sin too small to hinder prayer.

Disorder in Marriage Relationships (1 Pet. 3:1-7)

One can be faithful in church and active in Christian work; but when things are not right at home, prayer is hindered. One cannot be right in his relationship with God if his relationship with his spouse is wrong. Wives, if you cannot submit to your husband for *his* sake, do it for the Lord's sake and for the sake of answered prayer. The pattern for the marriage relationship is in the Godhead. "Let us make man in our image . . . in the image of God created he him; male and female created he them" (Gen. 1:26-27).

Husbands are to live with wives "according to knowledge"— knowledge that God has made the wife to be most comfortable when she can depend on her husband for love, protection, and provision. This does not mean that wives are inferior. The husband is to love the wife as Christ loved the church and gave Himself for it. When a wife receives this kind of love, she can respond in submission without risk. This principle is also mentioned in the Old Testament (Mal. 2:13-15).

SELFISHNESS—LACK OF GIVING

James 4:3 says, "Ye ask, and receive not, because ye ask amiss, that ye may consume it upon your lusts." It may not be that the thing we ask for is wrong, but that the reason we ask is wrong. We are to ask for His glory (John 14:13). One can pray selfishly even for revival or for the filling of the Holy Spirit. Remember that Matthew 7:7 (ask, seek, knock) follows Matthew 6:33, which tells us to "seek ye first the kingdom of God."

Luke 12:15 shows that the true purpose of prayer is not to obtain the things we want from God but to make us content with things He wants us to have. Self-examination is important, lest we pray with pretense. Abraham prevailed with God. Have you noticed how unselfish he was in the settlement with Lot? (Gen. 13:8-9).

Luke 6:38 indicates that we receive as we give. 1 John 3:22-23, which says that we receive because we keep His commandments, reminds us that His commandment is to love one another. And we show that love by supplying one another's need.

Philippians 4:19—"But my God shall supply all your need according to his riches in glory by Christ Jesus"—was given to those who had sacrificed to help Paul in his time of affliction and need. Twice they sent sacrificial gifts when he was in Thessalonica.

Proverbs 21:13 says, "Whoso stoppeth his ears at the cry of the poor, he also shall cry himself, but shall not be heard." It is not only selfishness in prayer, but a lack of generosity—a refusal to give to the poor—that will hinder us from receiving answers. This may be one of the least known of God's requirements because it touches money, but it's there—like it or not. In Acts 10 Cornelius's prayer was heard because of his generous giving.

Isaiah 58 is a precious chapter, listing numerous promises to those who give to the needy, and among them it says in verse 9, "Then shalt thou call, and the Lord shall answer; thou shalt cry and he shall say, Here I am."

Of course, there are other hindrances not mentioned here. This is not intended to be a complete list, but these are some that affect most of us.

SUMMARY

"After all that has been said, we see that everything can be summed up under one head. All hindrance to prayer arises from ignorance of the teachings of God's Holy Word on the life of holiness He has planned for all His children, or from an unwillingness to consecrate ourselves fully to Him. When we can truthfully say to our Father, 'All that I am and have is Thine,' then He can say to us, 'All that is Mine is thine' " (*The Kneeling Christian*, p. 127).

9

The Laws of Prayer

Jack Taylor

Jack R. Taylor is the president of Dimensions in Christian Living, Inc. He is a former Southern Baptist pastor and the author of several books on prayer, revival, and the Christian life. Mr. Taylor is a conference speaker throughout the United States and in other countries.

You cannot read the Bible, whether it is in Genesis or Isaiah or Matthew or Acts or the Revelation, without finding that God uses prayer in the implementation of His will. It is God's way of getting things done.

In Romans 8:25-32, Paul says these things about prayer:

But if we hope for what we do not yet have, we wait for it patiently.

In the same way, the Spirit helps us in our weakness. We do not know what we ought to pray for, but the Spirit himself intercedes for us with groans that words cannot express. And he who searches our hearts knows the mind of the Spirit, because the Spirit intercedes for the saints in accordance with God's will.

And we know that in all things God works for the good of those who love him, who have been called according to his purpose. For those God foreknew he also predestined to be conformed to the likeness of his Son, that he might be the firstborn among many brothers. And those he predestined, he also called; those he called, he also justified; those he justified, he also glorified.

What, then, shall we say in response to this? If God is for us, who can be against us? He who did not spare his own son, but gave him up for us all—how will he not also, along with him, graciously give us all things?

Prayer has to do with something you cannot see. We get excited about things we see, but it's time we got excited about things that are real even though we can't see them. The only thing that is real is that which survives time. When we pray, we are engaging in an eternal enterprise—something that will last.

This miracle of prayer, unlike other miracles that sometimes have to wait for Providence to move, is a continuing miracle. It is waiting for you right now. It is a miracle of power, a miracle of communication. When we pray, we are pushing beyond reason and stepping into transcendent realms of power. In prayer we can do more than *we* can do. We can be more than we are. We can know more than we know. I want to say three things about the miracle of prayer.

THIS MIRACLE COMMENCES AT THE POINT OF HUMAN NEED

Jesus accomplished the first miracle on the occasion of a deficiency in the wine supply. He raised a man who had been crippled for thirty-eight years, a well-established need. The disciples awakened Him in the boat in the midst of a problem.

WE ARE INFIRM

Notice the previously quoted passage from Romans: "In the same way, the Spirit helps us in our weakness" (8:26). Every miracle is God addressing Himself to a human need. Many times we hate to admit that we are weak, but if it didn't bother Jesus to admit that He was helpless without God, it shouldn't bother you. This is what He said: "The son can do nothing by himself; he can do only what he sees his Father doing" (John 5:19). Prayer is the means God has given us to walk from our weakness into His limitless power.

WE ARE IGNORANT

"We do not know what we ought to pray for" (8:26). But the Holy Spirit is with us, waiting day and night, ready to introduce us to the waiting miracle of prayer.

Any time we feel deficient in either strength or knowledge is the call to pray.

This Miracle Continues with the Partnership of the Spirit

The Holy Spirit takes up the other end of this matter of prayer and bears it to the Father. This is a real assurance. We often pray according to what we think is obvious, but what we see and think is not always from God. So in partnership with us, the Holy Spirit gently guides us.

It is most amazing to get into prayer and discover the Holy Spirit shifting the emphasis of your prayer. Not only does He intercede for us, but He intervenes and sometimes even interrupts.

This Miracle Consummates in the Purpose of the Father

Praying is how you get things done. It's not what you do, or your preparation; it is prayer itself that is God's method of getting things done.

Remember the Lord's Prayer: "Your kingdom come, your will be done on earth as it is in heaven" (Matt. 6:10). What we are doing in prayer is implementing the will of God on earth. We are praying heaven's plans down to earth. We are marching into invisible realms and bringing back reality.

Only within the context of Spirit-directed praying can "we know that in all things God works for the good of those who love him, who have been called according to his purpose" (Rom. 8:28). It is not just important that *God knows* that He will work all things together; it is important that *we know* that He is going to do that. It is the difference between victory and defeat.

So we see that this waiting miracle of prayer commences with a human problem (infirmity and ignorance); it continues in the partnership of the Spirit; but it consummates in the purpose of the Father. And understanding these things provides us with a perspective to appreciate the laws of prayer.

The Laws of Prayer

There are two ways of discovering laws: You can read what someone says about a law, or if you look long enough, you will find that someone took the time to study cause and effect. You can either read what Newton says about the law of gravity, or you can do what he did, and understand by observing.

Here are some laws of prayer. Read what I have to say about them, and go ahead and try to prove them wrong. For in so doing, I am confident you will prove them right.

Law 1: No believer's spiritual life will rise above the level of his or her praying. Your spiritual living level is the same as your praying level. Unfortunately, your spiritual life does not take off at the high level of the conferences you have attended or the lofty books you have read.

I used to say to myself, "I'm so glad for this meeting; I'll never be the same." And I wasn't . . . for maybe two weeks. Then I was right back to the level of my praying.

If you want a changed life, then ask God (and cooperate with Him) to change your prayer time.

Law 2: No church's ultimate effectiveness will rise above the level of its corporate praying. Whether in a church, a mission agency, or some other Christian institution, it's not enough to pray before committee meetings; it's not enough to punctuate the service with a few prayers. Everything we do must be pervaded with prayer. It's not enough to devise our own schemes. We must pray and then wait until we hear from God.

Everything we do must issue from a life of praying faith.

Law 3: No church's corporate prayer life will rise above the level of the prayer lives of its individual members. I've ministered on prayer around the world, and I've seen this rule working. I can speak to a group, and everyone will get excited about prayer. Everyone wants to be a part of some program, but I've found that a person who does not regularly pray—one who does not have a quality prayer life—will not remain excited about prayer.

It does no good to promote prayer at a corporate level if we do not first learn how to meet God personally in a regular way.

Law 4: No believer's prayer life will rise in quality above his daily time alone with God. Almost everything in me and in my background shrinks from something regular, but when my personal prayer time suffers, my whole spiritual life feels the effects.

If you've been looking for a reason for the frustration and failure in your life, you may have no reason to look any further.

Law 5: No believer's practice of prayer will be greater than his view of prayer. In other words, right now you are doing what you really believe to be the most important. What you are not doing is not important to you; that's the bottom line. If you are not giving priority to personal prayer, let's face it, you don't think it is that important.

For that reason, I challenge you to study prayer in the life of Jesus, to study prayer in the prophets, to study prayer in the early church, and to study prayer in the lives of the great men and women of church history. You will discover that they have one thing in common: they were people of prevailing, intense, regular, studious, committed prayer.

Constantly work on enhancing your view of prayer. Study books of prayer. Sit at the feet of people who are great pray-ers.

Law 6: Both private and public praise are indispensable factors in the prayer life. "Enter his gates with thankgiving and his courts with praise; give thanks to him and praise his name" (Ps. 100:4). Praise is the preface to the prayer experience.

There was no greater day in my life than when I began to discover that the best way to get into an atmosphere of prayer to God was through thanksgiving and praise.

Do you realize that there was a tribe in Israel whose name meant "praise"? Do you know where their position was when the children of Israel stopped in the wilderness? They were the tribe stationed nearest the entrance to the court yard of the Tabernacle. It was "Judah."

Memorize Scriptures of praise, and recite them often.

Law 7: The only way to learn to pray is to pray. You will not learn to pray by going to seminars or reading books or filling in the blanks in a workbook.

As soon as you can, get to a private place with God and say, "God, I'm so glad these things are true about prayer. I'm so glad that I have access to You. I'm so glad You have devised prayer. It is a wonderful thing. Would You forgive me for my negligence of my exercise of the greatest exercise available to me? Please get me so right with You that I get excited about prayer."

The only way to learn to pray is to pray.

Go to it!

10

Using Scripture as the Basis for Prayer

Jeannette Hawkinson

Jeannette Hawkinson is a traveling prayer representative for Campus Crusade for Christ. She is currently serving in Europe and resides in Germany. Before joining the staff of Campus Crusade in 1971, she was an executive secretary in the aerospace industry for fifteen years.

God waits for His people to pray so that He can show us His mighty works. "Call to me," He told Jeremiah, "and I will answer you, and tell you great and unsearchable ["mighty," KJV*] things you do not know" (Jer. 33:3). And the apostle James reminds us, "You do not have, because you do not ask God" (James 4:2). When we do ask, however, "the prayer of a righteous man is powerful and effective" (James 5:16).

What is *effective prayer*? Effective prayer needs to be in line with God's will and, therefore, in line with God's Word.

It is profitable to go to Scripture to learn to pray, for "all Scripture is God-breathed and is useful for teaching, rebuking, correcting and training in righteousness, so that the man of God may be thoroughly equipped for every good work" (2 Tim. 3:16-17).

We can learn a great deal about prayer by studying the prayers of God's people. After his conversion, Paul, for instance, was a man of fervent, unceasing, effective prayer. He and those whom he discipled were accused of turning the world upside down. I am convinced

*King James Version.

that that is in part because Paul discipled his converts in effective prayer.

In his letters to young churches, Paul encouraged them to "Be imitators" of him (1 Cor. 11:1, NASB*) and "to join . . . in following [his] example" (Phil. 3:17). Let's look at Paul's prayer life to learn more about how we can become effective in prayer.

PAUL: AN EXAMPLE OF EFFECTIVE PRAYER

Paul was already a man of prayer before his conversion. He did not have the whole Bible for reference as we do, but he was a Pharisee and therefore intimately acquainted with Scripture. But it was only after Christ appeared to him that Paul discovered who Jesus Christ is as revealed in the Old Testament.

PAUL'S FIRST PRAYER

Paul's first prayer to Jesus is found in Acts 22:8, when he met Him on the road to Damascus. Struck blind by a bright light, Paul cried out, "Who art Thou, Lord?" (NASB) I believe he continued to ask that question for three days as he meditated on Scripture in prayer and fasting during his blindness.

Later he spent three years in the Arabian desert. At that time he received the gospel message through a revelation of Jesus Christ. The whole time his heart attitude was, "Who art Thou, Lord?"

In order to learn to love and trust and worship God in a deeper way we, too, need to grow in our knowledge of Him. As we study the Word of God—God's revelation of Himself to us—we should always prayerfully ask, as Paul did: "Who art Thou, Lord?"

- Show me Your attributes.
- Show me Your character.
- Show me Your works.
- Show me Your promises.
- Show me Your principles.

New American Standard Bible.

PAUL'S SECOND PRAYER

Paul's second prayer was also a question. It was uttered still in the dust on the Damascus road: "What shall I do, Lord?" (22:10) Again, that must also be our prayer: "Lord, what shall I do?"

• Show me the conditions attached to Your promises.
• Show me Your commands.
• Show me Your will.

There are many other teachings and prayers of Paul which we can use as an inspiration for our own prayers. But his attitude in his first two prayers at the feet of Jesus Christ is especially significant in helping us know how we should approach Scripture and prayer.

HE TRAINED OTHERS IN PRAYER

As Paul closed his letter to the Colossian church, he wrote, "Epaphras, who is one of your number, a bondslave of Jesus Christ, sends you his greetings, *always laboring earnestly for you in his prayers*, that you may stand perfect and fully assured in all the will of God" (Col. 4:12, NASB; emphasis added).

I have asked myself, "How did Epaphras learn to pray like that?" That's how I want to pray, and that's how I want to train others to pray—to labor earnestly in prayer for others, that they might stand perfect and fully assured in the will of God.

At the time Colossians was written, Epaphras was a fellow prisoner and Paul's prayer partner. Tradition says he may have been one of Paul's converts in Ephesus. We do know from the first chapter of Colossians that the Colossians responded wholeheartedly to the gospel with understanding, and that it was Epaphras who evangelized them.

As I consider these few facts about Paul's disciple, I envision Epaphras responding to the gospel in Ephesus, then hearing Paul's teaching day after day. Then I see him praying with Paul, learning to pray like him: "Who art Thou, Lord? What shall I do, Lord?" I visualize them both praying fervently for the people in Epaphras' hometown of Colossae. Finally, I see Epaphras taking the gospel to them. When he did, prayer had enabled God to prepare the hearts of the Colossians, and as a result another city in that heathen world was turned upside down.

USING SCRIPTURE AS THE BASIS FOR PRAYER

I would like to disciple others in prayer, as Paul did with Epaphras, with the same kind of results. Just as Paul was able to say, "Be imitators of me," God wants *us* to set a Spirit-filled example in the way we live and the way we pray. For this reason, I like to use Scripture as the basis for prayer in order to pray effectively according to God's will.

I apply Scripture to help me pray by asking about a particular verse or passage: "What do the words tell me about God? What do they tell me about my relationship with God? And, what is God telling me to do?"

SCRIPTURAL INSPIRATION FOR PRAYER

When I choose a verse for meditation, I read it with two questions in mind: "Who art Thou, Lord?" and, "What shall I do, Lord?" Then I pray as God shows me the answer to those two questions.

For instance, if my reading is Psalm 145 (NASB), I read the first verse:

> I will extol Thee, my God, O King;
> And I will bless Thy name forever and ever.

Then I use individual words and phrases to inspire my own prayer time. The phrase "My God" encourages me to pray as follows:

> Heavenly Father, thank You that You are *my* God, my *personal* God. I worship and adore You. I praise You that You are the almighty and holy God of heaven and earth, and that there is no other God beside You, a righteous God and my Savior.

I am reminded that God is "King":

> Heavenly Father, You are the supreme ruler in the universe. I rejoice that I am a citizen of Your kingdom. More than that, I am a princess, a daughter of the King. Your kingship means that You are

sovereign in all that happens in my life, and all that happens in the whole world. Praise You, O King. Nothing happens that is not a part of your permissive will.

This verse says, "I will extol Thee":

O Father, I want to tell of Your goodness and mercy, compassion and lovingkindness. When I do that, Lord God, I exalt Your name. "I will extol Thee . . . forever and ever"! That is a promise I make to You, Father, but You know that sometimes I let other things interfere with the time I should be spending with You. Help me to be faithful to proclaim the greatness of God every day of my life. Father, my assignment for all of eternity is to praise Your name forever and ever. Help me to get a lot of practice while I am still here on planet Earth.

The last phrase reads, "I will bless Thy name":

Father, thank You that You have made Your names so real to me this last year. I have learned that You are Jehovah-Jireh, "the God who provides." Thank You that You have provided all I have needed in the past, and that You will provide all I need in the future. Father, when I become concerned about a need I have, please remind me of Your name, Jehovah-Jireh, the God who provides. Help me to be a blessing to You and to those around me by declaring, "My God is Jehovah-Jireh. He will provide."

I ask all these things in the name of my Lord Jesus Christ. Amen.

Many other truths may come to your mind as you think of God being King or blessing His name every day. But this is one example of how stimulating a single verse of Scripture can be in personal worship.

CONVERSATIONAL PRAYER USING SCRIPTURE

If you are praying alone, your prayers can be as short or as long as you wish. However, if you are meeting with several people to pray through Scripture in this way, I recommend that each person take a turn praying a single, short thought, leaving time for your prayer partners to add their thoughts on the same subject. Continue in this fashion with each person expressing a single thought on the same verse, until you sense that the Holy Spirit is guiding you to begin reading and praying from a second verse.

This type of praying is called "conversational prayer." It can be a great blessing when everyone participates while being sensitive to each other and to the Holy Spirit, rather than one person taking a long time with his own prayer.

USING SCRIPTURE FOR CONFESSION

As we spend time worshiping God through His Word, the Holy Spirit will often bring to mind an area of our lives that is not pleasing to God.

Isaiah 59 reminds us: "Surely the arm of the Lord is not too short to save, nor His ear too dull to hear. But your iniquities have separated you from your God; your sins have hidden His face from you, so that He will not hear" (Isa. 59: 1-2).

Reading this passage provides an opportunity to ask ourselves, "Is there a sin in my life that is separating me from God?" We should not assume that we have perfect fellowship with God and that He is pleased with our lives until we have prayed, as David did in Psalm 139, "Search me, O God, and know my heart; test me and know my anxious thoughts. See if there is any offensive way in me, and lead me in the way everlasting" (Ps. 139:23-24).

As we wait before God, the Holy Spirit will bring to mind any unconfessed sin or anything we need to make right with a brother or sister. When we have confessed the sin, then we can pray, claiming the promise in 1 John 1:9: "Thank you, Father, that You are faithful and just to forgive my sin and to cleanse me from all unrighteousness. Thank You that our fellowship is now restored. Help me to meet with the person whom I have offended and ask for forgiveness. In Jesus' name, Amen."

If we feel guilty after confessing our sin, then it's very likely that Satan is attacking us in our thoughts. He is the accuser and the father of lies. Sometimes he accuses us in our own words, such as, "It's no use. I'll never learn to be loving toward that person. Besides, he doesn't deserve it; it's just a waste of time."

We know in our heart that those words are lies. But they trip us up anyway. What can we do? We can turn to James 4:7 which reads, "Submit yourselves, then, to God. Resist the devil, and he will flee from you." In this verse we find the courage to pray, "Father, I submit myself to You and claim Your power in my life. Satan, I resist you and your lies in the name of the Lord Jesus Christ. Get out of here and leave my thought life alone."

We can also turn to Romans 5:5 which says, "God has poured out His love into our hearts by the Holy Spirit, whom he has given us." This encourages us to pray an affirmative prayer, claiming God's love in our heart as if we already have seen evidence of it working in our lives and transforming our attitudes. We can pray, "Thank You, God, that I love that person with Your love which you have spread in my heart."

USING SCRIPTURE TO FACE AFFLICTION

When I am experiencing persecution or affliction, I remember Romans 5:3 ("We know that suffering produces perseverance") and James 1:3-4 ("The testing of your faith develops perseverance") and find courage to pray something like this: "Father, I rejoice in my affliction. Thank You that I am learning to persevere. As I look to You for the strength to endure, I know something wonderful is happening. You are transforming me so that I will be perfect and complete, lacking nothing. So Father, by faith, I give You thanks in the name that is above all names, the precious Lord Jesus Christ. Amen."

USING SCRIPTURE TO PRAY FOR OTHERS

Many times I use Paul's prayers for the Ephesians or Colossians, and pray them for others, inserting their names. For example, this prayer is based on Ephesians 1:15-19:

Heavenly Father, ever since I heard about Nancy's faith in the Lord Jesus and her love for all the saints, I have not stopped giving thanks for her, remembering her in my prayers. I keep asking that You, the God of our Lord Jesus Christ, glorious Father, may give her the Spirit of wisdom and revelation, so that she may know You better. I pray also that the eyes of her heart may be enlightened in order that *she* may know the hope to which You have called *her*, the riches of Your glorious inheritance in the saints, and Your incomparably great power for us who believe.

USING SCRIPTURE TO PRAY FOR GOD'S WILL

When our prayers grow out of God's Word, we can know that we are also praying according to His will as revealed in Scripture.

For instance, Jesus made it a priority to pray that all who believe in Him "may be one, Father, just as you are in me and I am in you. . . . May they be brought to complete unity to let the world know that you sent me and have loved them even as you have loved me" (John 17:21, 23). We can make this a priority prayer as well, knowing we are praying according to His will for the church.

SCRIPTURE IS GOD'S COMMUNICATION; PRAYER IS OUR RESPONSE

As we search the Word of God day by day, our communication with Him will become more meaningful and more effective if we respond verbally (in prayer) to all that God shows us in His Word.

We began by praying, "Who art Thou, Lord?" and "What shall I do, Lord?" In that regard, learn to ask of God:

- Grant me understanding in the passage, Lord.
- Help me to learn more about You.
- Help me to see how this should influence my prayers for myself.
- Help me to see how to pray for others.
- Help me to pray appropriately for events in the world around me.
- Help me to see what action You would have me take after I have prayed.

As God reveals Himself and His ways to us, we can demonstrate our love for Him by being obedient. Jesus told His disciples, "Whoever has my commands and obeys them, he is the one who loves me. He who loves me will be loved by my Father, and I too will love him and show myself to him" (John 14:21). God was able to use the apostle Paul and his disciples in a dynamic way because Paul's attitude was always, "I was not disobedient to the vision from heaven" (Acts 26:19).

If we want to follow Paul's example, we will

- devote time to learning "Who art Thou, Lord?"
- continually ask, "What shall I do?"
- obey God.
- live our lives in such a way as to be an example.
- disciple and train others by the example of our life and our prayer.

11

The Necessity of Training Christians to Pray

Glenn Sheppard

Dr. Glenn L. Sheppard served on the staff of the Southern Baptist Home Missions Board, Atlanta, Georgia, as the special assistant to spiritual awakening with the Evangelism Section. He now travels worldwide, moblizing prayer movements.

About twenty years ago while I was a student in the United States, God touched me in a sovereign and unusual way during a brief period of revival that swept across the country. During the latter sixties and early seventies there was what was known as the "Jesus Movement." It grew during a time when there was great internal turmoil within the United States—racial disharmony, student unrest, and opposition to the Vietnam War.

I was a student during those days, and I, like many others, was ready to throw in the towel. I wanted to give up and walk away from my heritage as a Christian because I really did not know whether God worked anymore in my life personally. In the midst of that kind of desperation, God did an unusual work in my life and changed everything. He saved my life, my marriage, and the ministry that God had called me to as a young teenage boy.

I did not historically, intellectually, or emotionally understand anything about spiritual awakenings. I'd never heard of the great movements of God around the world or through history. I'd never experienced anything quite like it. But what happened in my heart so revolutionized me that I came to the conclusion that the greatest need in the world was for God to change people so they would never be the same again.

That kind of change comes only when people are filled with His Holy Spirit and walk in submission to His control. It cannot be done in the flesh of man. It cannot be accomplished by enthusiasm. It cannot be accomplished by organization. It only is accomplished when God's Holy Spirit begins to touch peoples' lives until it permeates the very society of which they are a part.

A Vision for the Power of Prayer

2 Chronicles 7:14 says, "If my people, who are called by my name, will humble themselves and pray and seek my face and turn from their wicked ways, then will I hear from heaven and will forgive their sin and will heal their land." The writer of the book of Proverbs reminds us that "where there is no vision, the people perish" (Prov. 29:18, KJV*).

There are places around the world where Christians are capturing this vision today. That's what's happening in Korea. That's what's happening in China. That's what's happening in South America, and in Latin America, and in portions of Africa. In many places around the globe people are beginning to fervently and desperately plead for the power of God to come and invade and touch their nations, to bind the power of darkness, to stop the flow of Satan, to resist the worldly bondage under which the church is struggling.

Someone asked, "Is it really necessary to train people to pray for this kind of spiritual awakening?" Yes! Unequivocally. It won't just happen spontaneously. Let me tell you what the disciples—those men who walked most personally with Jesus—did in the early days of their own ministry.

They had seen Him raise the dead and heal the blind. They had listened to Him preach the greatest sermon ever preached. They had watched as He walked across water. They had participated in things that would boggle the minds of anyone. And yet the only request they had was, "Lord, teach us to pray."

If the disciples of the Son of the living God needed instruction

*King James Version.

in prayer, how much more should we in the twentieth century say, "God, teach us to pray." We desperately in our need to know how to pray.

I have a dear friend who said to me something that frightened me. He was preaching in the church where I was pastor at that time. He was a well-known speaker, and he said these words to a congregation filled to capacity. He said, "God does not honor prayer." And in those moments my heart sank, and I thought that in his old age his mind had slipped. Then he added: "God honors desperate praying."

Then I began to understand the secret of the outpoured Spirit on the day of Pentecost. Those who were gathered there that Sunday had seen the Son of the living God go back into heaven. There was no way for them to do the thing He had told them to do—evangelize the world. They could not do it in their own power. And so it was out of that desperation that the Spirit was poured into their hearts two thousand years ago. Those believers who were filled with God's glory in that moment of prayer literally turned the world inside out.

Our most enthusiastic promotional efforts, our best organization, and the best minds in human history cannot do in a lifetime what one human can do in a twinkling of the eye when the Holy Spirit of God is upon that person. Yes, it is essential to teach people to pray.

As you begin to catch a supernatural vision for the power of prayer, I think you will begin to understand that Paul gave us instructions for a supernatural walk with God when he wrote to the church in Philippi and told them to do everything in prayer and in supplication. And then he told them that as they began to do this with thanksgiving, they would begin to experience peace about the will of God (Phil. 4:6-7), for God issues that kind of vision as people pray.

WHAT IS PRAYER?

Many Christians are so ignorant about how to pray that they are even uncertain about what it is. Here are a few definitions:

1. *Prayer is communication with God.* It's a dialogue between an individual who loves God and God Himself. Prayer is to verbalize,

to say to God, "You are everything. You are the Father, and I am your child. Oh Father, I trust You."

2. *Prayer is the breath of our spiritual life.* Without prayer, we are weakened. Prayer is to the spirit what oxygen is to our bodies. If you do not receive oxygen, you will die today. It doesn't matter how healthy you are. It is so tragic that there are peoples of the world who are dying because they are not in communion with God the Father; they are literally dying for the breath of God Himself.

3. *Prayer releases the power and the authority of God.* The Bible tells us, "Whatever you bind on earth will be bound in heaven, and whatever you loose on earth will be loosed in heaven" (Matt. 18:18). We see that we have the capacity literally to reach into the realms of heaven and touch the very hand of God Himself.

Consider for a moment some of the promises Jesus made concerning prayer. He said, "Ask and it will be given to you; seek and you will find; knock and the door will be opened to you. For everyone who asks receives; he who seeks finds; and to him who knocks, the door will be opened" (Matt. 7:7-8).

The Bible also tells us (in James 4:2) that we have not received because we do not ask. Every now and then I discover that I begin my prayer by saying, "Father, why don't you help me in this area where I desperately need Your assistance?" And then He answers, "Why son, you've not asked before. That's why I've not done anything." The Bible says, "Ask, and you shall receive."

WHO CAN PRAY?

We pray to God the Father, through the Holy Spirit and in the name of Jesus Christ. That is so we will have the capacity and the authority to touch the heart of God.

But people cannot address God as Father unless they are children of the Father, born again by the Spirit of God through faith in the Son of God. Until they have been born again, they can never be God's child.

That is the first prerequisite. As I've traveled around the world giving seminars on prayer, I've discovered in every prayer group that there are people who are a part of the church as an organization, but they are not part of the family of God. They have not been born of the Spirit of God.

The first and most important prerequisite to prayer is being born again.

OBSTACLES TO PRAYER

Two of the greatest obstacles to answered prayer are pride and unrighteousness in the life of believers. There are other hindrances that are just as bad such as disobedience, selfishness, and wrong motives. But I just want to deal with two about which Christians seem to be most ignorant: pride and unrighteousness.

Pride. Perhaps the most real obstacle to answered prayer in most churches today is pride, or the ego. We're more concerned with what others think of us than with what God thinks of us. When the Holy Spirit of God comes and crushes the ego of man and shatters his character and takes his pride away, God is lifted up, and man is abashed. And that is God's plan—to break us. That is why Paul said, "I have been crucified with Christ and I no longer live, but Christ lives in me. The life I live in the body, I live by faith in the Son of God, who loved me and gave himself for me" (Gal. 2:20).

Unrighteousness. Do you remember what the seraphim were saying when Isaiah had his vision of the Lord, high and lifted up in the temple? They were crying: "Holy, holy, holy is the Lord Almighty" (Isa. 6:3). Some might want to interpret God as being just a cuddly God. And He certainly is a God of love. But He is also a holy God. And He demands that we bear witness to His holiness by living lives of holiness ourselves. I believe that the greatest need in the church today—whether in the Orient, Africa, the Western nations, the islands in the oceans, or anywhere—is an awakening of righteousness among God's people. God's way is holy.

The greatest obstacle in the church today is the obstacle of sin in the lives of believers. That calls us to the Spirit-filled life. There is no exception. You do not live in the power of God's revival without being filled and walking continually in the fullness of God's Holy Spirit. There is no power in man's hands to do the work of God in his own ability. There is no mental activity or exercise which we can do. Only as the Holy Spirit comes and controls us, empowers us, and lives through us are we able to walk in the fullness of revival.

Several years ago I was in one of the western states of the United States, sharing a need. At the conclusion of the meeting, two very lovely women came to give me a small box. It was just a little box, and in it was a gift. I thought it was for my wife, so I was going to take it home to Atlanta, Georgia, and give it to her. But with a twinkle in their eyes, the women said, "That's for you."

"Do you want me to open it now?"

"Oh, yes. Right now."

So I opened it up and found a most unusual gift. In that little box was a little scrub pad, a Brillo pad—something you would use to scrub dirty pots and pans.

I looked at it, and then I looked up at the women and said, "What does this gift mean?"

Well, I have a beard, and with a twinkle in their eyes they said, "That's just what you look like."

I laughed at them. But then I said, "Lord, is there a message for me in their little gift?"

And here's what God's Holy Spirit very clearly said to me: "I am like a holy scrub pad with eyes. I can see where you are dirty, and I can clean you up and make you right with the Father."

If we would regularly pray, "Oh Lord, search me and try me and see if in me there be any wicked way in me," be sure that His holy scrub pad would scrub us clean. And when we are clean, we simply say, "Now, Father, in those areas where I have been hurt, in those areas where You have been pushed down because I have been disobedient, God, would You come and fill me and overflow me with Your Spirit."

There are two prerequisites for real prayer. One is that we must be born again. Second, in order to pray in the Spirit, we must be filled with the Spirit. Then we can commune with God the Father, Jesus His Son, and His ever-present Holy Spirit.

Psalm 85 summarizes the necessity for us to return to righteous living as a prerequisite for effective prayer. It reads as follows:

> You showed favor to your land, O Lord;
>   you restored the fortunes of Jacob.
> You forgave the iniquity of your people
>   and covered all their sins. *Selah.*
> You set aside all your wrath
>   and turned from your fierce anger.
> Restore us again, O God our Savior,

and put away your displeasure toward us.
Will you be angry with us forever?
    Will you prolong your anger through all generations?
Will you not revive us again,
    that your people may rejoice in you?
Show us your unfailing love, O Lord,
    and grant us your salvation;
I will listen to what God the Lord will say;
    he promises peace to his people, his saints—
    but let them not return to folly.
Surely his salvation is near those who fear him,
    that his glory may dwell in our land.
Love and faithfulness meet together;
    righteousness and peace kiss each other.
Faithfulness springs forth from the earth,
    and righteousness looks down from heaven.
The Lord will indeed give what is good,
    and our land will yield its harvest.
Righteousness goes before him
    and prepares the way for his steps.

Part Three

Prayer for
the Revival of the Church

12

What We Can Learn
from Past Spiritual Awakenings

Richard Lovelace

Dr. Richard Lovelace is professor of church history at Gordon-Conwell Theological Seminary in South Hamilton, Massachusetts. He is theological consultant and an executive committee member of Presbyterians United for Biblical Concerns and serves on the executive committee of Evangelicals for Social Action.

For several decades, I have been studying the history of spiritual awakenings and the theology of church renewal. I have also been working to bring renewal in the major American denominations, partly by training the new tide of young evangelical leaders pouring into these churches, and also by theological activism, helping the movements for renewal and reform which have now appeared in every mainline church from the Congregationalists to the Roman Catholics.

During this study and experience, a growing burden for specific aspects of awakening, reform, and renewal has taken possession of my heart and mind. If we are going to launch a world movement of prayer for spiritual awakening, our prayer agenda must have *content* or it will soon run out of steam.

J. Edwin Orr has remarked that evangelicals today typically confine their prayer to *projects*—an evangelistic crusade, a mission thrust, meeting a budget, etc.—and that God always answers these requests. In the eighteenth and nineteenth centuries, however, western evangelicals prayed for *general spiritual awakening in the church*—and God gave them exactly that!

We need to unpack the phrase "general spiritual awakening," to see some of the directions God had moved in past awakening eras, to see how renewal in the church has led to outreach in home and foreign missions, and to ask whether we ought to be praying for some of the same things to happen today. Although my examples draw largely from the history of awakenings in America and Europe, I am convinced by Scripture that their renewal elements also have pressing relevance to our prayer for the church in other parts of the world. And I am convinced that if we continue to ask God to give us these dimensions of renewal, He will give us exactly what we request.

What Is Spiritual Awakening?

First we need to define our terms. From analysis of Scripture, history, and the theology of revival forged by Jonathan Edwards, I have come to define spiritual awakening as the sovereign movement of the Holy Spirit within and around the church, in which the kingdom of darkness is progressively driven back and the kingdom of Christ established.

During periods of awakening, which I believe can last for decades, the flesh, the world, and the devil are challenged and partially expelled from the church; and the church aggressively takes ground away from the devil through missionary expansion and cultural transformation. I use *renewal* and *revival* as synonyms for this awakening process, though they may also be used to describe its permanent effects within the church and around it.

During periods of spiritual decline in the church, on the other hand, the flesh, the world, and the devil sweep into the church. Rising generations of Christians have a form of godliness but deny the power of Christ in their lives. The church becomes filled with unconverted members and leaders. Personal spiritual growth and sanctification are neglected. Doctrinal belief, which is essentially sanctification of the mind, becomes unclear or heretical so that the true gospel is not proclaimed, and false gospels abound.

Even those who remain orthodox are often full of spiritual pride and carnal zeal which divide the church rather than credibly challenging it to conversion. All sectors of the church become conformed to the world in various ways, adopting its idolatries. The devil, the "accuser of the brethren," whispers lies and slanders in the ears of believers to create unnecessary division. He also energizes false teaching or unbalanced theologies which are programmed to divide the church. The Body of Christ becomes crippled and powerless. Its witness is either paralyzed by the loss of gospel proclamation, or found lacking in credibility by the negative impact of its own corruption—for an unawakened church is a great monument to unbelief, which points the world so clearly *away* from Christ that it cancels every other effort to point *toward* Him. The greatest argument the devil has against the resurrection of Christ is the unawakened church.

TWO MODELS OF AWAKENING

How can "the invaded church," as theologian Donald Bloesch has called it, be awakened and revived? Prayer clearly plays a pivotal role in spiritual awakening.

Old Testament Model. In the Old Testament book of Judges, there is a repeated five-part cycle of spiritual decline and renewal. As new generations arise, (1) the people of God gradually fall away from loving and serving Him. As their hearts are emptied of the love and presence of God, (2) they begin to absorb the corruptions of the surrounding world, like a squeezed sponge thrown in a puddle. At this juncture, (3) God removes His blessing from them and they begin to experience hardship and defeat. Then, as (4) they groan in their hearts under these punishments, (5) He is again moved to pity, and raises up a new deliverer who can bring peace and the rule of God for one generation.

New Testament Model. In the New Testament, there is another kind of "prayer cycle" involved in pursuing mission, this time with three phases. The cycle begins with (1) *prayer* in the face of extreme difficulty or satanic counterattack (Acts 1:13-14; 4:24). (2) The church then *prospers* in its spiritual growth and outward extension (Acts 2:14-47; 4:32-35). (3) This expansion of the kingdom arouses satanic counterattack in the form of *persecution*, resistance expressed through the world and the flesh. At this point, the cycle must begin again with prayer, for if it halts in discouragement, the growth and outreach of the Body of Christ will be stifled.

When the church and individual Christians are *passive* with respect to the kingdom of God, they endure the five-part cycle of decline and renewal which was the characteristic way of life under the Old Covenant. When they became *active* in advancing the kingdom, in the New Testament pattern, the three-part cycle of prayer, spiritual growth, and satanic counterattack in Acts is the norm.

In either case, the course of individual and corporate spirituality does not run smoothly, but ebbs and flows. *This is because we are in a spiritual war*, fighting to liberate a planet occupied by the powers of darkness. The characteristic pattern of such a war is ebb and flow, advance and retreat under counterattack in a progressive series of pulsations moving outward until the earth is "filled with the knowledge of the glory of the Lord, as the waters cover the sea" (Hab. 2:14).

PRAYER, THE HALLMARK

In the midst of this kingdom warfare, prayer is the most natural expression of our dependence on the messianic Victor. He has won the ultimate battle. He alone can supply us with the resources to complete the task of spiritual liberation.

The clearest biblical portrait of an awakened church is the description of the early Christian community after Pentecost in Acts 2. A Norwegian authority on revival comments that the sound of rushing wind in this chapter suggests a kind of spiritual housecleaning, sweeping the forces of darkness back so that the church can move forward in an atmosphere of the Spirit's presence. The results are three: (1) The awakened church, filled with the Spirit, immediately manifests *a powerful dynamic of evangelistic outreach.* (2) *The unity of the body of believers*, shown in their caring for and sharing with one another, lends credibility to the church's verbal proclamation of the gospel. (3) Meanwhile, the spiritual vitality of the body of believers is sound and strong, so that *the Lord adds daily* those who are being saved, with no danger of quenching the newly kindled fire by the addition of dry wood.

In theory, we might expect the church of Christ to continue indefinitely in an awakened state, moving outward to conquer territory for Christ. After all, we now are led not by fallible human judges whose lives span only forty years, but by a King who is immortal, who "always lives to intercede" for us (Heb. 7:25). However, *following* this Leader is not a matter of simply obeying His orders, but of participating in His resurrection life through our responses of faith. This faith and sharing in the life of the risen Lord are most centrally expressed in dependent prayer.

The prayer cycle must never be interrupted by discouragement under loss—or complacency in apparent success—or the church's supernatural vitality will subside, and it will go back into the invaded state which characterized the people of God under the Old Covenant.

Prayerful dependence on the risen Christ is one of the most vital ways of participating in His life. But prayer itself should be focused on other key elements of life in Christ which are present in the book of Acts, and visible also in the history of spiritual awakenings. Let us look now at revival history, at Scripture, and at the present state of the world church, to see some of the dimensions of renewal which we ought to ask for in our intercessory prayer.

DIMENSIONS OF REVIVAL IN HISTORY AND IN SCRIPTURE

The unawakened mind of the non-Christian is somewhat like the eye of a person with glaucoma. Patients tested for glaucoma are shown a circle which represents their visual field and then asked to identify the places where they have blind spots within this field. The disease typically darkens the center of the field, while leaving some vision on the periphery.

The fallen mind's view of everything is darkened and distorted by sin, but it has a sort of twilight vision of many things on the periphery of life. In the inner circle of its most important concerns, however, it is in deeper darkness. It has at best only a dim apprehension of the grandeur of God, the depth of its own need, and the real significance of its relationships to significant persons.

PRECONDITIONS OF RENEWAL

In order to awaken human beings spiritually, God must bring them out of this darkness and show them His own character, their real nature as sinners, and the twisted human relationships in the center of their lives. The whole of the Old Testament is aimed at this target, seeking through the Law and God's mighty acts to reveal our sin and His holy justice and love. Isaiah's vision of God made him cry out, "Woe is me! . . . For I am a man of unclean lips, and I live among a people of unclean lips" (Isa. 6:5). The illumination of the mind's central darkness produces hunger and thirst for righteousness, thirst for a way to close the gap between our sin and God's glory, which cannot be satisfied until we know Christ. This awakening of the heart to God—and to our own true identity—I call "Preconditions of Renewal." They are

• an awareness of God's holiness (His justice and love)
• an awareness of the depth of sin (in yourself and the world)

As T. S. Eliot said, "Human beings cannot bear very much reality." We cannot gaze long upon the gap between our sin and God's holiness without grasping the central vision of Christ which bridges this gap. And therein is the hope for renewal. When Peter's audience in Acts 2 was "cut to the heart" by conviction of sin, they readily believed in the Messiah whose life, death, and resurrection brought forgiveness.

THE DITCH ON EITHER SIDE OF THE ROAD

But Paul's letters show that even the awakened church of Acts was battling invasions of darkness and assaults of unbelief and sin—specifically the opposing heresies of *legalism* (Galatians) and *licentiousness* (1 Corinthians). By the second century, Christians could speak of Jesus as the "new Moses who had brought a new Law." This ditch of works-religion into which the church had careened became more Christ-centered by the time of Augustine, but even this great theologian taught that we are *justified* by being *sanctified*—entering into a "state of grace" by an infusion of the life of Christ. Suspending our whole salvation on one dimension of our union with Christ, in the variable climate of our Christian experience, put a strain on the conscience of medieval Christians. Seeking for assurance of salvation, they built many makeshift bridges across the chasm between God's holiness and our sin: heroic works of ascetic self-denial, the intercession of the saints, and the church's priestly role and sacramental system.

Martin Luther brought spiritual awakening to the Western church through his discovery that we are really justified not by being sanctified but by accepting through faith the wholly alien righteousness of Christ. That brought freedom and release to individual believers and got the church back on the road. It gave a great release of creativity to the whole of Western society, since the energies formerly centered on earning salvation could now be devoted to lay vocations.

But later generations of Protestants plummeted into the ditch on the other side of the road, stressing justification without an equal emphasis on sanctification and Christian experience. This produced a dead orthodoxy, a merely "notional" belief in Protestant doctrine without ultimate concern for Christ and His kingdom.

PRIMARY ELEMENTS OF RENEWAL

In the seventeenth century, two new awakening movements blossomed, which got the church back on the path by balancing the stress on justifying faith with a stronger emphasis on sanctification, especially regeneration, its first stage. Those two "born again" movements, Calvinist Puritanism and Lutheran Pietism, also shared an experiential stress on other elements of Christian living grounded in Christ's atoning work: the indwelling presence of the Holy Spirit and authority in spiritual warfare against the powers of darkness. I call these four dimensions of union with Christ the "Primary Elements of Renewal":

- *Justification*: You are accepted in Christ
- *Sanctification*: In Christ you are free from the bondage of sin
- *The Holy Spirit Within*: In Christ you are not alone
- *Authority in Conflict*: You are in command in Christ

The central sleep of the human heart cannot be awakened unless we are "walking in the light" with respect to our own sin and God's holiness, and are claiming by faith all four of these dimensions of grace. Jesus has nailed our sins to the cross; has raised us up by His Spirit in power over our sins; has stripped principalities and powers, making an open show of them; and has empowered us to resist and displace those powers by our command. These four dimensions of renewal form the core of the gospel, the good news of our liberation from slavery to sin, the world, and the devil.

SPIRITUALITY FOR THE INDIVIDUAL

It might appear that with these four dimensions of "abiding in Christ" appropriated by faith, Puritans and Pietists would be filled with the Spirit, fully awakened, and able also to awaken the church and expand its missionary witness to the ends of the earth. Deep as their spirituality was, however—and it was far deeper both in mind and spirit than that of most Western evangelicals today—it was still totally centered on individuals. It was a church of redeemed nomads or atoms, with little appreciation for the missionary task and deficient concern for the unity of Christ's Body. Its models for renewal were drawn from the Old Testament—from the repeated renewing of covenants with God, not from the New Testament or from Pentecost.

The Reformers had concentrated on rebuilding the center of theology. In their struggle with Rome they had no leisure for missionary concern. One Reformer, however—Martin Bucer, who had been a mentor to Calvin and the Puritans—formulated the agenda for future spiritual awakening and missionary extension of the church. On the basis of Romans 11, Bucer taught that the church must continue being theologically reformed and spiritually renewed until the awakened church could reach every nation on earth for Christ. At this juncture, which Bucer called "the church's happy state" and "the fullness of the Gentiles," the fullness of the Jews would also take place—a great ingathering of God's covenant people, now convinced by the sheer beauty of the bride of Christ that Jesus is indeed the Messiah.

The Puritan and Pietist awakeners consciously aimed at fulfilling Bucer's agenda, but they found little power in the church to achieve it. As H. Richard Niebuhr has noted, the Reformers delivered Protestant lay people from the rat race of earning their salvation, but they did not articulate a theology of the kingdom of Christ that would give them a larger, God-centered goal of mission. Consequently they could easily be absorbed into a new kind of rat race: the quest for prosperity. Edmund Morgan comments that Puritan clergy talked about winning the Indians for Christ, but the laity did not grasp this focus of mission. Their model of Christianity was not the missionary church of Acts, but the Old Testament example of Abraham. They wanted to be pious enough to be prosperous, Cotton Mather wistfully lamented, "Piety hath begotten prosperity, and the daughter hath devoured the mother."

The result was a period of seventy-five years called "New England's spiritual decline," except that it was not limited to New England. The wind had gone out of the sails of all Western Christianity.

As he surveyed the lack of progress of the gospel in the whole world in the 490 days and nights he spent in prayer, Mather began to call upon the church to move to a New Testament model, and to call upon God for a new Pentecost, an outpouring of the Holy Spirit that would empower it for life and mission. This outpouring began in the year of Mather's death, 1727, with the Great Awakening.

THE GREAT AWAKENING

This revival brought an inflow of light into the church involving all the elements of renewal we have so far mentioned. In Jonathan Edward's church in Northampton, apathetic church members immersed in business were suddenly gripped by the significance of the doctrines they had been storing in their minds. As God poured out the Spirit of wisdom and revelation, the eyes of their hearts were enlightened. They saw the glory of God and their own deep sin, especially the sins of pride and envy and hatred and covetousness which bind the heart at its deepest levels. Above all, they were deeply convicted of their apathy toward God—convicted that they were not more convicted! And a miracle occurred in Northampton: New England's spiritual decline was reversed. People became so concerned about God, their own spiritual state, and the salvation of their loved ones that they were tempted to neglect their businesses out of concern for the church and mission. I would suggest to you that this is normal Christianity—though it is not very common in this age.

You can see that the Great Awakening involved a fresh concentration of light upon the elements of renewal we have so far discovered. But new dimensions of "abiding in Christ" were being pioneered in the European phase of the Awakening.

In the 1720s, Count Ludwig von Zinzendorf, trained by the Pietists, took their teachings a step further. In founding the renewal community of Herrnhut, he deliberately made it a microcosm of the shattered Body of Christ, offering shelter on his estate to many Christian refugees from the wars of religion. Moravian Hussites, Lutherans, Calvinists, and even Roman Catholics came together there. At first they were continually fighting with one another—and naturally so, since Lutherans were still praying for the destruction of Calvinists in the same way that Calvinists were praying for the destruction of Rome.

For three years the different sects in Herrnhut fought like cats and dogs. Zinzendorf responded by breaking the community down into small groups for sharing and prayer (landlords can do some things more readily than pastors) and escalated the volume of prayer on the Hutberg, the mountain of God's watch, until it was continuing around the clock. The eventual result was Herrnhut's "Pentecost" on August 13, 1727, at a sunrise service in which all present received a powerful filling of the Holy Spirit. The main evidence of this outpouring upon the community was the filling of members' hearts with fervent love for one another, leading to mutual forgiveness.

It was only at this point that Herrnhut began to be effective as a missionary community in an explosion of outreach which far surpassed earlier Protestant efforts. Two kinds of mission teams went out from Herrnhut: those planting the gospel in new areas and those taking the message of spiritual renewal to the centers of all existing denominations. The Pietist Spener had said that the fractured pieces of the Body of Christ could not be brought together until they were spiritually renewed. Zinzendorf set about promoting renewal, seeking to draw all denominations—including Rome—together in a loose but intimate network of communication. He did not aim at the destruction of the existing church bodies, but only at their closer linkage. He considered each denominational tribe to have a jewel of truth or life or worship to contribute to the Body of Christ, and he aimed, as Richard Baxter had, at "unity without uniformity."

THE RENEWED CHRISTIAN COMMUNITY

If we compare the experience of the awakened community at Herrnhut with the church in Acts, we find that there are three other elements of "abiding in Christ" which are also present in the early church described in Acts. All of these elements move beyond individual spiritual awakening to involve the corporate dimensions of "renewal dynamics."

1. *The commitment to mission.* We cannot really abide in Christ without following Him outwardly in mission.

2. *The prayerful dependence on the risen Christ.* We cannot do His works without depending on His strength.

3. *Community with other Christians.* We cannot remain healthy and alive without receiving grace from all the gifted members of Christ's Body, and contributing our gifts to them.

The explosion of Protestant missions began at Herrnhut. But its most significant achievements may have come out of the Wesleyan movement in England and America, which continued through the Second Evangelical Awakening of the early nineteenth century.

THE SECOND GREAT AWAKENING

The most powerful demonstration of the messianic kingdom we have yet seen may be the impact of the Wesleyan phase of the Great Awakening on the British empire. Beginning with the Wesleys in the 1730s, it continued in the Second Evangelical Awakening under the converted slave trader, John Newton, who organized an "Evangelical United Front" involving elements of almost every denomination in England.

A single Anglican parish in Clapham, near London, contributed business leaders and the parliamentarian William Wilberforce, who could reach the levers of power in the empire. Whereas modern laity may feel they are doing well to keep their own spiritual sanity and reach a few of their peers in personal evangelism, the Clapham laity set out to change the face of England. They attacked moral corruption until the dissolute Regency period yielded to the Victorian era. They attacked the abuses of the Industrial Revolution until child labor was abolished and public school for commoners became a reality. They lived out an evangelical theology of liberation, moving beyond the redemption of individual souls to effect the abolition of the slave trade and the release of slaves within the empire (at a cost of twenty million pounds to the British Treasury); deliverance from wage slavery on the home front; and the conversion of the British Empire from a pure instrument of colonial exploitation into a rail-system for the delivery of the gospel.

There was as yet no clearly articulated theology of the kingdom of Christ motivating this great surge of spiritual and social transformation. But its cutting edge was a laity detached from the struggle for success or survival in the "kingdom of self" and committed to establishing the reign of Christ through their vocations.

The Clapham leaders lived at a spiritual level considerably beyond anything we even suggest for laity today. They spent three hours daily in prayer—morning, noon, and evening. They were not just donating a percentage of their incomes to the clergy so that they could do whatever spiritual things would not too seriously rock the economic boat. They lived simply off a fraction of their incomes and ploughed the rest of their funds into the struggle against slavery, illiteracy, and degradation. Some of them lost their health and their fortunes before that struggle ended. Lord Shaftesbury, who fought long and hard against the evils of industrial capitalism in England, lived on the brink of poverty most of his life. These men and women were for the most part Tories and from the nobility—the equivalent of modern Republicans—but their very conservatism helped them to carry out reform once they saw that it was necessary. Most historians agree that the whole movement from Wesley through Shaftesbury delayed the Enlightenment in England, and avoided its political corollary, violent revolution.

This expression of the messianic kingdom was paralleled in the American phase of the Second Awakening. C. C. Cole has remarked that after the initial movement of widespread popular evangelism, the Awakening was built through five waves of subsequent activity:

1. A wave of development in home and foreign missions
2. A wave of popular Christian literature to nurture converts
3. A wave of establishing new educational institutions, or reasserting Christian influence in older schools, to consolidate and extend the Awakening
4. A wave of "reformation of manners," cleaning up moral corruption
5. A wave promoting peace and social justice, especially the great crusade for the abolition of slavery

Unfortunately, southern evangelical clergy and theologians lost their nerve, avoided challenging the economic concerns of the laity, and developed a doctrine now labeled as heresy by their descendants: "the spirituality of the church," or the notion that "the church should deal only with spiritual issues, and let political and social issues alone." Because of this heresy—because the Evangelical United Front broke ranks—Americans had to shed blood to abolish slavery in the great Civil War. Still, Alexis de Tocqueville and Philip Schaff agreed that nineteenth century America was the most Christianized society in the world, despite the fact that the church relied on spiritual influence and not political establishment to produce this effect.

The Second Evangelical Awakening may have been the finest hour of the Western church. The levels of prayer, unity, and truly holistic mission in this period of advancement were extraordinary.

THE THIRD GREAT AWAKENING

The Third Evangelical Awakening, which began in 1858, launched a great prayer movement of laity for general spiritual awakening and world missions. Around this time, however, American evangelicalism was losing its deep concern for theological integration and was moving into pragmatic anti-intellectualism. The Reformers and the Puritans had been Christian humanists, concerned to integrate biblical truth with discovered truth in the humanities and the emerging sciences. The Moravian Jan Comenius, the founder of western educational theory, had cherished the same ideal. So had Edwards, the Wesleys, Timothy Dwight, and later Abraham Kuyper. But American Christianity at the end of the nineteenth century was neglecting education. As Timothy Smith has recently said, while Protestants and Catholics were fighting one another, secular humanists took over the educational system. The result has profoundly debilitated Western Christianity during the twentieth century.

But is theological integration really part of revival? Are Spirit-led minds essential to a Spirit-filled church? The biblical answer is *yes.* The church in Acts would have been shattered in division and paralyzed in mission if God had not turned its worst enemy into its greatest theologian. Paul was able to lead the church between the Scylla and Charybdis of Christian life and thought: *destructive enculturation* (the accommodation to paganism which was threatening the Corinthian church), and *protective enculturation*, the frozen culture of the Judaizers which would have crippled missions by insisting that all Gentiles become culturally Jewish.

Because it had neglected the cultivation of Spirit-filled and biblically-based minds (the essence of Christian education), the Western church has been crippled by the twin plagues of Modernism and Fundamentalism, which are current forms of destructive and protective enculturation. The result has been division in the church, and limitation of evangelistic outreach. Only recently have we begun to learn that our Jewish converts should be allowed to remain culturally Jewish! This is one of the ironies of history, but also an indication that Martin Bucer's great dream of "the church's happy state" may be drawing near.

And so we come to see that there are four "Secondary Elements of Renewal" in the church. They are:

- *Mission*: following Jesus into the world, presenting His gospel in proclamation and in social demonstration
- *Prayer*: depending on the power of the risen Christ individually and corporately
- *Community*: uniting with the Body of Christ in micro communities and macro communities
- *Theological Integration*: having the mind of Christ toward revealed truth and toward one's culture

As you can see, these elements all extend the rule of Christ's kingdom beyond the individual Christian's heart, bringing order to thought and action and powerfully affecting the outside world.

If we can integrate these lessons of history concerning the "Preconditions of Renewal," the "Primary Elements of Renewal," and the "Secondary Elements of Renewal," we will have established a strong foundation for how we should pray for renewal in our day.

13

A Prayer Agenda
for the Next Great Awakening

Richard Lovelace

What God began building in past awakenings is a good sign of what He intends to complete today. Wholly new features may emerge if He grants us a worldwide spiritual awakening. But since the elements of renewal described in the previous chapter are central to the gospel and anchored in the life and mission of the early church, we can pray for their occurrence today with the assurance that they are critically important for revival and for mission.

HEARTS THAT ARE OPEN TO GOD

Before anything else can happen within the church, God must get our undivided attention. We need to sense our need for God. Can we pray with the hope that today's believers will be awakened from their sleepwalking, disengaged from the rat race for success and survival that the world has built, and turned humbly toward God? Yes, for this is the goal of biblical religion! Under the Old Covenant, the Scriptures were carried about in a box, the Ark of the Covenant, as the talisman that would bring Israel victory in battle because God's presence traveled with it. But God's real home is the human heart that is sensitive to His voice. "Heaven is my throne and the earth is my footstool; what is the home that you will build for me? . . . But this is the man to whom I will look, he that is humble and contrite in spirit, and trembles at my word" (Isa. 66:1-2, RSV*). God

*Revised Standard Version.

has promised to write His Word "with the Spirit of the living God, not on tablets of stone but on tablets of human hearts" (2 Cor. 3:3, RSV). For the heart of the New Covenant is this: "I will give you a new heart and put a new spirit in you; I will remove from you your heart of stone and give you a heart of flesh" (Ezek. 36:26). God has promised to turn the Body of Christ into a construction team which will build His temple of living stones. We should pray that all professing Christians will turn their hearts toward the Lord with a hunger to seek His will.

A New Awareness of God's Holiness and Our Sin

Turning our hearts toward God will result in an outpouring of the Spirit, illuminating our hearts and bringing deep conviction of the holiness of God and the depth of individual and corporate sin. We should pray that whole churches will suddenly become conscious of the sins they are tolerating, which are not just conscious acts of disobedience, but longstanding conditions of spiritual pride, jealously, envy, hatred, resentment, and strife, as well as doctrinal false teaching. We should pray that Christians will realize their sin is no rare and outrageous occurrence in their lives; for the "works of the flesh" are constantly among us, tolerated and virtually invisible. We should pray that *religious flesh* and *spiritual self-centeredness* will be revealed by the spotlight of God's truth. In America Christians are constantly preoccupied with their individual spiritual growth or even their health and wealth, and care nothing for the lost and hungry multitudes of the earth. As John of the Cross points out, every deadly sin has a spiritual form also: spiritual pride, spiritual gluttony, spiritual envy, and so forth. We must overcome this hidden gravitation toward self which afflicts even our spiritual lives, or we will never see an awakened church reach the world for Christ.

As church members and outsiders are brought under deep conviction of sin by the Spirit, they will be eager to hear the good news of Christ's saving work. We need to be sure that our proclamation of the gospel is clear and complete, including *justification, sanctification, the Holy Spirit's indwelling,* and *spiritual authority.*

How many of our people really understand that they are justified (accepted as righteous) not because of their experience, not because they were born again, but only because of the wholly alien righteousness of Jesus Christ laid to their account? How many of them know that they are involved in a lifelong process of sanctification in which God shows them areas of bondage to sin and helps them overcome these by Christ's power? How many of them know the Holy Spirit as a real power? How many can detect the characteristic strategies of Satan in tempting them, accusing them to drive them into discouragement and promoting lies and slander to divide the church! How many pastors are preaching a shallow version of the gospel which does not proclaim the full victory we have in Christ?

PRACTICAL TRANSFORMATION IN OUR LIVES

Not many of our people are even awake enough to have the center of their lives illuminated by the core of the gospel. But how many have gone beyond to reach for the corporate dimensions of life in the Spirit? How many are praying regularly for the kingdom to come among their families, their friends, their bosses, and their subordinates? How many are praying that their place of business will be honest and uncorrupted, and that its whole operation will be a blessing for workers, managers, consumers, the environment, and the whole human community? How many are praying, and also contributing, so that the gospel will reach all people groups, and all the earth be full of the knowledge of the glory of God, as the waters cover the sea?

INTEGRITY WITHIN THE BODY

We can pray that Martin Bucer's agenda of global *inreach* and *outreach* will be achieved in the church. Bucer, you will remember, attempted to encourage the Puritan and the Pietist to pay attention to more than individual piety but also to mission. These goals are mutually dependent. *We cannot achieve world evangelization without an awakened church,* because the church (not just its message, or individual Christians) is "Exhibit A" for the truth of the gospel. Unfortunately, at the moment, it is the biggest piece of evidence on earth that Jesus is *not* Lord. We should especially pray for troubled spots like Northern Ireland and South Africa, where strong commitment to the Bible is combined with unconscious disobedience to its commands.

A Renewed Missionary Spirit

Ralph Winter's work has made American Christians aware that they enjoy a disproportionate share of *everything*—not only of the world's energy usage and gross national product, but of exposure to the gospel. As we might expect, the huge majority of committed and nominal Christians are in North America, Europe, and other parts of the world colonized by Europe. These areas also have some "unreached peoples" who are culturally distant from the Christians surrounding them. But the majority of unreached people are in the Muslim world or in areas dominated by older living religions in the Asian heartland or in the Middle East. That is to say, most Christians are saturated by the gospel while many non-Christians have never heard the good news.

The aim of Protestant world mission during the last three centuries was the expansion of Christian witness until all the earth should be full of the knowledge of the Messiah, "as the waters cover the sea." But if Dr. Winter's research were graphically portrayed as this world viewed from space, it wouldn't show a little gospel everywhere. Rather, the predominating ocean areas would represent deep ignorance, not knowledge. Three centuries of expanding missions, and the earth is still a sea of ignorance!

We should pray that many young Christians will give several years abroad as tentmaking missionaries and that older Christians will take early retirement to go to Third World countries which need their skills and would be glad to receive the gospel also when they realize that it is Christ who has sent them to meet their practical needs.

The Anointing of the Laity

We should pray that the laity, the sleeping giant of the church's power, will experience the release and enabling of its leadership gifts. Richard Hutcheson has said that in every great spiritual awakening, the clergy retire to the coach's box, and the lay people get out onto the field and play the game. This was especially true in the Second Evangelical Awakening, where lay people like William Wilberforce and Henry Thornton changed the whole shape of English life. In the Second Vatican Council, Cardinal Suenens moved that the church be defined primarily as *the people of God* and only secondarily as the hierarchy. Now Pope John Paul II states that social change can best be promoted, not by an activist clergy, but by an awakened laity.

THE SOCIAL DEMONSTRATION OF THE GOSPEL

We should pray for the social demonstration of the gospel, especially in countries where there are large numbers of Christians. J. Christy Wilson has said that the Arab world is unlikely to receive the gospel from Americans when all they know of us is our drunken businessmen and our X-rated films. We must launch crusades to roll back the tides of pornography, abortion, and other socially destructive forces in ways which will not sacrifice freedom of expression.

We must also pray that hunger and other forms of social injustice—the disease centers which communism can infect—will be healed. It is my conviction that multi-national corporations, transformed by Christian workers and managers who will put their jobs on the line to witness for Christian principles, may be able to do far more than governments to end social injustice. Businesses often manage to accomplish what they attempt; governments, for some reason, seldom do.

The model of Campus Crusade's Christian embassy in Washington is instructive. Those leaders discovered that they could not do evangelism credibly with Third World diplomats unless they responded to their concerns for hunger and development in their home countries. The Crusade leaders introduced them to businessmen in this country who could help meet their needs, and *then* they found the diplomats open to listen to the reasons behind their help and their Christian hope.

A BURDEN TO ENTER INTO INTERCESSORY PRAYER

This may sound circular: pray that more will pray. But don't dismiss this point too quickly. Prayer as a serious task is important. In the last century, throughout the eras of spiritual awakenings, prayer escalated—from quarterly concerts to weekly meetings to the daily noontime prayer among laity. But in this century among

Western churches, prayer has been drastically weakened while we work at projects for the Lord.

Intercessory prayer has become vestigial in the churches—a ritual which baptizes meetings as they begin and buries them when they end—because it is focused not upon the whole panorama of God's work in the world, but on stifling particularities. How many pastoral prayers have you heard which really embraced the scope of God's work throughout the planet, probed the concerns of His kingdom in the whole nation, and adequately dealt with local concerns beyond the needs of your own congregation? Our worship services are now monuments to our spiritual self-centeredness as a result of the impatience many people have felt when their pastors have tried to "pray around the world." It is a wonder that any pastoral prayers ever rise higher than the ceiling, when they so rarely embrace anything beyond the walls.

In the late twentieth century, the Pentecostals have become a "third force" in world Christianity, not because their doctrine is perfect, but because they have given themselves to the praise of God and to intercessory prayer. If we are to be delivered from attempting only what is predictably achievable, while others "expect great things *of* God and attempt great things *for* God"—to quote the great missionary leader William Carey—we must return to a proper regard for prayer.

An increase in the volume of prayer may not be as important as refinement in the agenda for intercession. God, as Jesus tells us, is not impressed by the multitude of our words (Matt. 6:7-8). He does respond, however, when we ask those things which are closely related to the interests of the kingdom of His Son. *He is not looking for perfect Christians, but for those who are deeply attentive to His holy purposes.* "This is the one I esteem: he who is humble and contrite in spirit, and trembles at my word" (Isa. 66:2).

Some years ago my wife and I began to pray together with a deliberate aim to develop intercession that was kingdom-centered rather than self-centered. One useful exercise was to pray according to the daily news. Often in prayer groups it helps to perform this simple exercise. Take the main section of the daily paper and tear it into single pages. Give each person a page, and ask him or her to read it, looking to the Holy Spirit to light up prayer concerns in the news of the world. Then hold these before the Lord in prayer. A little experience with this technique will show you how often we ignore God's power to change world events and meet deep human needs, both spiritual and social.

If we are to "expect great things and attempt great things" in this global way, we must surely enlarge the place of praise and worship in our prayer. Only a faith grounded in a deep awareness of God's glory, power, and grace will give us courage for the tasks the coming Great Awakening may involve.

THE DEVELOPMENT OF CHRISTIAN COMMUNITY

We must pray for the development of congregations which are full of cellular groups for prayer, sharing, support, and pastoral help. This means recapturing the experience of true Christian community. In the Herrnhut model, community was strongly concerned with encouraging unity among Christians at levels beyond the local congregation. We must pray for what I call regional ecumenical renewal, in which all the churches in a given area begin to plan and cooperate and share their gifts across denominational lines.

Paul regarded all the congregations in an area as the church in that region, and I am convinced that God still looks at things this way. How can we read 1 Corinthians 1-3 without realizing that Paul would be appalled at our dividing up into teams named after favorite theologians, forms of polity, or doctrinal convictions? What gifts for the whole body are locked up when we isolate all the Pentecostals in one church, and all the Calvinists in another? Often the churches which have most to offer in sharing sound doctrine avoid contact with weaker churches in their area. But Paul teaches that the cure for our being "blown here and there by every wind of teaching" lies not in separation from those less pure but in the drawing together of believers and the "speaking [of] the truth in love" (Eph. 4:14-16).

We must also encourage prayer for the renewal movements of inreach which God has now given us in every mainline denomination including Rome. Why should nominal Christians be ruled out of the great missionary movement of our time? How can the descendants of past awakening movements, whose forefathers were in covenant with God, hear the awakening message of the gospel unless it comes to them in culturally familiar clothing? Christ told us to forgive and to love our enemies and to pray for their recovery from sin and

falsehood. Should we not pray for fellow sinners among the Orthodox, the Roman Catholic Church, and even the World Council of
Churches?

A STRONGER CHRISTIAN EDUCATION

Finally, we should pray for the strengthening of Christian education and theological integration among evangelical churches—
and we must be willing to pay for this as well as pray for it.

When Communists want to subvert a nation, they first infiltrate
its schools. Do they know something we don't know?

A Christian periodical recently urged us to "pray for another
Abraham Kuyper." We should pray for one hundred Kuypers, and
one hundred Edwardses—for great theological minds which are
filled with the Spirit, in touch with our cultures but not duped by
them, and able to meet the issues of our time with biblical answers.
We need minds which can design theological containers big enough
to unite all Christians without quenching any gifts or insisting that
all manifest the same gifts. We need systems which will harness
together those burdened for evangelism and those burdened for
social action without restricting either concern. We need theological
activists who will evangelize the historic churches for orthodoxy,
and experts at apologetics who will not just defeat their opponents
with arguments but convert them with kindness and love.

In short, in order to have global spiritual awakening, we must
have a massive infusion of the mind of Christ, delivering us from
conformity to the world and transforming us by the renewing of our
minds. May God give us grace, understanding, and persistence to
pray for this and every other scriptural dimension of global spiritual
awakening, in order that the world may be reached with the gospel!

14

Twelve Fruits of Revival

J. Edwin Orr

Dr. J. Edwin Orr was a part-time professor of the history of awakenings and the dynamics of missions at Fuller Theological Seminary School of World Mission from 1966 to 1987. He was an ordained Baptist minister, noted author, and a traveling lecturer in 150 of the world's 160 countries. He died in May, 1987.

Revival is the renewal of spiritual life in the body of Christian believers, paralleled by their awakening to the spiritual need in the community. This results in greater evangelism, the teaching of disciples, and reforms in society wherever Christians exercise influence.

The awakening among the believers is due to the outpouring of the Holy Spirit, whereas the evangelism, teaching, and reforms are the response of believers.

THE CHURCH GROWS NUMERICALLY

Church growth is one of the primary fruits of authentic revival.

Following the soundest evangelical awakening in American history, in which more than a million converts were added to four million former members of the evangelical churches, an observer, A. P. Marvin, declared in 1859 that "the chief value of every great work of the Holy Spirit is to be sought, of course, in the number of souls that have been converted, and the increase of spiritual force in the body of Christ."

The first outpouring of the Spirit occurred at Pentecost, when in one day about 120 believers experienced an enduement of power and their number grew to 3,120—which Dr. Donald McGavran has considered "very satisfactory church growth." This was followed by a continued expansion of the Christian faith.

Spiritually vital statistics for the Church of England in the eighteenth century are lacking, but by 1740 the number of Free Church permanent places of worship had dwindled to 27, temporary chapels to 506. Sixty years later, there were 926 permanent and 3,491 temporary churches—an astounding more than 50 percent and 100 percent per annum increase respectively. This, of course, was attributed to both the First and Second Awakenings, with a severe recession between them. More specifically, the First Awakening added thirty thousand converts to Congregational membership in New England; 150 new churches founded in twenty years.

Before the Second Awakening, Wesleyan Methodist church growth had dropped to less than 1 percent, but following the phenomenal revival of 1792, it rose to an unsurpassed 13 percent in 1793. Baptists shared in this revival. Likewise, in the United States decline was followed by remarkable growth. In the resurgence of 1830-42, the number of American Methodist members increased from 580,098 to 1,171,356 in two years. Baptists and others also increased in membership.

During the 1857-58 Awakening in North America, some Canadian denominations quadrupled their number of converts. In the United States, the Methodist Episcopal annual increase in membership more than doubled; Baptist intake of members rose by 140 percent, while the baptisms of believers rose by 84 percent. Presbyterians quadrupled their 1857 figures in 1858 and doubled again in 1859. Congregationalists welcomed treble family growth. The Episcopal confirmations increased by 40 percent in two years, while the Lutheran figures almost trebled.

In the 1859 Awakening in Britain, Baptists added 100,000; Congregationalists, 135,000; Methodists, 200,000. Estimates for Anglicans and Presbyterians raised the total to a million. In Australia, denominations gained in proportion to their evangelical strength; and in South Africa, Dutch Reformed and Methodists alike inscreased in numbers.

A critic of the Welsh Revival of 1904 complained that after five years only 75 percent of those who joined the historic denominations were still in membership—some being "lost" to Pentecostalism and to mission halls, others to emigration. Most recent studies in church growth showed that five historic denominations had increased 20 percent in three years to 687,473, losing less than 2 percent in the next three. The Free Church membership in England reached an all-time high in 1907, exceeding Anglican totals for Easter communicants for the first and only time in history.

That church growth follows revival on the mission fields can be demonstrated by looking at Polynesia in the 1830s. In Hawaii there were 577 church members. Prayer began in 1835, revival followed in 1837, and in five years, 27,000 converts were added to membership, 19,679 being in good standing after twenty years' natural attrition. Other revivals in Africa and Asia caused extraordinary church growth.

It is useful to contrast Japan, considered a very resistant field, to Korea, a very responsive field. In 1883, an intense revival began in Yokohama, Japan, marked by tears, brokenness, confession, restitution and reconciliation; in five years adult membership increased from 4,000 to 30,000. The decade of the 1890s showed decline, but in 1900 began Taikyo Dendo, and 40,000 Japanese evangelicals became 65,000 within a year. In 1914, Taisho Dendo produced 27,350 inquirers, but not as much church growth as previously.

It has been suggested that the 1907 Pyongyang Revival occurred after church growth in Korea was already underway, and that it therefore could not have been a cause of church growth. This misinterprets the events of the first decade of the twentieth century in Korea. The revival commenced, not in Pyongyang in 1907 but in Wonsan in 1903, with prayer, confession, and restitution. The prayer movement that followed in 1905-1906 was described as a "spreading fire, a continuing awakening" in both North and South, bringing many thousands into the church. The extraordinary events which began in Pyongyang in 1907 were a catharsis of the mass of new converts, accelerating church growth. The revival declined by 1910, when it was replaced by the Million Souls Movement in which 15,805 converts were won. It is possible to have church growth without revival, of course, but it is unusual to have revival without church growth.

In more recent times, the Revival of 1952 in Brazil increased Presbyterian (IPB) intake nearly three times and Baptist baptisms 66 percent, while the Assemblies of God seemed unable to calculate gains for three years. In Nagaland, a state of India, 100,000 Christians celebrated their centenary in 1972. In 1976, in an obscure village, revival began, increasing membership to 212,000—a third of the population—within seven years.

THE SPIRIT ANOINTS ALL

The Spirit's outpouring at Pentecost affected all of the believers. It moved some prepared leaders whom we know by name, but it affected a host of anonymous saints as well. Likewise, it is clear that the great awakenings since then have not been the work of any one famous man. Rather, from a host of revived folk God has chosen one or several humble instruments to extend the work. Who would have chosen a student working his way through college to move the multitude on both sides of the Atlantic? . . . But such was Whitefield. Who would have selected a cobbler to spearhead a missionary movement that became worldwide and ever extending? . . . But such was William Carey. Who would have picked a shoe salesman to inaugurate a movement of citywide evangelistic enterprise? . . . But such was D. L. Moody. And who would have called a dairy farmer's son to preach to the millions with a simple gospel? . . . But such was Billy Graham.

CHRISTIAN BROTHERHOOD IS SPREAD

It is sometimes said that revival results in schism and in separation. This is seldom true of the results of a genuine outpouring of the Spirit before opposition to the movement develops. The Lollards wished only to reform the Roman Catholic church in England, but when several hundred were burned alive, they began to feel less than welcome in the established church. Luther's reform also resulted in a separation, but that was scarcely Luther's fault. Wesley in his eighties was still urging his followers to remain within the established church, but his directions were scarcely possible to maintain in the face of official hostility.

There were lesser separations in the early eighteenth century, but the causes lay in earlier repression of revival developments. The disruption of the Church of Scotland followed the 1839 Revival, but it was caused by the gross abuse of secular patronage, not by the revival. When the Awakening of 1857-58 occurred in North America and the Revival of 1858-60 occurred in Great Britain, they caused no schisms. In fact, the American movement produced the greatest demonstration of brotherhood and cooperation since the early church. At first, at least, revival produced brotherly love among Christians. That deteriorated only when forces arose to oppose and divert the revival.

BELIEVERS PRAY IN THE SPIRIT

Undoubtedly, the First Awakening increased the volume and quality of prayer among all participating. The Second Awakening was preceded in Britain by the "union of prayer" in which William Carey was active, and in the United States by the "concert of prayer" promoted by Isaac Backus. The 1857-58 Revival was phenomenally marked by prayer—whole denominations committed to prayer, the churches filled, and even theaters and public halls packed out at noontime. By prayer the movement spread in 1958-60 to the British countries. The Welsh Revival of 1904 arose and continued in prayer meetings. The Korean Revival of 1903-1909 began in little prayer meetings and climaxed in vast assemblies. Even the recent Naga Revival began in concerted prayer. History is silent about any great revivals that did not begin in prayer.

NEW SONGS ARE GIVEN

Isaac Watts, author of hymns as varied in expression as "When I Survey the Wondrous Cross" and "Joy to the World, the Lord Is Come," provided much of the hymnody for the First Evangelical Awakening. Charles Wesley's hymns were fully in vogue by the time of the Second Awakening. There were no such giants in the movement of 1857-58, but the revival popularized Charlotte Elliott's "Just As I Am, Without One Plea" and Joseph Scriven's "What a Friend We Have in Jesus," and a chorus of new songs arose.

For instance, Anna Warner produced a hymnbook in 1858. It has been long forgotten but not the song she wrote for the burgeoning Sunday schools in the revival, "Jesus Loves Me, This I Know, for the Bible Tells Me So," designated by a German theologian as the greatest ever written. Up until 1858, a blind girl, Fanny Crosby, had been writing secular songs, sentimental and sweet; after 1858, she wrote "Sweet Hour of Prayer" and "Jesus, Keep Me Near the Cross," the major themes of that Awakening. And Fanny Crosby soon became the most prolific of all of the American hymnwriters.

Likewise a sixteen-year-old lad in Montreal, converted in the same revival, wrote, "My Jesus, I Love Thee, I Know Thou Art Mine." The revival overtook P. P. Bliss, who was teaching music in Pennsylvania, and made him a mouthpiece of folk singing. Much the same could be said of the worldwide Awakening of the early 1900s, when vast crowds were singing "Channels Only, Blessed Master" and "O That Will Be Glory for Me." In India's Kerala, the Awakening of 1873 and subsequent revivals provided the Malayalam lyrics sung to this day, and this example could well be multiplied throughout the world. Even the hippies converted in the Jesus Movement produced songs and choruses sung everywhere by all denominations.

Children Come to Christ

The Sunday school movement got its start during the stirrings which led to the Second Awakening. Every awakening since that time has accelerated the work of Sunday schools by burdening parents for the salvation of their children, by raising up teachers willing to give their time, and by drawing in the children. In 1857, American Episcopalians reported 95,559 in Sunday school; in 1858, 109,349; in 1859, 117,612—a 22 percent gain, four times the biological growth rate of the period. Presbyterians announced that Sunday schools in almost every presbytery were flourishing; every denomination gained.

New Workers Volunteer for Ministry

Revival produces an immediate increase in the number of those volunteering for ministry, and it crowds out the colleges and seminaries with candidates for ordination. This was seen during the 1857-58 Awakening, where the seminaries—denominational and union—were overcrowded. Traditionally at that time the Ohio Episcopal Kenyon College enlisted 40 to 140 students. However, in the following year candidates for orders in that denomination increased to between 233 and 291. This was typical of most denominations.

Not only have world evangelists arisen from great revivals, but each movement in the various fields has called forth indigenous evangelists. Not only have effective evangelists produced great revivals, but revivals have produced great evangelists. The evangelism of Taikyo Dendo in Japan in 1901 was carried on by national evangelists. The Chinese revival of the decade raised up outstanding Chinese evangelists, such as Wang Chang-tai and Ding Li-mei, a pattern repeated in the 1930s in the ministry of Sung Shanchieh, Wang Tsai, Gih Tsu-wen, and a host of others. The 1903-09 Revival in Korea raised up not only evangelists, but missionaries to nearby countries.

John Wesley's use in the eighteenth century Awakening of lay preachers and lay exhorters is well known, but other denominations were scarcely affected until the 1957-58 Awakening in North America and the 1859-60 Revival in the British countries. Bishop Warren Candler noted that the revival "inaugurated the era of lay work in American Christianity." And the Lutheran *Evangelical Quarterly* declared that the revival brought a "modern era of revivals, missions, and benevolent institutions" with consecrated laymen taking their rightful role and position in the church.

BIBLES AND TRACTS ARE DISTRIBUTED BROADLY

Active promoters of the Second Great Awakening formed the British and Foreign Bible Society, followed by societies in United States, Scandinavia, and other countries. The same was true of the Religious Tract Society, and the movement for publishing and circulating Christian literature. And each subsequent work of the Spirit has been followed by a great acceleration of such enterprises.

In the 1858 Revival, the American Bible society reported the lowest level of donations and legacies for five years, due to the disastrous bank panic, yet reached record highs in sales in both 1858 and 1859. This prepared the way for the enormous circulation of Scriptures maintained throughout the Civil War. In Britain, the 1859-60 Revival expanded Bible circulation in Ireland and Scotland and brought about great developments in England and Wales.

It would be indeed difficult to discover a national or local revival in any decade or continent which did not greatly increase Bible distribution. In some such movements in recent times, not only were the stocks of Scripture exhausted, but shipments were rushed from a dozen countries speaking the same languages.

New Missionaries Volunteer

The Moravian missionary movement, which started in 1727 with a prayer vigil that lasted one hundred years, grew out of the eighteenth century Awakening. It was not until the Second Awakening—from 1792 onward—that foreign missions became a general practice in all the evangelical denominations. William Carey, an initiator of the Union of Prayer that preceded the revival in Britain, became one of a noble band of pioneers who reached all the continents. The movement of the 1830s accelerated mission pioneering and brought local revival to various fields.

Out of the 1857-60 Awakenings came an extension of activity by all of the existing mission societies, together with the founding of interdenominatinal societies such as the China Inland Mission by Hudson Taylor, a worker in that revival in London. So thorough was the 1860 Revival in Jamaica that the London Missionary Society withdrew, as did the American Board from Hawaii, turning over the work to indigenous workers. By the time of the 1905 worldwide Awakening, the revival spawned phenomenal awakening in many fields—Korea, India, Chile, and most of Africa. The pattern is still repeating itself.

The Moral Life of the Land Is Uplifted

Early efforts promoting temperance in, or abstinence from, alcoholic drinking arose from the Second Awakening. In 1858, whole towns were purged of grogshops and saloons. Every revival movement has made its impact on addiction. For instance, hundreds of drinking saloons went bankrupt during the Welsh Revival of 1904. And the effect of the Jesus Movement on drug addicts is well known.

Much the same could be said about debauchery and prostitution. Britain was the industrial workshop of the world in the first half of the nineteenth century, but the prostitution disgracing its cities and towns received a setback in the 1859-60 Revival—a midnight meeting movement evangelizing women of the street. This was followed by Josephine Butler's campaign for the repeal of government patronage of prostitution and licensing of vice.

SOCIAL REFORMS ARE LAUNCHED

Social reform may be carried out by Christians only when they, as citizens, exercise influence in the place of power. A missionary or pastor whose ministry is appreciated by a hereditary tribal chief may achieve more for reform of society than millions of believers repressed under an atheist dictatorship.

This may be illustrated in the fact that the abolitionists of the slave trade were almost all activists in the Evangelical Revival renewed at the beginning of the nineteenth century. The so-called Clapham Sect, mostly evangelical Anglicans, persuaded great men in places of power to join them in their grand objective. Likewise, a generation later, Sir William Fowell Buxton—another evangelical—mobilized opinion in Parliament to proclaim an emancipation of the slaves in every country of the Empire. Parliament was supreme. And had the United States been a unitary republic rather than a federation of equal states, evangelicals might have been able to persuade Congress to abolish slavery before the Civil War.

Reform of prisons, indescribably foul at the time, was a result of the Evangelical Revival in Britain. Such activists as John Howard and Elizabeth Fry in the nineteenth century succeeded in accomplishing the separation of the sexes, classifying criminals, useful employment, secular education, and religious instruction, to restore criminals to society. Theodor Fliedner in Germany, duly impressed, built a home for discharged women prisoners, another for men, another for orphans, a hospital for the sick, and an asylum for the insane, thus impressing the German authorities. In turn, Florence Nightingale learned nursing there and became a ministering angel to wounded soldiers and the founder of modern nursing.

Kenneth Scott Latourette in his weighty volumes confessed that there was not enough space to list more than a few of the reforms impelled by evangelical motivation. Ashley Cooper, Seventh Earl of Shaftesbury, converted in the times of revival before Waterloo, described himself as "an Evangelical of Evangelicals," and continued to be active in evangelism throughout the movement of the 1830s, in 1859, and in Moody's great campaigns of the 1870s. Until he initiated his reforms, workers were caught on a treadmill of industrial drudgery that kept them straining for sixteen hours a day.

He introduced the ten-hour day, the Saturday half-holiday, minimum Sunday work; he and his supporters introduced legislation to abolish the use of women in coal mines, of children in cleaning factory chimneys, and of the insane in exhibitions. He promoted public parks, playing fields, gymnasia, garden allotments, workmen's institutes, public libraries, night schools, and other civic benefits.

After the 1858 Awakening, social action was soon applied to the needs of soldiers, the wounded, and prisoners of war; but also to minister to the needy in cities of the United States. Following the 1859-60 Revival, "the major part of the great growth in voluntary charity" reached its peak in Britain in 1860s and 1870s, "inaugurated, manned, [and] also financed by revival converts and sympathizers"—a prime vehicle being the Salvation Army.

David Lloyd George, the British Prime Minister, declared that "the movement which improved the condition of the working classes, in wages, hours of labor, and otherwise . . . is due to the great religious revival of the eighteenth century." But most of these reforms were achieved in subsequent revivals.

EDUCATION IS IMPROVED

The first necessary step of social reform is the education of the masses. The first American universities were founded by Puritan settlers, the next in the eighteenth century Awakening, after which the denominations affected by subsequent revivals founded hundreds of colleges, while supporting popular education.

Following the Second Awakening, evangelical missionaries pioneered popular, monitorial education in Latin America, and helped set up Argentina's teacher training colleges. Presbyterians penetrated Brazil in 1859, and set up schools from kindergarten to university, followed by other denominations. A Brazilian historian, Fernando de Azevedo, said that for a long time these schools "were among the few innovating forces in education" and are now recognized as the forerunners of the Brazilian system of education.

In India and southern Africa, evangelical missionaries possessed advantages in their right of appeal to the source of power— the British Parliament. so they pressured the East India Company to provide schools for Indians; however, after forty years they themselves operated as many or more schools with similar totals of pupils. After 1859, their enterprise founded India's medical system of hospitals. Even during World War II, 90 percent of all nurses in India were Indian or Anglo-Indian Christians. Much the same was true of Southern, East, and West Africa, where evangelical missionaries sent out by the revivals pioneered not only education, but medical services. Even today, various African nationalist leaders were mission-trained.

What of countries that were independent of colonialism but nonetheless were penetrated by the gospel? The opening of Japan to the West occurred in times of revival and was followed by the evangelical pioneers who not only communicated the gospel but opened schools—one of which became the Imperial University. Japan already possessed its own system of education, but there was a craving for Western education. Within thirty years, the missionaries had established 250 churches with twenty-five thousand members, and one hundred schools. Neesima established Doshisha, a Christian university.

A convert of the 1859 Revival in Wales, Timothy Richard went to China as a missionary. He proposed founding colleges in the capital cities of the eighteen provinces. His opportunity came when he persuaded the authorities to use 500,000 taels of indemnity money for the establishment of the University of Shansi, so influencing Chinese higher education. Missionaries established universities in Canton, Shanghai, Nanking, and Peking; and in provinces such as Shantung, they accomplished this on limited budgets.

In summary, it could be affirmed that the outpouring of the Spirit has been God's greatest method of reviving the Christian constituency and extending the growth of the church throughout the world. It has taught believers to pray and to witness; it has recruited candidates for the ministry and mission field and for social action; it has expanded Sunday schools and founded Bible societies; it has produced a wealth of hymns and spiritual songs. And, wherever permitted, it has tackled social evils providing education and social advantage, tackling drug addiction and prostitution, confronting child exploitation, reducing workers' hours of labor, providing Christian leadership in affairs of state and industry—a light to the nations and the way of salvation.

15

The Necessity of Unity in the Body of Christ

Joy Dawson

Joy Dawson serves on the staff of Youth With A Mission. Her Bible teaching ministry takes her to many nations on every continent of the world. Her deep prayer life and intense knowledge of the Scriptures gives depth and authority to her messages.

Unity in the body of Christ will only be experienced when we understand what unity means from the divine perspective. The standard of this unity is uniquely found in John 17:11, where Jesus prays that "they may be one as we are one." Therefore, biblical unity—the unity that God is talking about—is nothing less than what might be called Trinity Unity—the unity that the Father and the Son and the Holy Spirit experience at all times. We need to know what their relationships are like because that is what we're supposed to experience here on earth.

CHARACTERISTICS OF THE RELATIONSHIP AMONG THE MEMBERS OF THE TRINITY

Although the relationship among the members of the Trinity cannot be fully articulated by man, some elements of that relationship can be enumerated.

1. The members of the Trinity are equal in authority but different in function.
2. They complete each other in ministry function but never com-

pete. We are often not aware of where one starts and another ends. There is a total blending of the three.
3. They have absolute truth in their relationship and therefore have absolute trust.
4. They glorify one another and serve one another.
5. They have singleness of purpose.
6. They have absolute holiness in their relationships—therefore the ultimate enjoyment of one another.
7. They are an invincible team which has an eternal, indestructible kingdom; therefore, they are the ultimate in effectiveness.

From Jesus' prayer in John 17 we understand that this Trinity Unity is a powerfully convincing proof to the world of the fact that God the Father sent God the Son to the earth in the Person of the Lord Jesus Christ.

In other words, the unity of the Body of Christ should convince the world of the deity of the Lord Jesus Christ and the total commitment of the Godhead to every disciple of the Lord Jesus Christ. The power and the force of this unity cannot be hidden. It ought to be increasingly obvious to the non-Christian. The source of our unity is the same glory God the Father gave to His Son, and it shines through us: "I have given them the glory that you gave me, that they may be one as we are one" (John 17:22).

Awareness of this unity should in turn strongly motivate the non-Christian to commit his or her life to the Lord Jesus Christ.

SEVEN PRINCIPLES OF TRINITY UNITY

1. *It is possible.* We seldom attempt anything unless we believe it is possible. Jesus prayed we would experience this kind of unity; therefore, it must be possible, and we must believe in its possibility.

2. *It applies to all believers.* We must want to experience this full unity with every child of God—not just those with whom we feel comfortable. Paul wrote, "We ought always to thank God for you, brothers, and rightly so, because your faith is growing more and more, and the love every one of you has for each other is increasing" (2 Thess. 1:3).

3. *We must ask for it.* James 4:2 says, "You do not have, because you do not ask God."

4. *We must receive it by faith.* Hebrews 11:6 says, "Without faith it is impossible to please God."

5. *We must submit to the Spirit.* We must submit to the Person of the Holy Spirit who alone can work unity in us and through us. Romans 5:5 says, "God has poured out his love into our hearts by the Holy Spirit, whom he has given us."

Dr. A. B. Simpson has said, "The Holy Ghost kindles in the soul the fire of love . . . the flame that melts our selfishness and pours out our being in tenderness, sacrifice, and service. And the same fire of love is the fusing, uniting flame which makes Christians one, just as the volcanic tide that rolls down the mountain fuses into one current everything in its course."

6. *Humility is essential.* We must realize that true humility of heart is the only condition in which unity will work. Such humility is the basis of all true love. All lack of love is based on pride. All coldness is rooted in pride. We're only as loving as we are humble. Philippians 2:1-4 puts it this way:

> If you have any encouragement from being united with Christ, if any comfort from his love, if any fellowship with the Spirit, if any tenderness and compassion, then make my joy complete by beng like-minded, having the same love, being one in spirit and purpose. Do nothing out of selfish ambition or vain conceit, but in humility consider others better than yourselves. Each of you should look not only to your own interests, but also the interests of others.

7. *We must submit to God's ways of love.* There are certain ways of relating that will work and other ways which won't work.

- We must be called of God to the group or relationship. The most spiritual person in the world who joins your group outside the call of God will, in time, become a source of disunity.
- We must have the same vision and purpose. It is the responsibility of spiritual leaders to seek God's face and God's vision for the group they have been called to lead. Vision is not the program; the program fits the vision.

  The vision is the most far-reaching purpose in the heart of God as to the reason He brings a group into existence. The leaders should also be constantly asking God, "Is there more vision You want to give us?"

  The vision must be clearly defined and declared. The program must always be a means of fulfilling the vision.

- All members of each group must be functioning in the right ministry gifts as outlined in Ephesians 4:11-12; 1 Corinthians 12:28; and Romans 12:6-8—apostles; prophets; evangelists; pastors; teachers; ministries of helps, giving, hospitality, writing, and so forth.

We must recognize each other's ministries, make room for them, submit to them, know what our own ministry is (and what it is not) so that we can learn and receive from others. Humility is the basis for this.

• We must always have the right attitude toward God. We should constantly be giving Him love, thanks, and praise—without resentment or murmuring.

• We must also have the right attitude toward others. Reserves must be dealt with. God's standard is to "love one another with a pure heart fervently" (1 Pet. 1:22, KJV*).

According to Psalm 133, the result of unity is inevitable. God bestows His blessing! It says:

> How good and pleasant it is
>   when brothers live together in unity!
> It is like precious oil poured on the head,
>   running down on the beard,
> running down on Aaron's beard,
>   down upon the collar of his robes.
> It is as if the dew of Hermon
>   were falling on Mount Zion.
> For there the Lord bestows his blessing,
>   even life forevermore.

Unity here is likened to the anointing oil poured on Aaron's head. We may fail to appreciate the imagery, but that oil was very costly, very holy, and very fragrant.

CHARACTERISTICS OF BIBLICAL UNITY

IT IS COSTLY

Biblical unity is not "peace at any price." It requires openness and brokenness. We have to become good communicators and, when necessary, deal in love with situations that are often painful.

*King James Version.

We must humble ourselves before others and extend forgiveness. We must love unconditionally.

IT REQUIRES HOLINESS

Biblical unity is based on the biblical standards of holiness. That includes holiness in thought, word, and deed. It also requires quickly repenting of all that does not meet those standards.

IT IS FRAGRANT

Biblical unity is fragrant. It is delicate. It is beautiful. It is pleasurable. By contrast, we are unable to enjoy each other where there is unresolved sin in a relationship.

This wonderful unity is like the dew on Mount Hermon. In arid Middle Eastern lands, dew is absolutely essential for life. The quality of our spiritual life will be determined by the quality of our unity with all other members of Christ's Body.

This kind of unity is also very powerful for the advancement of the kingdom. Jonathan and his armor bearer had unity, and a remarkable phenomenon took place. Two men killed twenty in the area of one acre of land and spearheaded a mighty advancement in the cause of the kingdom of God (1 Sam. 14:1-15).

We, too, can outsmart the devil every time we fulfill these conditions of Trinity Unity love.

PRAYER AND BIBLICAL UNITY

We need to follow Jesus' example and make prayer for unity in the Body of Christ a top priority, for John 17 clearly states that unity is a key to world evangelization.

We need to pray for a great release of the Holy Spirit's power to convict us of our pride and to produce the humility of heart needed in all of God's children. That will help us to see our need for each other and especially the need to learn from each other, so that we can truly say that we "in honour [prefer] one another (Rom. 12:10, KJV).

We also need to pray that God will expose satanic activity among spiritual leaders. Often Satan's subtlest tactic is to cause disunity over minor issues.

We need to pray that spiritual leaders will see the need to become loving intercessors for other spiritual leaders, which is a powerful weapon against division.

16

Once Begun, How Can Revival Be Maintained?

Peter Beyerhaus

Dr. Peter Beyerhaus, from East Germany and a former missionary to South Africa, is currently a professor at Tübingen University and director of its Institute of Missiology and Ecumenical Theology. Almost every year since 1971 he has been following-up on invitations to visit various countries. This has brought him into vital contact with churches, missions, and theological training institutions in all parts of the world.

Many of us feel that revival has already begun to come to us these days. And we pray that the Holy Spirit will cause it to grow into a mighty revival that will move the world.

But if that kind of revival is coming, let us also pray that it will not be short-lived. Church history identifies many revivals by their length. There have been great revivals with long-term blessings that were appreciated for generations. Others were more spasmodic: they came, they disappeared, and maybe they appeared in another place, but there was no continuity. Some burned out after a very short while; others ran wild.

So if revival is starting among us, what is it that will result in "the continuation of revival"?

We should not approach the subject with a nostalgic attitude to believe that the very first appearances, those ecstatic emotional effects, must constantly persist. It's tempting but shortsighted to think that if the emotional ecstasy passes, so has the revival. Continued revival means that the awakened new life remains with us and that this new life is continuously renewed in each member of the Body of Christ and that this new life spreads through us to others.

As it says in John 7:38, "Whoever believes in me, as the Scripture has said, streams of living water will flow from within him." Spurgeon describes such a revived church in the following way: "It's a church that is marked by its desire constantly to hear and to share the Word of God. A revived church is a church whose members are marked by a deep conviction of their sins and a longing for grace. A revived church is a church who is grateful to Jesus Christ for the redemption and bursts out in praise and thanksgiving. A revived church is a church that is aware of God's holy presence in our midst which is filled by a deep Christian love where the members have a sense of unity and a missionary urge."

Now, for this to become a reality, we must constantly remind ourselves of three things. First, what is the origin of our spiritual life? Second, what are the dangers to it? And third, what is our responsibility to maintain this reality of new life?

WE MUST UNDERSTAND THE ORIGIN OF OUR SPIRITUAL LIFE

Our world is desperately yearning for real life—life that is lasting, life that is meaningful, life that gives fulfillment and joy. And we know that there are many treacherous answers that promise to give life but lead to death. They urge salvation through Eastern religions, mystic cults, or self-realization. All of these offer no real life to modern man. The Bible gives a very clear answer in contrast.

1. *Jesus Christ is the source of the church's new life.* Jesus Christ, risen and ascended, is the fountain of continuous revival. The Bible first of all makes it clear that the loss of life is the predicament of the whole fallen world. In our rebellion we cut ourselves off from God, the origin of life.

But on the very day that the human race fell into sin and lost the life, God already had in His mind and His heart of Fatherly love a grand program to restore that life. And the clue of this program to restore life is Jesus Christ, who in all eternity enjoys that divine life that unites His three blessed Persons of the Trinity—Father, Son, and Holy Spirit. Though Christ came to us as a humble man, He had in Himself that life. When the disciples heard Him preaching, they said, "Lord, to whom shall we go? You have the words of eternal life" (John 6:68). He restored the life of dying people by His miracles, but the greatest mystery is that He sacrificed His own life in order that we could live. Out of His resurrection came the new life for all the world. And when Jesus Christ had risen and ascended to His Father, the first thing He did was to send the promised gift of the last times: the Holy Spirit that made life available to everyone.

2. *The church is the vehicle for sharing this new life.* Now we encounter another mysterious design in God's plan. Jesus Christ decided that it should be His disciples in the church who would become the vehicle of all the life He wants to offer to dying man. What a tremendous privilege to be the Body of Christ filled with His life and to be able to share that life. But that task can only be fulfilled if we remain in constant communion with Jesus, who is the origin of salvation, and follow His example in sacrificing our life for God. We can do all this if we become a church marked by continuous revival. How can a Christian or a church want to do anything but live in continuous participation with Christ's life in a ministry?

What is the reality? Far too often many churches and many individual Christians lose their vitality. They make a good beginning, but they relapse into a state of coolness. There is, of course, a reason for it. The enemy of God, who is the enemy of man, does not want to lose his influence. However, he cannot interfere directly with our divine life if we remain branches in Jesus Christ. The Lord Jesus said, "No one can snatch them out of My Father's hand" (10:29). So Satan tries to counteract our life in the ministry. That is one reason we so often lack true vitality. We have lacked spiritual watchfulness and therefore we have given opportunity to Satan to wedge between us and our ministry.

WE MUST BE AWARE OF HINDRANCES TO OUR EFFECTIVENESS

We must remember the three factors which influence our personal spiritual lives and our lives as a part of the church: the divine, the human, and the demonic.

1. *The neglect of the divine factor* is the first reason we so often become spiritually poor in this life. When we do not experience true communion with God, the process of His reviving us is

halted. We abandon our first love for God. There is no longer that fervent prayer which urges us to share our divine life with others, and that can start in a very subtle way. Even a church which is very active and fights the enemies of God and endures persecution can nonetheless lose its first love. That is the reason the Lord wrote to the church in Ephesus, "Yet I hold this against you: You have forsaken your first love" (Rev. 2:4). When we become careless in using the means of grace and careless in sharing God's life with others, Satan will use that blockage in our relationship to God and we will no longer revive the church.

2. *The human factor* also affects our life. Satan seduces even the Christian to develop self-conceit. Even in a church marked by revival, our old nature wants to serve itself. Even in revival, the human factor can take center stage. Too much importance is paid to the leaders. We indulge the dark coat of the evangelistic creature and we deprive God of His glory. Rivalry arises amongst the revival leaders, we take pride in our particular traditions, and there is strife among the revivalists. Yes, my dear friends, even we so-called evangelicals are often tempted to put ourselves in the place where God should be.

Another way the human factor enters in is that the people in the pew enjoy their emotions and their tears too much. Sometimes they feign what is not genuine or let themselves become sentimental rather than be moved by the Holy Spirit. Feelings become more important than a conscience genuinely convicted of sin.

3. *Satan is the third factor,* and he is even more dangerous. When Satan discovers that the human factor has become important in a revival, he uses it to enthrone himself. Satan is the master in imagination, and he uses his terrible skill to imitate a true Christian revival.

The imitation of supernatural manifestations and miracles is often unperceived by many people. But that is the key to the strange and terrible inroad of spiritualistic manifestations among some of the most surrendered souls in the church.

This is the reason that even in the middle of a revival we are warned, "Beloved, do not believe every spirit, but test the spirits, whether they are of God; because many false prophets have gone out into the world. By this you know the Spirit of God: Every spirit that confesses that Jesus Christ has come in the flesh is of God, and every spirit that does not confess that Jesus Christ has come in the flesh is not of God. And this is the spirit of the Antichrist, which you have heard was coming, and is now already in the world" (1 John 4:1-3, NKJV*). Now our time, dear friend, is a period of increased spiritual warfare. Satan knows that his time is short. And it seems that in the time in which we are privileged to live, both the risen Christ and Satan are doubling their effort to prepare for the final battle.

We should read about the battle which is raging between Satan and Christ for control of the church. We should again and again return to the seventh epistle in the book of Revelation, which ends with this appeal: "He who has an ear, let him hear what the Spirit says to the churches" (Rev. 3:22). We have to remember that indeed God in His providence does allow the enemy to put His church through the test. As the Lord Jesus said to Simon Peter in Luke 22:31, "Simon, Simon! Indeed, Satan has asked for you, that he may sift you as wheat. but I have prayed for you, that your faith should not fail; and when you have returned to Me, strengthen your brethren" (NKJV). So not even the most beloved disciple, not even the most beloved church can stand in this fight, unless the Lord Himself prays for us.

We Must Embrace the Prerequisites for Revival

We see that Jesus Himself sets an example for us in that He does pray and intercede for the continuous revival of His loved ones. But He does not want to perform this high priestly ministry alone. He has invited us to join Him.

Indeed, dedicated prayer is the indispensable condition for maintaining a continued revival. We have reminded ourselves of our great endowment and vocation to be bearers of new life to a dying world. We have also been shaken by realizing the severe danger of losing our momentum in sharing this new life. And now we need to learn that true revival may continue or even start afresh in a remarkable way.

1. *God wants to revive us.* Some may ask, "Do we actually need a revival? Are we not witnessing many encouraging signs,

*New King James Version.

activities, and conferences, which are expanding the kingdom of God? Are we not daily developing new strategies to evangelize the world?" All these things are true indeed, and we are grateful that the Lord has blessed us. But when I look at the world scene of Christianity, the evangelical scene included, I see that we are still missing one important thing. I do not really see the Holy Spirit breaking through and bringing the church to its knees in confession and repentance.

In former ages when the church was revived, there was a marked spiritual upheaval in the whole society. That occurred because nonbelievers were impressed by the change in the lives of the Christians. Even hardened people—criminals and those who were constantly attending the pubs—were breaking down in prayer and reforming their lives under the influence of the Holy Spirit. Whole societies were purged. Do we really see this happening today? More commonly we see immorality spreading more wildly and even affecting Christian families. Why do so many young people seek their satisfaction in drugs and in Eastern cults? Shouldn't we as Christians give that life to them?

I think that we have yet to see true revival in this age. But God does want to revive us.

What does this mean? First of all we have to remind ourselves that it is God Himself, not we, who will accomplish revival. True revival always comes from God when He sends His Holy Spirit to convict of sin. As it is promised in Zechariah 12:10, "And I will pour out on the house of David and on the inhabitants of Jerusalem the Spirit of grace and of supplication; then they will look on Me whom they pierced; they will mourn for Him as one mourns for his only son, and grieve for Him as one grieves for a firstborn" (NKJV).

God wants to give revival to the humble and contrite. When we are ready to confess our sins and to turn away from the world and self-satisfaction, we will prepare the way for the outpouring of His Spirit. God gives revival in answer to prayer. All historical revivals were given in this way. Do we have enough of such prayer?

2. *God seeks intercessors.* God seeks intercessors because this world is filled with perishing people—three billion souls are perishing. The Lord is seeking those who will plead for perishing souls that they should not be lost. And far too often, He cannot find intercessors.

The Lord says to Ezekiel in Ezekiel 22:30, "So I sought for a man among them who would make a wall, and stand in the gap before Me on behalf of the land, that I should not destroy it; but I found no one" (NKJV). God seeks intercessors because He has great riches to give. Has God already exhausted His riches and His spiritual blessings? He gave His Son to the world. He gave His Holy Spirit. He gave the age of Martyrs. He gave us the Reformation. He gave us evangelical revival. He gave us the great missionary movement. But God has *not* exhausted His possibilities. He is still a rich God—but who will claim these riches by intercession?

God seeks intercessors because He gave us a powerful instrument in this gift of prayer. Do we realize its power? Do we handle it correctly? Do we establish prayer ministries in our congregations? Why do the churches engage in all types of activities and even dabble in politics instead of making prayer their main concern?

Let intercession spring up in your personal life. Help intercession become a major ministry in your home congregation and in your denomination.

3. *God blesses the self-surrendering prayer.* What kind of prayer brings down new revival because it reaches the throne of grace? It is a prayer of surrender and meditation and repentance. It is prayer that magnifies God's grace and claims His promises. It is prayer that joins the praying ministry of Jesus Christ, the High Priest, and is done in the Holy Spirit. It is prayer that is done intelligently, strategically, perseveringly, and maybe most importantly, in a united spirit.

In my study at home I have one photograph, which is the dearest one in my whole house. I brought it with me when I came home from my second visit to Korea in 1974. I call the picture, "The Praying in Korea." It is of an aged Korean lady, deeply bowed in prayer. She is closing her eyes, but you can feel that something is pulling out the soul of this lady. Rain was pouring down terribly hard the day I took the picture, and the lady was completely soaked. But she didn't notice the rain because her mind was at home with Christ. I think that picture was taken the night before EXPLO '74 started. When we arrived we were told that there was a great prayer meeting being held all night by Korean ladies. We were not actually invited to go there because the prayer was to be all in the Korean language, but my friend and I went anyway, in order to see what was happening. We saw that the whole former airport was covered with praying Korean ladies. Of course there was no translation, but I think I understood what was prayed.

I sensed the mood in which that prayer was done. It started in a very low-key, humble way, and then it went almost into weeping. The spirit of imploring and interceding was poured out. Suddenly again the tone changed, and it became full of joy. Again and again I heard one single Korean word that I recognized: "Thank you, thank you."

What had happened? These ladies had already received the fulfilling of their prayer. That is what I mean by praying in a spirit of surrender and giving glory to God.

I conclude by inviting you to join such a movement of prayer. In the words of the prophet Hosea:

> Come, and let us return to the Lord;
> For He has torn, but He will heal us;
> He has stricken, but He will bind us up.
> After two days He will revive us;
> On the third day He will raise us up,
> That we may live in His sight.
> Let us know,
> Let us pursue the knowledge of the Lord.
> His going forth is established as the morning;
> He will come to us like the rain,
> Like the latter and former rain to the earth.
>   (Hos. 6:1-3, NKJV)

17

Group Praying in One Accord

By Evelyn Christenson

Evelyn Christenson is the author of What Happens When Women Pray *and has conducted seminars all over the United States and in several countries on the subject of prayer. She is organizer and chairman of the board of United Prayer Ministries, a nonprofit corporation based in Minnesota. Evelyn has helped organize citywide prayer chains in many cities throughout the United States.*

Most of us agree that praying in one accord is important if we want God to answer our prayers. However, sometimes we do not realize that various factors other than genuine differences of opinion destroy our unity. In many cases these factors stem from our prayer times being too disorganized.

When I was doing research about prayer, I discovered that a large percentage of Christians seldom or never prayed aloud in the presence of others. Many were afraid to try because they felt so inadequate when they heard more experienced Christians praying. Therefore, I encourage the more experienced Christians to alter the form of their prayers so that the less experienced people will not feel intimidated.

Disorganization and intimidation do not build a spirit of one accord. We need a few guidelines. And that is what I want to share with you. I call them the "Six S's Method of Group Prayer."

To make these elements work effectively, the prayer group leader is responsible to see that all the members abide by the rules. Otherwise the prayer meeting may become a gossip session or a coffee party. The leader's job is to teach new "pray-ers" how to pray and to guide the veteran pray-ers so that they won't intimidate the new people and defeat the purpose of your group.

S-1: Subject by Subject

Praying about only one subject at a time helps produce praying in one accord. While one member leads audibly on a subject, all others are praying silently instead of planning long prayers in advance. Then all members have the privilege of praying audibly about additional aspects of that subject if they wish. Avoid vain repetitions.

Leaders should set the example of staying on the subject when they pray. Example is one of the best teaching methods in praying.

When new people are learning to pray in public, they usually don't have too much trouble with this method. However, many veteran or experienced pray-ers find it difficult to avoid wandering into new subjects. If you have a problem with others not observing this rule, pray about it, and watch as you let the Lord take care of it.

You should explain that as the group's leader, you will be the one to introduce new subjects of prayer when a previous one has been adequately covered. You can do so by:

- Announcing a new subject. This is a must if the group is large. Also it is very helpful in guiding inexperienced pray-ers.
- Leading out in prayer on a new subject when you feel that everyone is finished praying on a previous subject. It is also useful to pause between subjects to let the mind switch gears.

Later, as your group practices together, other members can lead to the new subject when all are finished praying on a previous one.

S-2: Short Prayers

Short prayers are the secret to success in group praying. If someone mentions every aspect of a subject when he prays, others feel there's nothing left that needs to be said. However, when each participant restricts what he or she says to just one or at the most a few sentences, it allows everyone a chance to take part.

Matthew 6:7-8 says, "And when you pray, do not keep on babbling like pagans, for they think they will be heard because of their many words. Do not be like them, for your Father knows what you need before you ask him." As a leader, it is your responsibility to see that your members pray short prayers. Remind the group of all the neglected requests because of the long prayers on a few subjects. It may be necessary to speak to some individuals privately.

Above all, as a leader keep your prayers short. Others will be willing to follow your example. You as a leader aren't there so they can hear your lengthy prayers but so that you can encourage all to pray. Every member should have the privilege of praying the same length of time.

As new pray-ers join your group (after you have graduated to more complex praying) it probably will be necessary to drop back to this simple rule to ensure the untrained ones' participation in prayer and their continuation in the prayer group. Remember, it is the leader's responsibility to help all participants feel comfortable.

S-3: SIMPLE PRAYERS

Simple prayers will enable the shy and untrained to speak from their heart. Avoid high-sounding words and theological phrases. Again, you as the leader will help keep the prayers of your group simple by leaving your high-sounding, theological phrases at home in your prayer closet.

If this is not done, new group members may never come back after concluding that they don't know the language you are speaking. As a leader, encourage newcomers, rather than discouraging them with your vocabulary.

As your group matures in prayer, you won't be inhibited by this rule.

S-4: SPECIFIC PRAYER REQUESTS

Take the time to have someone record specific prayer requests, and then record specific answers in the days and weeks that follow. This will be a great encouragement to continued and enlarged praying.

Keep a record of requests in a book. Record all requests with the date requested and then the date answered in a column or page next to the request. This will be a great tool in teaching how long God waits to answer, how He answers, and how He answers all things for our good.

Your members will themselves see the value of prayer as they note the answers to their prayers.

If your prayer group starts to fall apart or members lose interest, review your specific answers to your specific prayers. Renewed enthusiasm is assured.

S-5: SMALL GROUPS

"Praying in one accord," usually works best in small groups because such groups allow an intimate oneness in the presence of Christ. It is much easier for a newcomer, a shy person, or someone untrained in prayer to pray in a small group. Large groups require real courage.

It is also easier for you as a new leader to begin by leading a small group. If the group gets too large, you may want to divide using separate rooms, drawing apart in small groups in the same room, or starting a new group. Don't underestimate the value of a small group. It can be the turning point in your spiritual life.

Remember Matthew 18:20, "For where two or three come together in my name, there am I with them." The presence of Christ is experienced in small groups just as well as in large ones.

As you practice the presence of Christ, keep in mind that Christ died, was buried, rose again, forty days later ascended from the planet earth bodily, and now sits at the right hand of God in the place of authority and honor as our Savior. However, by the Holy Spirit, He will be in the room with you, and we do experience the thrill of His presence as He promised.

The only thing to remember is that a person cannot experience the presence of Christ if he or she is not a member of the Body of Christ. Matthew 18:20 was promised to Christ's followers only. Be alert as a group leader for the unusual opportunity of guiding any unsaved group members into a personal relationship with Christ.

S-6: SILENT PERIODS

Silent periods during a prayer session are a privilege and a blessing. Don't panic if there is a lull. Prayer is a two-way conversation with God, not just talking *at* Him but talking *with* Him. If there is a period of silence, just listen, for God may be speaking to you.

It is helpful if you explain this to the group so that others aren't made uncomfortable by lulls. Actually, the leader is responsible to wait in silence long enough for God to speak to members of the group. They need to expect to hear from Him.

There are two specific times when you as a leader should encourage some silent time:

• Before starting audible prayer. Help your group to turn off the world from which they have come and silently draw near to God before any audible prayers are uttered. However, there is one caution: Warn members against popular meditation methods which are not prayer but just ways of opening one's mind to any spirit.

• Between prayer subjects. Don't deprive members of hearing God's voice in two-way conversation with Him, and don't deprive God of the opportunity of bringing answers to mind by rushing on to the next prayer request.

By following these simple guidelines, I believe that you can guide groups into a new and exciting experience of praying in one accord.

18

A Pastor's Perspective
of Building a Praying Church

Paul Cedar

*Dr. Paul Cedar is presently the pastor of the Lake Ave-
nue Congregational Church of Pasadena, California, with a
membership of more than forty-five hundred. He is also the
president of Dynamic Communications, Inc. and an ad-
junct professor of evangelism for Fuller Theological Seminary, leading seminars and workshops for local churches,
pastors' groups, and business leaders. Cedar is the author
of six books, including* Sharing the Good Life! *and* The
Strength of Servant Leadership.

The church was born in a prayer meeting (Acts 1:14). The
commandment of our Lord was that they should gather together in
prayer, waiting and seeking Him until He empowered them with the
Holy Spirit. They did that. Do you remember the astounding results
of the coming of the Holy Spirit? There was a sound like a mighty
wind and flames of fire on the heads of the believers, filling their
hearts and lives with the Holy Spirit. He absolutely transformed the
lives of the apostles and that little band of 120 people who had
gathered together to wait for the Lord.

Before Pentecost Sunday, there had been much fear and resistance. But now there was great power, great victory, and great
courage. Peter stood in the streets of Jerusalem along with all the
apostles and the band of the faithful believers, and they proclaimed
the gospel of Jesus Christ. In one day the church grew from a little
circle of 120 people to an assembly of 3,120 people.

Prayer was the key to the coming, the filling, and the empowering of the Holy Spirit. Throughout the New Testament we can see the centrality of prayer.

I am a pastor of a very wonderful church, and I praise God for the privilege to serve as I do. Presently, we are suffering from a very marvelous problem. We are filled to overflowing. We have three morning worship services that are now full. We have a television overflow room, and we have our adult classes, youth classes, and children's classes filled. We don't have any more room. It would be easy for us to just assume that all we need to do is build more buildings.

But by God's grace we have decided to do something else: set aside a period to pray and fast and seek the will of God. In that period, we are setting aside all of our agendas, all of our preconceived ideas, all of the little camps into which we so easily divide. There are always little camps in the church—"We ought to build this," "We shouldn't build that," "We should do something else"—instead of the common denominator of just seeking the Lord.

At this point, I admit that I honestly do not know what God is going to call us to do. but I am grateful that we are opening the doors of our hearts and lives as a church. If I as a pastor, and the members on the pastoral team and all of us whom God has called to leadership, humbly seek God, He will direct us, guide us, and provide for us. And we will have the unity of the Holy Spirit.

My commitment as a pastor is to so follow Christ that I can invite my people to follow Christ together with me, that we may grow to become more and more like Jesus Christ Himself. That is the model in Ephesians 4:11-13. I remind you that God gave leadership gifts to the church so that all the saints would be equipped, that all would be involved in ministry together, that the body would be built up, that there would be a unity of faith and a unity of the knowledge of Jesus Christ, and that we would all grow to maturity.

Then Paul gives a measurement for that maturity. It is an astounding measurement. We are to measure ourselves by nothing less than the full stature of Jesus Christ Himself. That is central for those of us who would like a life of prayer. We read in 1 Thessalonians 5:17 that we should pray without ceasing, that we should be communing with God constantly.

We used to have about twenty people attending our regular Wednesday prayer meeting; now we have several hundred, plus we have several other prayer events. Here is how Lake Avenue Congregational Church began to be transformed into a praying church.

Our Leaders Were Committed to Prayer

The first step was to get our committee and board members to commit themselves to participate in our weekly all-church prayer meetings.

I proposed to the leadership of the church and then to the congregation as a whole that we move our board meetings and our committee meetings to one single night of the week—that night being Wednesday night. The reason was so that while all those leaders were at the church, they could take time out of their meetings to participate in our regular Wednesday evening all-church prayer meeting. Then they would return to their committees and complete their business.

Now I know that every week there will be several hundred people in our all-church prayer meeting because the leadership has made a commitment to take time from our business meetings and spend it together in prayer. When the pastoral team and the church leaders committed themselves to congregational prayer then—and then alone—were they ready to begin to expect the rank and file members of the body to come.

One of the other things we've done regarding our Wednesday night prayer meeting is this: We have nearly one thousand people who meet in small weeknight groups. I have encouraged all small groups of the church to cancel one meeting a month and instead come to the church on the night of our all-church prayer meeting.

Scores of those people are now coming to our Wednesday evening meetings once a month. In order to allow for continuity of their meetings, when the congregation as a whole breaks into small groups within the larger assembly, I encourage the people from the weeknight groups to break into their own small groups for prayer. If they want to continue to meet for another half hour or hour following our prayer time for sharing and fellowship as a small group, they have the opportunity to do so.

We Set Aside a Quarterly Week of Prayer

We set aside one week a quarter for what we called a "week of prayer," including an all-night Wednesday prayer meeting. There again, we gather all of the congregation together for prayer.

In addition, we established what we called a "round-the-clock prayer chain" during the whole week. We allowed people to sign up for various periods around the clock for seven days.

Our particular church, though it was a large, influential, evangelical congregation, had never set aside a day of fasting and prayer as a church. But we started to do this. As you may have guessed, it turned out to be a tremendous source of blessing. I find that the people of God respond wonderfully to structure when we provide it. We need to provide regular times and regular meetings for prayer.

WE HELPED FAMILIES TO PRAY

We need to help our families in their prayer times and family devotions, and even help them pray together as families around meals.

We need to teach husbands and wives how to pray with one another. We need to help people to spend time in prayer with God each day. I find that few people are effective in corporate prayer who haven't first learned how to be faithful in their personal prayer. Prayer is not optional, but neither is it easy. Therefore, our communication with God must be made central in our lives.

WE GAVE SPECIAL INSTRUCTION IN HOW TO PRAY

Some time ago Dick Eastman came and conducted a school of prayer for us. Nearly one thousand people came and spent an entire day learning how to pray. We are already planning another school of prayer for the coming year. I believe that we need to stay on the offensive. Prayer is a spiritual battle. Satan will do anything he can to keep the church from prayer. We need to plan special occasions to focus on prayer that will motivate, equip, encourage, and help us as a church, as families, and as individuals.

WE ENCOURAGED PRAYER FOR THE OUTREACH OF THE CHURCH

I believe we need to set up special prayer groups in our churches to support in prayer the various outreach activities of the body. Let me give you two examples that are taking place in our church. I am so grateful for both.

AN OPEN MINISTRY OF PRAYER

We have developed a prayer room ministry that takes place following each of our Sunday services. At the close of each service, I give an invitation for people to come to our prayer room. We have a ministry team composed of members of our pastoral staff and lay leaders who are willing to pray with people about almost any concern. We believe in anointing with oil and praying for healing, and that is part of that ministry. We believe very deeply in praying for personal needs. We believe very deeply in praying for members of family and for friends.

I cannot begin to tell you of the tremendous blessing this prayer ministry has been as literally hundreds of people each year are now being ministered to through this service of prayer. It is simple, it is very low profile. There's nothing emotional about it. In fact, people do not come forward until after the benediction. They are given instructions as to how to reach the prayer room, but they must take the initiative to get there themselves.

I encourage you, whatever your theological persuasion, to consider this kind of prayer ministry.

SUPPORT FOR THE WORSHIP SERVICE

The other example is a prayer ministry with which I have nothing to do. It was begun in the hearts of some lay leaders, and it has been a spontaneous movement of the Holy Spirit. We now have a prayer team of several hundred people who take turns praying every Sunday during the three worship services. Usually about a dozen people out of the total large group go to the prayer room and pray during the entire worship hour. I cannot tell you the value of that ministry.

I want to remain open to the Spirit. The correct strategy for Lake Avenue Congregational Church may not be the correct strategy for your church at all. But I believe that by some means we all need to give priority to prayer in our churches.

Part Four

Prayer and Regional Evangelization

19

Strategy for Developing a Prayer Movement in Each Region

David Bryant

David Bryant serves nationally as Mission Specialist with Inter-Varsity Christian Fellowship, USA. He has promoted biblical vision and practical strategies to thousands of students and lay people across the United States through his World Christian Conferences. He is a member of the Intercession Working Group of the Lausanne Committee for World Evangelism.

In 1724, Jonathan Edwards, a Puritan preacher in New England, wrote a book with the following lengthy title: *A Humble Attempt to Promote Explicit Agreement and Visible Union of All of God's People in Extraordinary Prayer for the Revival of Religion and the Advancement of Christ's Kingdom on the Earth.* That's a mouthful, but in it Edwards reveals exactly what he saw in a passage of Scripture as the prescription for launching a spiritual renewal in his generation.

The passage was Zechariah 8:18-23. Keep in mind some of the words of Edwards' title, and I think you will understand how he found those ideas in this passage.

> Again the word of the Lord Almighty came to me. This is what the Lord Almighty says: "The fasts of the fourth, fifth, seventh and tenth months will become joyful and glad occasions and happy festivals for Judah. Therefore love truth and peace."
> This is what the Lord Almighty says: "Many peoples and the

inhabitants of many cities will yet come, and the inhabitants of one city will go to another and say, 'Let us go at once to entreat the Lord and to seek the Lord Almighty. I myself am going.' And many peoples and powerful nations will come to Jerusalem to seek the Lord Almighty and to entreat Him."

This is what the Lord Almighty says: "In those days ten men from all languages and nations will take firm hold of one Jew by the hem of his robe and say, 'Let us go with you, because we have heard that God is with you.' "

We see in these verses from Zechariah what I might call the anatomy of a movement of prayer. And these words were spoken to a very specific situation. They were spoken to some forty thousand faithful people—a remnant—who had come out of captivity back to their homeland for one purpose: they had come to rebuild the temple.

But fifteen years later when Zechariah came on the scene, this remnant had become so discouraged for various reasons that they had given up.

Maybe you've felt something like that when you considered the task of motivating people for prayer. If so, these words are for you.

The movement these faithful people had undertaken is very similar to trying to launch a movement of prayer. And in the anatomy of this movement I see four characteristics: (1) The attitude of the people involved. (2) The agenda that is addressed. (3) The impact of the movement. (4) And finally, the ignition that gets it started.

Each one of these four characteristics is very practical to remember and apply as we plan for prayer mobilization.

THE ATTITUDE OF THE PEOPLE

There are three important characteristics of the attitude of the people.

1. *Joyful prayer.* I know the importance of prayer and fasting, but here Zechariah tells the people to quit fasting and start feasting.

You see, they were commemorating in four separate fasts during the calendar year the four major sieges of Jerusalem. In other words, for seventy years they had lived in defeat. But God was ready to do a new work in their midst. As a sign of that, Zechariah says, "It's time to pray with celebration and with praise, because God is on the move to do all that He has promised."

2. *Urgent prayer.* The second thing that marked their attitude was that it was a prayer movement full of urgency. Notice the phrase, "Let us go at once." Immediately. There was no time to delay. I believe that urgency was there for two reasons.

One, there was a holy desperation. The temple lay in ruins. God's name was being blasphemed among the nations. The time had come to call His people to prayer before the eyes of the nations, that the nations themselves might come to seek Him as well. It was a sense of holy desperation. Isn't that true for today?

But also there was a sense of holy anticipation. God was ready to move. Don't we feel that today, too? And if He was ready to do what He promised, for example, through His prophet Isaiah—to do the grand and glorious things in people and throughout the nations as He said He would do—then can we expect any less? Zechariah says, "Go at once to seek the Lord."

3. *Laborious prayer.* It was an attitude and a prayer movement in travail. Where the Bible says they were "to seek the Lord Almighty and to entreat Him," we find two Hebrew words that are used elsewhere in the Old Testament to describe a woman in childbirth.

This is a prayer movement that is travailing. And yes, there is agonizing and there is warfare in prayer. It's hard work. But there's also glory and beauty in a movement of prayer, like a woman who is giving birth to a child, bringing forth something new and fresh and alive. It is similar to what we read in Romans 8 about all of creation groaning and travailing to be released from its bondage of decay. Aren't we also groaning and travailing for the day of renewal, and even more for the day when we will experience the full redemption of our bodies and the time when the Spirit draws alongside our weak universe and such weak people as we, and He helps us? But even when the Spirit intercedes, He too groans. He knows what God has in His heart and would like to perform in His church and in His world, and the Spirit desires it with everything in Him. He is God. He leads His people to travail in the same way. It's hard work!

THE AGENDA OF THE MOVEMENT

What is the primary task for this movement of prayer? The call that goes out is: "Let us go at once to entreat the Lord and to seek the Lord Almighty." Literally in Hebrew it says, "to seek the face of the Lord." There are many places in the Old Testament where the phrase to "seek the Lord," to "be in the presence of the Lord," to "stand before the Lord," really originates in the Hebrew from the idea of coming before the face of the Lord. His face is what I stand before in prayer.

In fact, that phrase is often used of the ministry of the Levites in the Tabernacle and in the Temple. They were "before the face of the Lord." Here is a prayer movement that has one basic prayer request: "Father, would you show us Your face?"

The writer of Psalm 67 understood that. He said, "May God be gracious to us and make his face shine on us"—that's spiritual awakening—"that your ways may be known on earth, your salvation among all nations"—that's world evangelization.

When you consider God's answers to every prayer request you have ever prayed and every prayer request that has ever been lifted to the Lord in a movement of prayer, you will see that God has shown more of Himself than had been seen before, either by His church or by His world. All of God's answers to prayer are summarized in one thought: He has revealed His face.

Whatever we do in mobilizing a movement of prayer, this must be the clear focus: that the earth will be filled with the knowledge of the glory of God. As the waters cover the sea, we must seek His face, revealed to His church and to His world.

The Impact of the Movement

Look again at Zechariah 8:23. It says, "This is what the Lord Almighty says: 'In those days ten men from all languages and nations will take firm hold of one Jew by the edge of his robe and say, "Let us go with you, because we have heard that God is with you." ' "

That was a movement of prayer which had international repercussions. And I believe that such a movement of prayer is erupting today. It has international repercussions in two ways.

1. *It establishes credibility for the gospel.* Observers will say as they did in Zechariah's time, "The Lord is among them. They have found Him. We see Him in their midst. And the beauty and glory and wonder and healing and life that we see in Him in their midst draws us out to seek Him ourselves as unbelievers, and we come to those who have found Him and say, 'We're laying hold of you. We want to

know Him as well.' " That's credibility for the message.

Can there be any more powerful incentive for evangelism than that the glory of God be so real and tangible in the midst of His people that the nations flow to us and seek from us a way that they can know Christ, too?

2. *It creates accessibility.* The other part of the impact of this movement of prayer is that it opens access to God for all. Somehow, something happened in the vision in Zechariah 8. Whereas there were only forty thousand in the audience with whom he shares his vision, by the time he ends his vision we find that there were Jews— that is the praying people—scattered throughout every language and nation, and they become accessible to those who do not yet know the Lord.

Notice the ratio of ten to one in Zechariah. There were ten unbelievers who are able to reach the robe of one believer, one of these praying people, and ask that person to lead them to the Lord. Ten to one!

Do you know that today there are approximately 2.5 billion on the face of the earth who cannot hear the gospel? They are totally unreached. The gospel is not accessible to them as things stand. But, worldwide, it is estimated that there are about 250 million evangelicals—that is, Christians who love the Lord Jesus enough that they want to share Him with others.

At this very moment in history, the ratio is exactly what it was in the book of Zechariah—a ratio of ten to one.

A movement of prayer, marked with feasting and urgency and travail that focuses on God revealing His face to His church and to His world, will become a movement of prayer that has international repercussions because it will give credibility to the message about God's Son, and accessibility to the messengers who are thrust out of that movement of prayer to share Christ with the world.

You can expect that in any movement of prayer you help to mobilize—whether in your church, in your city, in your nation, on your continent—if it is true to the vision of Zechariah, it will have those characteristics.

THE IGNITION FOR THE MOVEMENT

How does such a movement get started? What sparks it?

Let me review for you Zechariah 8:20, "This is what the Lord

Almighty says: 'Many peoples and the inhabitants of many cities will yet come, and the inhabitants of one city will go to another and say, "Let us go at once to entreat the Lord and to seek the Lord Almighty. I myself am going." ' "

One city was going to another, calling the people to come and experience what they had found, to come with them and seek the Lord together. There's something in the words of Jonathan Edwards' book title: *A Humble Attempt to Promote a Movement of Prayer.* . . . What point was he making by choosing those words?

There's something important about the humbleness of starting where you are. Some time ago my wife and I made a covenant together to spend five minutes a day before we retire in the evening down on our knees and praying for one thing and one thing only: that God will reveal His face to His people and to the nations. Though we pray for many other things together at other times during the day, at that point we pray for just that one thing.

I can say that what God has done in our relationship as husband and wife to unite us in love for Christ and in service to Him, is far beyond anything we had ever experienced. It arises out of those five minutes a day that together we have given to seek God's face.

That's the place to begin if you are married. It might take other forms. It might be one Sunday school class going to another Sunday school class in your church and saying, "Why don't we set aside one class a month and meet together for the hour to pray for a spiritual awakening and for world evangelization?"

Or it might be one church in a city going to a church of a different denomination, and saying, "Come, let us seek the face of the Lord." I've seen God do that to some degree in my hometown of Madison, Wisconsin, the past few years. Churches going to other churches.

Could one city go to another city and say "Come, let us seek the face of the Lord"? In the Los Angeles area, churches in one city are going to churches in another city and saying, "Come, let us seek the face of the Lord together."

Could it ever come to the place, as Zechariah suggests it might, where one nation would go to another and say, "Come, let us go at once and seek the face of the Lord?" Well, that happened when the church in Korea invited churches from around the world to assemble for the International Prayer Assembly. It's continuing to happen as various groups have sensed a movement of the Spirit of God summoning us to serve what He is bringing forth in prayer in His church.

Many of us have found ourselves in one way or another saying to others, "Come, let's join together from different nations; let's covenant with each other so that in the days and months and years to come, we will be better servants to a movement of prayer in the church."

What is the igniting spark for that kind of impact in mobilizing prayer? Ultimately, if this movement of prayer is to take place, there must be individuals who express precisely what the people expressed in Zechariah when they said, "I myself am going." *That's* the humble spark that sets the blaze. If in your church, your city, or your nation, you cannot find others to begin praying with you for spiritual awakening and world evangelization, you must begin alone. You must have the conviction that God has spoken clearly enough to you, that even if no one else goes to seek the face of the Lord, you will say, "I myself am going."

But I know and you know that God is already touching many lives, and they're just waiting for someone to draw alongside them and say, "Let's go together and seek Him together."

20

Changes in the Muslim World

Gottfried Osei-Mensah

Gottfried Osei-Mensah was executive secretary of the Lausanne Committee for World Evangelization for many years. Previously, he was pastor of Nairobi Baptist Chruch, Nairobi, Kenya, for three years, served as traveling secretary of the Pan African Fellowship of Evangelical Students, and was a sales engineer for Mobil Oil, Ghana, Ltd., before entering the ministry.

One in every five persons in the world today is a Muslim. Yet Christians, on the whole, know very little about their Muslim neighbors or the religion of Islam.

As long as we remain uninformed, we cannot pray intelligently or effectively for a real break-through in sharing the good news with Muslims. Islam, therefore, remains perhaps the greatest single challenge to the gospel in this generation. The concentration of Muslim populations is in the so-called "resistant belt" stretching from Senegal in West Africa, through North Africa, the Middle East, the Arabian Peninsula, all the way to Bangladesh and down to Indonesia. But significant communities of Muslim peoples are scattered all over the world. A growing number of Muslims now live in Western countries as a result of recent migration.

THE CHALLENGE OF ISLAM

The impact of the increasing self-awareness of the Muslim peoples is felt by the rest of the world in many areas of life:

209

- *Economically*, the oil-producing Muslim nations are now capable of holding the rest of the world at "gunpoint," and have done so. The use of the "oil-weapon" has seriously affected the economies of many Western nations; but the effect on the non-oil-producing developing countries has been devastating.

- *Politically*, access to vast oil wealth has given unscrupulous Muslim dictators the capacity to interfere in the affairs of other nations. This they have done by financing dissidents and supplying international terrorists with arms. Even respectable governments have been tempted to turn a blind-eye to the suppression of human rights due to the promise of lucrative profits related to the petroleum industry.

- *Socially*, the tendency of most Muslim immigrants to avoid integrating with the peoples of their host country has created problems. Sizable Muslim immigrant communities in some Western countries are demanding a right to special schools and other social amenities for their culture and religion. The resentment felt by their indigenous neighbors is understandable.

- *Religiously*, the Muslim world no longer pleads to be left alone by other proselytizing faiths. Resurgent Islam has itself become intensely evangelistic, and desires to convert the whole world to Islam. Muslim strategists see the spiritual vacuum created by secularism in the West and the quest for spiritual solidarity in the developing countries as their opportunity to strike. Concrete plans have been made to convert Europe and Africa to Islam in this generation. Already strategic use is being made of schools, hospitals, the media, and other Islamic institutions.

The Attraction of Christ

The challenge of Islam is considerable; but that is only one side of the story. The other side is the unprecedented attraction that the Lord Jesus Christ has among many Muslim peoples today and their openness to hearing the good news of salvation through Him. This openness to the gospel has occurred in many areas.

- The Isawas of Northern Nigeria are traditional Muslim scholars who specialize in the study of references to Jesus (Isa) in the Koran. In recent years they have turned to Nigerian evangelists to learn more about the Savior from the Bible; some have been converted.

- The Fulani and other West African Muslim peoples have learned about the Lord Jesus mainly through Christian radio broadcasts and the practical love of Christian workers, especially during the recent droughts. They have become open to the good news!

- Similarly, Afghan refugees in Pakistan camps have turned to Christ in large numbers as a result of their experience of the love of Christ through the sacrificial service of Christian relief workers.

- From Egypt, Indonesia, and the Muslim immigrants in Germany and Australia come reports of wonderful conversions as Muslims' eyes are opened to the Lord Jesus Christ through the Scriptures and the loving service of Christians.

But the instances are many, too, where missionaries have faithfully taught and sacrificially served for years without seeing much fruit.

THE CALL TO PRAYER

Because of the hardships that the policies of some Muslim governments tend to impose on the rest of the world, feelings toward Muslims are on the whole, negative. Some Christians even find theological and historical justification for their antipathy toward Muslims. But it is clear that the command to proclaim the saving love of Christ to people of all the nations includes the Muslims as well.

In his recent book, *The Supremacy of Jesus*, Bishop Stephen Neill writes: "It is a fact of experience that, when Muslims have become Christians, the starting-point of their quest has, in many cases, been found to be some act of service rendered by a Christian to a Muslim, who had no claim whatever to any such act of service, the action going far beyond what could ordinarily be expected as between friends."

Therefore, the primary objective of our prayer for the Muslim world must be that Muslims may come to see the Lord Jesus Christ in all His love and power to save, through His Word and the sacrificial service of Christians. This primary objective can be broken down to three targets toward which we must aim our prayers:

1. That Christians (worldwide) may be sensitive to the spiritual needs of Muslims and accept their own obligation to show Christ's love to their Muslim neighbors. Therefore, we must pray for the work of Christian institutions whose ministry is to help Christians to develop their knowledge of the Muslim religion. Examples of these kinds of institutions are: the Samuel Zwemer Institute, the Henry Martyn Institute, Gairdner Ministries.

2. That existing opportunities to witness for Christ among Muslims may be creatively used to the full, both in Muslim lands and among the diaspora; therefore, we must pray for effective radio broadcasts, quality correspondence courses, and the distribution and use of literature. We must also pray for the discreet witness of Christ's presence through Christian engineers, architects, oil workers, medical personnel, business people, teachers, lecturers, and relief workers serving in Muslim lands. Pray, too, for Christian social workers and volunteers called to teach English, French, or German to immigrants in their homes.

3. Finally, that the Spirit of the Lord may create and deepen a widespread spiritual hunger for Christ among Muslim peoples all over the world. And that that would lead to a large-scale harvest among Muslims and the establishment of an appropriate witness for the Lord Jesus Christ throughout the Muslim world.

It is a big challenge. But "is anything too hard for the Lord?" (Gen. 18:14)

21

The Need for Prayer in Muslim Evangelism

Kundan L. Massey

Kundan Massey and his wife, Iqbal, began Campus Crusade for Christ's campus ministry in Pakistan in 1959. He is the former Director of Affairs for the Middle East.

Prayer in evangelism is not a secondary thing but is the most important thing. It is the foundation for the entire work of evangelism. John Wesley said, "God does nothing apart from prayer and everything by it." S. D. Gordon said, "The real victory in all service is won beforehand in prayer. Service is merely gathering up the results." Those views are the deep conviction of my heart, too.

When Jesus drove out an evil spirit that the disciples had been unable to dislodge, they asked why they couldn't. "He replied, 'This kind can come out only by prayer' " (Mark 9:29). Samuel Chadwick stated, "For this task we need the supernatural power; that supernatural power comes with prayer and fasting. Also there is no power like that of the prevailing prayer of Abraham pleading for Sodom; Jacob wrestling in the stillness of the night; Moses standing in the breach; Hannah intoxicated with sorrow; David's heart broken with remorse and grief; Jesus in sweat of blood. Add to this list the records from the church and always there is the cost of passion unto blood. Such prayer prevails. It turns ordinary mortals into men of power. It brings power; it brings fire; it brings rain; it brings life. It brings God."

We serve a God who answers prayers. Jesus is sitting at the

right hand of God as our High Priest answering prayers. God works. A prayer can become a nation-shaking, history-making, world-moving affair. "Call to me and I will answer you and tell you great and unsearchable things you do not know" (Jer. 33:3). It is not that our prayers are so mighty but that God promises to show great and mighty things. Our God is the living God with whom nothing is impossible. He is the Almighty and can change the course of history and the hearts of people, and He is able to transform the life of a nation.

THE SCOPE OF ISLAM

The Muslim religion has become the fastest growing religion in the world. Its missionary efforts, zeal, and the commitment of its people to the cause of Islam are amazingly contagious. There are 750 million Muslims in the world. One of every six human beings scattered all over the whole world is a Muslim.

THE NATURE OF ISLAM'S REVIVAL

A few decades ago it seemed that in many parts of the world Islam was a dying religion. But that is not the case today. New life has come to Islam. Muslim missionaries are being trained in Pakistan, Egypt, etc. and are being sent to convert pagan peoples and ignorant Christians.

All this effort is being funded by the oil rich countries in the Middle East. Political and even military power are sometimes used to advance the cause of Islam. The strong Muslim nations that are becoming independent are encouraging religious devotion in order to unite and inspire their people. To some Muslims, converting Muslims to Christianity is considered a political rather than a religious offense.

More and more Muslims are traveling to the West. People who a few years ago lived in goatskin tents and rode camels across the sand dunes are suddenly buying Mercedes cars, televisions, video machines, and even American banks. The world of Islam is in the news today more than ever before, while the rest of the world collectively holds its breath each time the OPEC nations meet. Demonstrations and riots in Iran, Egypt, and Pakistan by Muslim conservatives demanding a return to traditional ways, a cry of

"Back to the basics," shows the world a militant revival and resurgence of Islam.

ISLAM IS A RELIGIO-POLITICAL SYSTEM

Islam is not only a personal religious faith, but it is also a religio-political system in which religion and state are united. The laws and rules of Islam are both civil and religious. Islam includes all aspects of life—personal, social, economic, cultural, religious, and political. The law of their faith tells the Muslim man and woman what their duties are in all areas of their life on earth.

THE NEED FOR MUSLIM EVANGELISM

The Great Commission was given for the whole world. Lord Jesus commanded us to proclaim the gospel of Christ to everyone everywhere (Mark 16:15).

God loves everyone in the world (John 3:16).

God wants to save Muslims, too. Christ died for them also. God loves the Muslim world. The Muslim world is hard; it is a big mountain to be moved. Muslim response to the gospel has been very little; very few conversions occur because of the persecution.

Dr. Samuel Zwemer often preached from Luke 5:5. "Master, we've worked hard all night and haven't caught anything. But because you say so, I will let down the nets." Yes, the Christian workers have toiled for centuries among Muslim people with only nominal results. There have been different conferences and seminars throughout the years to find new methods and tools to reach the Muslim world. But the time has come to let down our nets with prayers of faith into the deep. Jesus said that what was impossible for men was possible with God. With God all things are possible. We need prayers of faith in Muslim evangelism, prayers of compassion, and most of all persistence in prayer. That is the answer for Muslim evangelism.

RESISTING SATAN

Prayer is a communication between finite man and his sovereign God. But don't forget that there is a third party who gets involved whenever we are trying to advance the kingdom of God. He is the old deceiver, Satan. Daniel 10 reveals this fact. Daniel was a man of prayer and faith. He prayed a stirring prayer. Remember, that prayer was made with fasting, and he prayed with great burden and mourning of his heart for three weeks. He waited for the answer but no answer came. One day passed; one week passed, then two weeks, even three weeks. This was most unusual for Daniel. As a man of prayer, his prayers were usually answered when he prayed. But Daniel didn't doubt God. Daniel didn't stop praying; he continued his prayer with the same zeal, compassion, burden, and persistence. The answer came on the glorious twenty-first day.

The angel told Daniel that God's answer had been sent the first day the prayer was offered. But that third party person, Satan, stepped in the way; and he and the angel became engaged in prolonged battle lasting more than twenty days. Had Daniel not been persistent in his praying, the battle would have ended, his prayer unanswered.

But prayer continued day by day and the hindering spirit was removed. The lesson from Daniel's life is simple. Satan is a real person, possessing awesome power to fight prayer. So when we pray, it's not just man and God. Into the scene comes another party, one seeking to block the answer. Philip Henry prescribes "Pray alone, let prayer be the key of the morning and the bolt at night."

PRAYER AND ACTION IN MUSLIM EVANGELISM

Mark 9:29 in the *Living Bible* says, "Jesus replied 'Cases like this require prayer.'" Muslim evangelism is one of these cases. Islam is Satan's fight against the deity of our Lord. He is blocking the ways, hardening the hearts, and closing the doors. But God is almighty and powerful. The prescribed formula is *prayer*... prayer of faith and persistent prayer, along with our efforts and action.

As we noted earlier, Luke 5:5 says, "Master, we've worked hard all night and haven't caught anything. But because you say so, I will let down the nets." But what was the Lord's bidding or command? Luke 5:4 says, "Put out into the deep water, and let down the nets for a catch." That is the action to which we are called. Let us continue to go into the deep for Muslim evangelism. Who has commanded it? The Lord, our Commander-in-Chief. The Great Commission is His command; our work is to obey. His promise is "Lo, I am with you always (even in the deep)." Convicting and converting is the work of the Holy Spirit.

COMPASSION IN PRAYER FOR MUSLIM EVANGELISM

Several young Salvation Army Officers asked General Booth, "How can we win the lost?" Booth's return letter said only, "Try tears." The psalmist made a worthy statement concerning emotions, "The sacrifices of God are a broken spirit; a broken and a contrite heart, O God, you will not despise" (Ps. 51:17).

Spurgeon's pleading cry was "Oh, for five hundred Elijahs, each one upon his own Mt. Carmel, crying unto God, and we should soon have the clouds bursting into showers."

It is time for more compassion, more love for the Muslim world, more prayer, more constant, incessant mention of the cause of Muslim evangelism in our prayer. Then the blessing will be sure to come. Today we do not have enough broken hearts in church pulpits or the pews. We talk about the neglect of the past, we talk about difficulties and dangers, but we don't shed tears of compassion for the Muslim world.

LOVE FOR THE PEOPLE OF ISLAM

It is easy to think of Muslims as enemies to overcome rather than as lost children of God to be sought and saved.

Islam has denied the basic truths of Christ's deity for thirteen hundred years. It also denies His death on the cross, His resurrection, and His glorification. It has pushed Him off the throne to seat another in His place. But that does not mean the command of the Great Commission does not apply here. It does. The greatest command of God is to love God with all our heart and with all our mind. But it also includes the command to love our neighbor. We need to present the truth with love.

Emphasize the uniqueness of Christianity. God is love, and we love each other because of God's love. Witnessing in love usually brings results. Many converts have come to the saving knowledge of Christ through the loving attitude of Christians. The growth of the church in Mali is an example of that fact.

Someone told me that it was the tears of one Christian friend that led him to become Christian. Muslim evangelism needs prayer with the fervor called for in Isaiah 41:21: " 'Present your case,' says the Lord. 'Set forth your arguments,' says Jacob's King." In other words, God has invited us to "Come argue the case with Me. Tell Me why you ask for this." Are we ready to do it?

Prayer according to God's will is answered. Muslim evangelism is His will. We see that in the Great Commission. God doesn't want anyone to perish. The lack is not in the cause but in the prayer support for this difficult cause of Muslim evangelism.

Let us make it a priority in our prayer.

22

Organizing a National Prayer Movement

Vonette Bright

Dr. Vonette Bright is the wife of Dr. William R. Bright and is co-founder with him of Campus Crusade for Christ International. She is the founder of the Great Commission Prayer Crusade, a movement which seeks to unite Christians around the world in prayer. She also serves as the chairperson of the Intercession Working Group of the Lausanne Committee for World Evangelization.

I believe prayer is the most important facet of Christian work and worship and yet many times the most neglected. If we are going to see anything vital accomplished for God, it is going to be as a result of prayer.

Christians from various parts of the world have begun to see changes in their countries as a consequence of a greater prayer emphasis. I believe this is true in the United States and feel that Korea is perhaps among those countries most changed.

WHAT HAPPENS WHEN PEOPLE PRAY

Revival results from prayer. So many times we think that evangelism is going to bring about revival. But that rarely happens. Prayer produces revival, and revival always produces evangelism. The steps are usually as follows:

1. A concentrated prayer emphasis
2. Evangelism

3. Increased literature distribution
4. Improved theological training
5. Church growth with a biblical emphasis
6. Education
7. Social awareness
8. Social action and change

The Scripture says that God hears and answers if we pray according to His Word (1 John 5:14-15). The Bible is full of evidences of answered prayer as a dramatic working of God. But these examples are not limited to events thousands of years ago.

• In Korea, the government passed a law compelling one partner in marriage to remain in the country at all times. Of course, this greatly hindered Koreans in spreading the gospel abroad. Christians united in prayer, and a few weeks later the law was changed, enabling couples to leave Korea as missionaries.

• In the United States, we have what is called a National Prayer Committee, which prays specifically for our nation. On September 7 and 8 of 1982 much time was spent together in intense prayer specifically for the decisions rendered by the Supreme Court. The following day, President Reagan gave a speech in Kansas City calling for spiritual awakening . . . using the same words the Committee had used. The Committee also prayed that the "Year of the Bible" would pass Congress, and it did in October 1983.

• In a Middle Eastern city, the Bible Society headquarters was closed, making it impossible for Christians to have a space large enough in which to meet. As a result of specific prayer, the authorities changed their minds and allowed it to reopen.

During the last several years we have seen unprecedented numbers of Christians united in prayer in many countries, meeting the conditions for God to send revival to individual lives and nations. 2 Chronicles 7:14 says, "If my people, who are called by my name, will humble themselves and pray and seek my face and turn from their wicked ways, then will I hear from heaven and will forgive their sin and will heal their land." We are claiming that promise in many countries. Since God has honored our small efforts, what will He do if we really give prayer priority in our lives?

But if we are going to see churches aflame with righteousness, cities saturated with the gospel, and the application of scriptural principles around the world, it will take a dramatic act of God and complete commitment on our part. We must be ready. We must be willing to saturate our cities with prayer. That may mean sacrifice on our part. I have begun to pray for a compelling spirit of prayer, so compelling that I can do nothing else. And that is my prayer for all believers.

What Would a National Prayer Movement Do?

If we did commit ourselves to prayer in this single-minded way, and began national prayer movements throughout the world, what would they look like?

1. They would inform Christians of issues for which to pray.
2. They would encourage them to take a stand for moral and spiritual values.
3. They would enable people that are involved in the prayer movement to unite in asking God's direction to turn the tide of atheism, materialism, and secularism in their country.

Dr. McFarland, an education consultant for General Motors, has said that "every person, no matter in what remote area of the world he might live, influences 160 people in his lifetime." That's something to think about. How are you influencing that 160 or more in your lifetime? One of the greatest influences you can have on the life of another person is by praying for them. Prayer is our greatest resource but often the most neglected. Begin by praying for yourself. Then pray with your family or with a partner. Pray about common concerns within your church, community, and city. Pray specifically for your national leaders, your government, and your national sins.

Why Should We Unite to Pray?

The Scripture indicates that every time God's people unite together in prayer, He answers. Every example in Scripture shows how He hears our prayers. He answers. He delivers. He provides. He empowers, and He does whatever is needed.

The common denominator is a united prayer effort. An example is in Acts 4. In fact, it was that passage that burdened my heart to first get involved in prayer. As I saw the conditions in my country and wondered what the answers were, my heart cried out, "Why doesn't somebody do something?" At first I sought other Christians who were involved in attempts to take action, but I found their actions to be futile. I was often disappointed with what I thought were small results or even negative results. Then one morning during my early devotional time I came across that passage in Acts 4. Beginning in verse 24 it says that the believers were united together in prayer. And it recounts the prayer. The disciples named before the Lord the conditions of the day. Then they asked for boldness and for the resources to meet those conditions.

Acts 4 says the believers were of one heart and mind. That's so important in the local church. But it's also important in the city. If the believers in a city can be of one heart and mind, if the believers in a nation can agree together and be of one heart and mind in prayer, and if the believers all around the world can be of one heart and mind, what prayer power can be mustered to change the world!

Terrorism, persecution, crime, corruption, drugs, immorality, divorce, war, poverty, racial conflict, political strife, hunger, and disease—these things are threatening to destroy our civilization. But Christians can be used of God to change these conditions by praying for God's direction and by using their influence in their homes and communities to reverse these trends.

How to Begin a National Prayer Movement

First of all, you must be called of God. You may make yourself available. However, you can't just decide that it is something you would like to do or an influence you would like to exert. Prayer must be vital in your personal life. You must have walked with the Lord long enough to be a mature believer.

Then, convinced of God's call, seek counsel from the Christian leadership of your nation. Seek to gain their support and their advice. You can carry a leading role of authority only if it's given to you on the level at which you serve.

Begin by contacting denominational leaders. Contact directors of Christian organizations. Contact the leaders of other prayer movements in your country. And seek to bring representatives of those groups together. Explore the formation of a network in your nation. This consultation may take place at a planned conference or an event where Christians from around the country have already come together. Together seek the Lord to see what He would have you do.

SELECTING LEADERS

If you feel that God is leading you to begin a national prayer movement, ask God to show you who the leaders should be. I suggest that the inner circle of leadership not be more than twelve people. Beyond that, a board of reference could include as many people as you desire. Seek people who are Spirit-filled and are known to have influence. Choose a cross-section of the Christian body, and seek ways in which you can complement each other.

Foster a national prayer movement to unite the Body of Christ. Let your aim be to accelerate the cause of revival and world evangelization.

On the other hand, sometimes coming together for prayer and support for a particular event is a good way to get started. An example is uniting together to pray for an evangelistic crusade, a consultation on evangelism, a city or a nationwide evangelistic thrust, or a concert of prayer.

The National Prayer Committee in the United States came together as a result of an American festival on evangelism. Some of us had been exploring the possibility of a national movement since the early seventies. We were asked to plan the prayer support for that event in 1980-81. Then we were asked to be the support for a National Day of Prayer in the United States. Thus God gave us a national influence through prayer. It was not the government which initiated this role. Rather, it was initiated by Christians who were concerned about a greater national prayer emphasis and who asked us to take action. All we had to do was volunteer our services.

I suggest that you plan to meet together as a national committee once or twice a year. You will need to challenge business leaders, churches, and others to help support your movement financially. Each member of your committee should share equally a sense of responsibility for the movement of prayer.

CITYWIDE STRUCTURES

It is useful to establish a pastors' advisory committee in your city. The composition of the committee might be similar to that given in Figure 1.

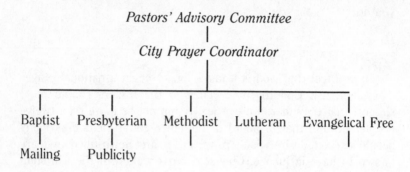

Pastors' Advisory Committee

City Prayer Coordinator

| Baptist | Presbyterian | Methodist | Lutheran | Evangelical Free |
| Mailing | Publicity | | | |

Fig. 1.

In forming a pastor's advisory committee, you'll find that people will have confidence in what you are doing and the pastors will guide you in a citywide movement. Then the city prayer coordinator can choose persons who would represent different denominations in the city.

For example, one person would be responsible for contacting a representative for all the Baptist churches in the city; another for all the Presbyterians, and so forth.

There are other responsibilities that need to be carried out, such as mailings or publicity. If the pastors' advisory committee doesn't seem to be responsive, or doesn't seem to start out that way, then prayerfully seek other people of like mind.

You do not have to start large. Begin with just a few people; then expand your influence. You may find you have just one denominational coordinator. In such cases you can form a steering committee that will be responsible for publicity and for various things that need to be done.

ESTABLISHING UNITY

From time to time prayer movements run into problems as different denominational groups tend to impose their doctrinal views or practices on others of different persuasions in the movement. To avoid this, it is often useful to make a point of agreeing to set aside your different doctrines or controversial practices in order to unite together.

You don't have to agree doctrinally to be able to pray as Christian brothers and sisters. But you must be very sensitive to each other's actions. If certain groups feel too uncomfortable together, choose a way to arrange for them to meet separately while maintaining a unity of purpose.

I usually recommend that all the groups agree on some basic statement of faith in order to have a foundation of unity from which to build. Here is a sample that you might use or adapt.

A Sample Statement of Faith

The sole basis of our belief is the Bible, God's infallible written Word. We believe that it was uniquely, verbally and fully inspired by the Holy Spirit, and that it was written without error (inerrant) in the original manuscripts. It is the supreme and final authority in all matters on which it speaks.

1. There is one true God, eternally existing in three persons— Father, Son, and Holy Spirit—each of whom possesses equally all the attributes of deity.

2. Jesus Christ is God, the living Word, who became flesh through His miraculous conception by the Holy Spirit and His virgin birth.

3. He lived a sinless life and voluntarily atoned for the sins of men dying on the cross as their substitute.

4. He rose from the dead in the same body, though glorified, in which He lived and died.

5. He ascended bodily into heaven and is now at the right hand of God the Father where He is the only mediator between God and man.

6. Man was originally created in the image of God. He sinned by disobeying God; thus, he was alienated from his Creator.

7. The salvation of man is wholly a work of God's free grace and is not the work, in whole or in part, of human works or goodness or religious ceremony. God imputes His righteousness to those who put their faith in Christ alone for their salvation, and thereby justifies them in His sight.

8. It is the privilege of all who are born again of the Spirit to be assured of their salvation from the very moment in which they trust Christ as their Savior. This assurance is not based upon any kind of human merit, but is produced by the witness of the Holy Spirit, who confirms in the believer the testimony of God in His written Word.

9. The Holy Spirit has come into the world to reveal and glorify Christ and to apply the saving work of Christ to men. He convicts and draws sinners to Christ, imparts new life to them, continually indwells them from the moment of spiritual birth and seals them until the day of redemption. His fullness, power, and control are appropriated in the believer's life by complete surrender and faith.

10. Every believer is called to live so in the power of the indwelling Spirit that he will not fulfill the lust of the flesh but will bear fruit to the glory of God.

LOCAL CHURCH STRUCTURES

In a church, the burden for prayer must begin with the pastor. Ideally a prayer coordinator would serve under him. But sometimes that does not happen, and it's just a matter of a small group of believers in the church banding together to pray. Seek a person who would be a part of your group and be responsible for the prayer groups of the women, the men, the youth, and the various other groups in the church. The structure might resemble the arrangement in Figure 2.

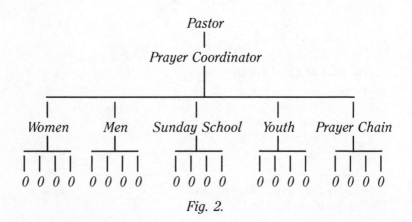

Fig. 2.

How to Start a Prayer Group

The key to starting a prayer group is to begin with prayer! Ask God to lead you to the people who will form a compatible group.

You do not have to have a large group in order to begin. Two people can begin to meet and pray while trusting God to enlarge the group.

The most natural place to begin looking for people to join your group is right in your own sphere of influence; for instance, neighbors on your street or block, people you work with or have worked with, people in your church and others whom God brings to mind. Make personal contact with each person. As you talk with these people, be sure to guard against the mind-set that everyone you contact will have the same personal convictions you do in regard to prayer. Often very dedicated Christians for one reason or another do not feel the need to be a part of a prayer group. Avoid making people feel pressured to become a part of your prayer group.

ESTABLISHING A STRUCTURE

If your group is growing too large to maintain its intimacy, or the time limit does not allow the opportunity for everyone in the group to pray, ask God to raise up another leader from the present group and divide into two groups.

It is a good idea to have a designated amount of time to pray. Individuals with busy schedules are more likely to attend and participate in a prayer group that begins on time and ends at a designated time.

Select an appropriate location to meet regularly. Choose a place that will be as free as possible from interruptions.

FORMING A LOCAL PRAYER CHAIN

If you are going to organize a local prayer chain, choose a prayer site for exclusive use of the 24-hour prayer ministry—for instance, a room at the church or in a home. If you are unable to secure a prayer site for the prayer chain, individuals on the chain may pray at home or at some other place where they can pray in a quiet place free from distractions.

Begin to fill prayer shifts with one or two persons for each time slot according to the division of the prayer chain time.

Select one person to record prayer requests and keep an updated list in the prayer room.

HOW TO SUSTAIN A PRAYER MOVEMENT

In efforts to unite individuals and groups to pray, it has been discovered that people are relatively quick to marshal together for urgent, crisis, or emergency issues. However, after a few meetings, the interest of many wanes because persistent prayer seems mechanical, repetitive, and unspiritual. Analyzing the problem in personal and group prayer, the conclusion has been reached that one of the greatest needs for our day is to teach people *how to pray.* Satan is eager to bring an effective prayer movement to ruin. Following is an outline of the vital elements necessary to keep the movement alive and growing.

I. Be sure that all the participants in the prayer movement understand how to effectively communicate with God:
    A. They should evaluate their relationship to God.
        1. God listens when His children pray: "The Lord is watching His children, listening to their prayers" (1 Pet. 3:12, TLB*).
        2. The unbeliever has no assurance that God will answer his petitions other than his plea to be saved. "We know that God does not listen to sinners. He listens to the godly man who does his will." (John 9:31).
        3. You become a child of God by receiving Jesus Christ: "But as many as received Him, to them He gave the right to become children of God, even to those who believe in His name" (John 1:12, NKJV*).
        4. If one is not sure of his relationship with God, make sure. He needs to receive Jesus Christ as his personal Savior.
    B. Be sure there is no unconfessed sin.
        1. God requires a clean heart. Sin short-circuits our relationship with God: "If I regard wickedness in my heart, the Lord will not hear" (Ps. 66:18, NASB*).

*The Living Bible
*New King James Version
*New American Standard Bible

2. Some hindrances of prayer to consider:
   a. Selfishness, wrong motives (James 4:2-3)
   b. Lack of compassion (Prov. 21:13).
   c. Lack of domestic harmony or peace with mate, children, relatives (1 Pet. 3:7)
   d. Pride (Job 35:12, 13)
   e. Disobedience (1 John 3:22)
   f. Lack of faith (James 5:15)
   g. Unforgiving spirit (Matt. 5:23-25)
   h. Failure to ask according to God's will (1 John 5:14)
   i. Failure to know God's Word and abide in Christ (John 15:7)
   j. Hypocrisy (Matt. 6:5)
   k. Wrong attitudes, e.g., impure thoughts, jealousy, guilt, worry, discouragement, critical spirit, frustration, aimlessness, etc.
   l. Loss of first love (Rev. 2:4)
   m. Lukewarmness (Rev. 3:16)
   n. Critical attitude (Matt. 7:1-5)

C. Confess all sin God brings to mind.
   1. God promises to cleanse and forgive: "If we confess our sins, He is faithful and just to forgive us our sins and to cleanse us from all unrighteousness" (1 John 1:9).
   2. Thank Him that He has forgiven all of your sins as He said He would. The very act of saying "thank you" demonstrates faith. Faith pleases God.
   3. Do not let the memory of confessed sin trouble you again. You are clean in the sight of God.

D. Appropriate the filling of the Holy Spirit by faith.
   1. Claim the promises of God by faith.
   2. The Holy Spirit enables you to pray effectively.

II. Suggested Activities
   A. Obtain a map of your city.
      1. Divide the city into regions.
      2. Develop prayer groups according to regions.
      3. Organize churches for prayer by regions.
   B. Organize a pastors' prayer group.
   C. Conduct occasional seminars or training sessions on prayer.
      1. Dynamics of prayer workshop

2. Concerts of prayer
3. Citywide prayer rallies
4. Obtain and circulate materials on prayer

Remember, prayer calls God's power into action!

Prayer is the Christian's most powerful weapon against wickedness and the powers of darkness; yet prayer is so often relegated to an insignificant role—probably because people do not know how to pray.

The late Dr. Charles Malik, a former president of the United Nations General Assembly (1958-59), once made this statement: "It is given to a great people once only in history to help decisively in saving the world." And I believe that praying Christians are among those people today. If missed now, this opportunity may never be given to us again. But if we seize the opportunity before us, we will honor the Lord Jesus Christ until the end of time.

23

The Value of a Whole Nation Praying with One Accord

Kyu Nam Jung

Dr. Kyu Nam Jung is a professor at the Asian Center for Theological Studies and Mission.

In their times of greatest peril, the Israelites sought to find the best way to deliver their nation. Sometimes they turned futilely to the power of foreign allies. But effective help came only when the godly people of the nation recognized their powerlessness before a crisis and sought the Lord together.

One of the most striking examples of a nation praying with one accord is shown in 2 Chronicles 20:1-30. The formidable invasion of the Moabites and Ammonites and some of the Edomites into Judah created a situation of great danger for the Israelites.

When Jehoshaphat, the king of Judah, confronted this crisis, he turned to the Lord. And in so doing, he took these actions:

1. *He proclaimed a fast* throughout all Judah. All Judah was standing before the Lord, with their infants, their wives, and their children.

2. *He praised the Lord* for His lovingkindness shown to the people of Judah.

3. *He confessed* that the whole nation was powerless before the greater power of the enemy and that they were completely dependent upon the Lord.

In response to this nationwide prayer by all Judah, the Lord responded graciously. The Lord assured the people of Judah that they would be saved from the invasion of the enemy. God made the battle of Judah His own battle. The people of Judah would see the salvation of the Lord on their behalf. In so doing, God completely destroyed the enemies of Israel, annihilating the invaders from Moab, Ammon, and Mount Seir. God let them be destroyed by their own swords in such a way that there could be no question that it was God who fought for Judah. Furthermore, the people of Judah became very rich because of the abundant spoils, goods, garments, and other valuable things left by the enemy.

The nationwide prayer of Judah turned a national crisis into a blessed opportunity to see a divine miracle and receive abundant spoil. The people of Judah had a great experience of salvation from the peril and distress that the nation had faced.

Along with this example of the effectiveness of a whole nation's prayer in one accord, there are other examples in Scripture:

1. *Judges 20:17-48.* The sons of Israel and all the people prayed against the tribe of Benjamin by fasting.

2. *1 Samuel 7:5-11.* Under the leadership of Samuel, all the people of Israel gathered to pray at Mizpah.

3. *Esther 4:4-17.* Esther and the people of Judah in the capital city of Susa prayed together for three days by fasting—not eating or drinking, night or day.

4. *Jonah 3:4-10.* All the people of Nineveh from the greatest to the least believed in God, put on sackcloth, and fasted—not eating or drinking.

5. *Joel 2:15-17.* Joel asked the people of Judah to have a solemn assembly of prayer by fasting.

THE CHARACTERISTICS OF PRAYING IN ONE ACCORD

1. *Everyone participates.* All the passages mentioned above portray a whole nation praying with one accord, involving everyone—a truly nationwide gathering of prayer. For example, the prophet Joel says in Joel 2:16, "Gather the people, consecrate the assembly; bring together the elders, gather the children, those nursing at the breast. Let the bridegroom leave his room and the bride her chamber."

2. *Fasting is important.* When the whole nation prayed with one accord, it was a prayer with fasting. Fasting gave expression to grief (1 Sam. 31:13; 2 Sam. 1:12; Neh. 1:4) and penitence (1 Sam. 7:6; 1 Kings 21:27; Joel 2:15).

3. *Divine guidance is sought.* The Israelites sincerely sought divine help or mercy in the whole nationwide prayer (Judg. 20:28; 1 Sam. 7:8; 2 Chr. 20:12; Joel 2:17; Jonah 3:8).

4. *Repentance is essential.* The people not only repented of their national sins when they gathered together before the Lord, but they repented of their personal sins, as well (1 Sam. 7:6; Joel 2:12, 13; Jonah 3:8).

The Benefits of Praying in One Accord

The biblical writers witness that when a whole nation prays with one accord, God is pleased to give them:

- Salvation from invasion by enemies (2 Chr. 20).
- Deliverance from divine wrath (1 Sam. 7; Joel 2).
- Spiritual and physical riches (2 Chr. 20; Joel 2).

In the times of great peril, the whole nation's prayer with one accord is the best means to get divine help and mercy. Indeed, as James says, "The prayer of a righteous man is powerful and effective" (James 5:16). In the same vein, I believe that a nationwide prayer effort accomplishes much. The effective prayer of a nation can change the impossible into the possible.

Part Five

Prayer Strategy for
World Evangelization

24

Concerts of Prayer
for Global Awakening

David Bryant

*David Bryant serves nationally as mission specialist
with Inter-Varsity Christian Fellowship, USA. He has promoted biblical vision and practical strategies to thousands
of students and lay people across the United States through
his World Christian Conferences. He is a member of the
Intercession Advisory Group of the Lausanne Committee for
World Evangelism.*

In September, 1857, a man of prayer named Jeremiah Lam-
phier started a prayer meeting in the Dutch Reformed Church Con-
sistory in Manhattan. In response to his advertisements, only six
people out of a population of one million showed up. But the
following week there were 14, then 23. This was the beginning of
the Great Awakening of the mid-1800 s which resulted not only in
revival worldwide, but also in great missionary advances.

In January 1981 three people of prayer called for "Concerts of
Prayer" involving Christians throughout the city of Madison, Wisconsin. Out of a population of 200,000, again six people showed
up! But their number increased. Why did they come? Out of the
conviction that the church worldwide is on the verge of another
great awakening—and to prepare for it in united prayer. So once a
month, an interdenominatinal group of lay people, students, missionaries, and pastors gathers for prayer that anticipates a coming
global awakening.

Internationally, concerted prayer is emerging in Christ's church worldwide, with visible results. Hundreds of national prayer mobilizers met at the International Prayer Assembly for World Evangelization in Seoul, Korea in 1984 under the banner of "Seeking God's Face for a Movement of Prayer for the World."

More than a decade ago, Sam Shoemaker wrote of our situation in his book *With the Holy Spirit and With Fire*: "What we are feeling for, imagining, longing for, really praying for, is a worldwide awakening in the power of the Holy Spirit. This alone would be enough to meet our needs, to use our resources, and to incorporate our little personal stores of faith in a movement greater than anything the world has ever seen."

GLOBAL AWAKENING

The greatest barrier facing the church regarding world evangelization is not external; it's internal. We have paralyzed faith. Why? I see six reasons:

1. *It's our nature.* We're caught up with selfishness. We each know that inside.
2. *We lack the facts.* Many of us need a clearer vision of Christ's global cause.
3. *We compartmentalize our faith.* In our discipling efforts, missions is seen as one of twenty-three major items, each totally unrelated to the others.
4. This fragmentation causes *psychological fatigue.* We're overextended and we're tired.
5. There is *lack of group prayer.* Without it, our faith cannot "breathe" as it must.
6. Most importantly, *we lack models.* We see few individuals who show an unselfish obedience to a clearly integrated vision, who pray corporately and relentlessly, and who bring the rest of us with them.

What can set us free? The answer is clear: we need a new work from God! We need spiritual awakening!

WHAT IS SPIRITUAL AWAKENING?

Do you remember waking up this morning? The noise of the alarm clock, the smell of coffee, the patter of feet, thoughts of the day's activities—all these invaded your awareness until you reached a point of no return. It was time to get up, get ready, and get on with the day.

A similar process occurs with a God-given awakening. The Spirit quickens the church with new pulsations of vision and faith. The church cannot turn over and go back to sleep; it must shake itself, get up, and get on with what is on God's heart, get on with God's new day for the world (see Isaiah 60:1-3).

Awakening is God reintroducing us to Jesus. We see His fullness in new ways, so that we trust Him in new ways, so that we love and obey Him in new ways. Consequently, we move with Him in new ways that lead us together to fulfill His global cause.

During an awakening, God asks us, "Is my Son the Lord of heaven and earth? Is He the Lord in this generation, able to overcome challenges to His worldwide purposes? Is He the Lord of His church? Is He the Lord through His church, able to empower her and work through her to fulfill His global cause?"

Christians begin to respond, "Yes, He is! And He is also Lord of my life and through my life, without limits, to the ends of the earth." All of that and more is awakening. In short, it is God leading His people into the full light of a decisive devotion to Jesus Christ.

ANOTHER GREAT AWAKENING?

Yes. Many believe we are on the verge of such a new global awakening. I've talked with historians, mission strategists, and national leaders from various countries who believe we may witness a "shaking" in this generation that will impact the ends of the earth.

There are three good reasons we can expect such an awakening:

1. *It is the divine pattern in Scripture* (read Judges or Haggai; read of John down at the Jordan, or read Jesus' words to the church in Sardis in Revelation 3:1-6) and in history (many church historians mark at least four major awakenings in the past three hundred years). God revives a new generation to carry His purposes forward in the earth. Usually He does this in four phases:

- a movement of united prayer;
- the restoration of devotion to Christ;
- the revitalization of present ministries;

- and, finally, the expansion of God's saving work where it had not come before.

If God has done it before repeatedly, He can do it again—today.

2. *There are signs of dramatic preparations* for such revival: the strength of the evangelical movement worldwide, world level consultations to develop strategies for total world outreach, the rise in numbers of missionaries from the Third World (more than fifteen thousand to date), the upswing of interest in world missions among collegians—to name a few. If God is building this "fireplace" to project the heat of the gospel to the ends of the earth, can the "fire" be far behind?

3. *We face a desperate need* for awakening: the world rests on the brink of moral bankruptcy, nuclear holocaust, and international famine. Above all there are still 2.5 billion people currently beyond the reach of the gospel with no churches among them to witness to them within their own culture and language. The church stands helpless before this scenario unless God's love and power are poured out in an unprecedented way on His people everywhere.

CONCERTS OF PRAYER

A. T. Pierson said, "There has never been a spiritual awakening in any country or locality that did not begin in united prayer." The late J. Edwin Orr concurred: "History is full of exciting results as God has worked through concerted, united, sustained prayer."

WHAT IS A CONCERT OF PRAYER?

Extraordinary prayer is not defined by how long we pray or how often, but rather by whether or not we do pray, if we pray for those things most on God's heart, and if we do so together—"in concert"—in Jesus' name.

As in the historical "Concerts of Prayer" that preceded other great awakenings, we (to use the words of Jonathan Edwards) "make a humble attempt to promote *explicit agreement* and *visible union* of all God's people in *extraordinary prayer* for the *revival of religion* and the *advancement of Christ's Kingdom* on earth." Or, to put it in other terms: we pray for fullness in Christ's body to accomplish the task before it, and we pray for fulfillment of God's purposes among all nations throughout that body.

A concert of prayer is nothing less than a call for the whole church to unite in a ministry of intercessory prayer for both itself and the whole world, and to do so around the whole counsel of God. A united movement of prayer, expressed in local concerts of prayer, must address the two great sweeps of Scripture: spiritual awakening and world evangelization.

DEVELOPING A CONCERT OF PRAYER

If in fact God is raising up a prayer movement as a prelude to a great new work of His kingdom worldwide, then we as His people need to be in it *together.* We need to coordinate our efforts to participate and serve what is emerging. Above all, we must gather God's praying people together. We must help them find one another and accomplish the crucial work God has given to them (and to us).

The following is a framework for developing concerts of prayer:

1. Leaders from the major denominational, campus, missions, and renewal groups—at both the local and national levels—should work together to build a grass-roots consensus and environment for revival, spiritual awakening, and the advancement of Christ's kingdom nationally and worldwide.
2. We work together by assisting and encouraging a sustained, united concerted, interdenominatinal movement of prayer within local communities throughout our country.
3. More specifically, we as leaders should commit ourselves initially to two years of cooperative effort in mobilizing "concerts of prayer" in mutually agreed-upon target communities. From our individual constituents within each community, we should pull together those who have already evidenced a growing concern for revival prayer and for the worldwide advancement of Christ's kingdom. And then we should directly encourage this concerted prayer for a period of two years.

WHICH ISSUES DO YOU PRAY ABOUT?

Those involved in concerts of prayer have dealt with concerns such as the following:

Revival, Awakening. Prayer concerns in the category of revival and awakening have to do with spiritual fullness.

- That God would give an *awakening* to His whole church, helping us to know Christ well enough to trust Him, love Him, and obey Him in ways that move with Him in the fulfillment of His global cause in our generation.
- For God to raise up *prayer bands* of world Christians on our campuses worldwide, in our churches and in our mission agencies.
- For new awareness of God's *holiness*, and the church's need to be holy as He is holy, if we are to have significant impact for His glory on the world.
- For a fresh sense of God's *love* for the world, and a rekindling of our love for Him. We need to be filled with Christ's love.
- For *reconciliation*, so that Christians become transparent before Him and before each other, and in repentance and forgiveness, band together for the cause of Christ.
- That God would renew our *world vision and faith* to move forward to reach the nations.
- That the church would awaken to Christ's universal *authority*, the basis of her commitment to the world missionary movement.
- For *gratitude* for all God has already done for us personally and collectively, that we would delight to bring what we have found to those who have never heard the gospel.
- For a sense of *accountability* to Christ to share our lives with the billions locked in extreme spiritual and physical poverty; that we would repent of hoarding the gospel, and release its full impact of love and justice worldwide.
- For *pioneers of faith* to lead the church to embrace the new things God wants to do through us in this generation; for visionary leaders to take His people into the ministry of redemption and healing among all nations and people.
- That God would give churches and teams around the world *new dreams* and visions of specific missions to the world.
- That God would fire commitment to Christ's global cause among the hundreds of thousands of *Christian students* worldwide, and

prepare them to assume leadership and to sacrifice as they carry out that commitment.

- For the church to have *victorious optimism* in keeping with God's love and purposes for the whole earth, and to step forth boldly in that light.

Advancement, Missions. Prayer concerns in the category of advancement and missions have to do with fulfillment.

- For *God to be glorified* throughout the earth, among all people everywhere. Tell Him what it will mean to you personally when He is thus glorified.
- For an intentional, sacrificial penetration of major human barriers worldwide, that *churches be planted* within every people group (providing God's kingdom a base of operation in each group) in this generation.
- For *spiritual hunger* among Muslims, Chinese, Hindus, Buddhists. That those who have yet to hear may find a new sense of God's reality and an awakened desire to seek Him.
- For *Satan to be bound* and truly routed, that Christ's victory on the cross would break Satan's hold on nations and cultures.
- For *world leaders and governments*, and for the outcome of *world events*. All of these can directly affect the free course of the gospel within a nation or within a people group.
- For major *global issues* which impinge upon a breakthrough of the gospel, and are a part of the moral darkness that must be penetrated (e.g., global hunger, nuclear proliferation, political and economic repression).
- For God's people everywhere to *see those around them* whose ways of living differ significantly enough to cut them off from a normal witness of the gospel—to recognize them and to reach them.
- That God would give to the church the gift of *"apostles"* (1 Cor. 12:28). We need hundreds of thousands of new cross-cultural messengers, missionaries, and "tent-makers" to be sent out by the churches around the world. Ask God to give the church wisdom

to know who these people are, to set them apart for the work to which He has called them, and to send them forth by a movement of prayer and sacrifice.

- For *churches within every country*, that God would raise up a new missionary movement from every nation and people group in which communities of disciples already exist.

- For *specific missionaries*. Pray for those you know personally and those you learn about in other ways, including the more than fifteen thousand from Third World churches. Pray for those working among a particular people group that you also desire to see reached.

- For those peoples and places *where doors are open*, allowing hundreds of more laborers to enter.

- For all *current efforts to research and formulate mission strategy*, to effectively deploy a new generation of missionaries.

- For *America as a major sending base* of missionary personnel. Of the eighty thousand Protestant missionaries worldwide, almost sixty thousand come from North America. Pray that God would revive the church in our nation so that the base of Christians here, containing 80 percent of the evangelical resources of the world and 70 percent of its trained Christians, might continue a God-given ministry to the earth's unreached.

- For the unreached *"nations" in America*. The unique U.S. ethno-cultural panorama includes ethnic groups speaking more than one hundred languages. At least three million have no knowledge of Christ and no one near them who is culturally like them to tell them. Tens of millions among the urban poor of our cities are completely out of touch with witnessing Christians. There are three hundred thousand international students here, as well.

- For God to raise up a *movement of "senders"* world-wide—people who know for certain that God has called them to send out a new force of cross-cultural witnesses and who embrace their assignment with the same vision and sacrifice as those who actually go.

- That individual churches around the world will *adopt* some of the earth's unreached people groups as their long-term focus for prayer and action.

KEEPING A BALANCE OF PRAYER

As these issues are covered during a concert of prayer, balance is sought. For example, many of our concerns have both local and global dimensions. Both are addressed. We fight the tendency to concentrate on either dimension to the exclusion of the other.

We also need to keep the balance between:

- rejoicing in what God is already doing (or promises to do);
- repenting for the things in us and in the church at large that hinder or ignore what God wants to do;
- asking for specific concerns under fullness or fulfillment.

Finally, we resist the tendency to pray for fullness issues to the neglect of fulfillment; we cannot pray only for those things that are closest and most directly related to our own felt needs. Concerts of prayer stretch our faith in Christ.

A CHALLENGE TO PRAYER

Surveying the Moravian Movement on the 250th anniversary of its "Hourly Intercession," an editorial in *Christianity Today* (Feb. 18, 1977) presented the challenge boldly:

> Whoever believes the Biblical record must agree that weak and ineffective Christians and a faltering Church are characterized by *prayerlessness.*
>
> It is fair to say that the Moravian's prayers along with those of others played an important part in making the 19th century the greatest of all centuries since Pentecost for the Christian faith. Nothing like the magnitude of the Christian advance between 1727 and 1900 is happening today. And nothing like that will happen unless God's people get back on their knees.
>
> We can be very grateful for what God has done in our day in response to the little prayer that has gone forth for such efforts as the Lausanne Conference on World Evangelization, for example. But at the same time we must consider the long range; such a project will have little lasting effect unless it is suffused with persevering prayer.
>
> Perhaps the time has come to pick up the challenge of the Moravian Brethren and begin another hundred-year prayer effort.

We challenge the Lausanne committee for World Evangelization to find 24 men and 24 women around the world who will pray around the clock, every day, each for one hour, for world evangelization. We challenge the National Association of Evangelicals to do the same.

We challenge every stumbling denomination to start such a prayer effort for renewal and for dynamic power.

We challenge the World Council of Churches to make Geneva a center for prayer with the conviction that prayer alone will do more to right the world's wrongs than any amount of social and political action that is *not* made in persevering prayer.

God called special servants of His among Moravians to give themselves to this prayer ministry. Surely there are 48 believers around the world whom the Spirit of God will lead to devote themselves to this prayer effort. And they will be able to pray others into the same ministry until there is an unbreakable chain of hundreds of thousands of believers who will not stop shaking the gates of heaven until the churches are revived and the Gospel of Jesus Christ is preached to every creature.

I, too, am looking for bands of forty-eight (and more) in city after city, made up of students, lay people, pastors, and missionaries willing to commit one night every month (in Edwards' words) to "explicit agreement and visible union [concerts] in extraordinary prayer for the revival of religion [fullness] and the advancement of Christ's kingdom on earth [fulfillment]."

Does anyone want to start something?

25

The Relationship Between Prayer and World Evangelization

Harold Lindsell

Dr. Harold Lindsell is editor-emeritus of Christianity Today *and a former professor of church history and missions. He is as well the author of several publications.*

Before we can fully discover the relationship between prayer and world evangelization, I believe we need to understand afresh the role of the gospel of Jesus Christ in the plan of God for the ages, for there can be no evangelization if there isn't a gospel.

THE ROLE OF THE GOSPEL

THE GOSPEL IS THE GOOD NEWS

The good news of the gospel can be summarized in four great truths:

1. Jesus died for our sins.
2. He arose again from the dead.
3. He ascended into heaven.
4. He is coming again.

Now the gospel of Jesus Christ needs to be understood in relationship to the sinfulness of man. All men are born in sin. All men are lost. There is only one way in which the condition of men can be changed, and that is by the gospel of Jesus Christ. "There is no other name under heaven given to men by which we must be saved" (Acts 4:12).

The gospel does contain some bad news: All men are separated from God. But it is primarily good news. The good news is that through Jesus there is salvation and reconciliation with God, and the good news is also that the gospel is to be preached to all men everywhere.

THE COMMISSION TO SHARE THE GOOD NEWS

This idea of preaching the gospel to all men everywhere is not just some idealistic suggestion as though it would be nice if everyone heard the gospel. It is not just someone's justification for foreign travel. It is a *command* in the Bible. In fact, many do not realize that the Holy Spirit saw fit to record the Great Commission for us in the Scripture no less than five times:

1. In Matthew 28:18-20, Jesus said, "All authority in heaven and on earth has been given to me. Therefore go and make disciples of all nations, baptizing them in the name of the Father and of the Son and of the Holy Spirit, and teaching them to obey everything I have commanded you."
2. In Mark 16:15, we read, "Go into all the world and preach the good news to all creation."
3. Luke 24:46-49 reports Jesus saying: "This is what is written: The Christ will suffer and rise from the dead on the third day, and repentance and forgiveness of sins will be preached in his name to all nations, beginning at Jersulaem. You are witnesses of these things. I am going to send you what my Father has promised; but stay in the city until you have been clothed with power from on high."
4. In John 20:21, the Bible quotes Jesus as saying: "As my Father has sent me, I am sending you." (Jesus was the first missionary; He came the furthest distance to preach, and as the Father sent Him, so He sends you and me.)
5. The fifth time we read the Great Commission is in Acts 1:8 when Jesus was about to ascend into heaven. The very last words that He spoke were: "You will be my witnesses in Jerusalem, and in all Judea and Samaria, and to the ends of the earth."

Repeating that five times tells you how important the preaching of the gospel is. All churches and indeed all Christians are obligated to do their part in taking the gospel to all the world.

THE GOSPEL AND THE END OF THE AGE

We must also understand the gospel in light of what we call the doctrine of eschatology, the understanding of the end times.

The church has been looking for the second coming of Jesus Christ for two thousand years. And yet Jesus still has not come. Why has Jesus not come again? The Lord Jesus gave us the answer to that question. In Matthew's gospel, Jesus said, "And this gospel of the kingdom will be preached in the whole world as a testimony to all nations, and then the end will come" (Matt. 24:14). Jesus has not yet come because the gospel has not yet been preached to the whole world.

The interesting thing about that statement is this: Jesus did not say this gospel of the kingdom *should* be preached unto all the world; He said this gospel *shall* be preached to all he world. This is a prophetic statement of what must take place.

And yet from this perspective we all bear a responsibility for hastening the day of the Lord. In Romans 10:14-15 we read: "How, then, can they call on the one they have not believed in? And how can they believe in the one of whom they have not heard? And how can they hear without someone preaching to them? And how can they preach unless they are sent? As it is written, 'How beautiful are the feet of those who bring good news!' "

Taken together we see that the world will not end until the gospel is preached to all the nations, and that can only happen when we do it. Jesus has no hands except your hands. He has no feet except your feet. He has no tongue except your tongue.

WHO WILL BE THE WITNESS?

Who is going to take the gospel of Jesus Christ to the end of the world? You and I are the ones who are going to have to do it. There are three things that Jesus Christ wants you and me to do:

1. *He wants us to go.* And when Jesus said go, He said to His disciples, "Start at Jerusalem." Begin where you are right now. If you are a Korean and you can't preach the gospel in Seoul, Korea,

you won't be able to do any better in the United States of America. Crossing an ocean won't make you better at preaching the gospel if you won't do it where you are. We must remember that God has called all of us to preach the gospel. But not all of us are sent to the ends of the earth to do it. And that's why Jesus told us something else we need to do.

2. *He wants us to give so that others can go.* If I can't go myself, I must do something to help other people go. It takes money to preach the gospel to the ends of the earth.

I'm a Southern Baptist; there are 14.6 million Southern Baptists in the United States. Southern Baptists send out more missionaries than any other denomination in the United States. But it is with sadness that I confess what we do financially. The average Southern Baptist in the pew gives only around $6 a year for missions. Six dollars a year isn't much of a priority for sending the gospel to the ends of the earth.

3. *He wants us to pray.* If we want others to give as well as to go, we're going to have to pray for open pocketbooks. While I have mentioned this last, it is really first. For it is something all of us ought to do, and all of us can do, even when we cannot go or give.

Why do I say that whether you go or whether you give, you still ought to pray? I say it because prayer is absolutely essential to the effective preaching of the gospel of Jesus Christ. You see, it is the Holy Spirit of God, who calls people to the work of ministry, to the preaching of the gospel, to giving, and to praying.

Jesus said, "The harvest is plentiful but the workers are few. Ask the Lord of the harvest, therefore, to send out workers into his harvest field" (Matt. 9:37-38). Do you see what that is saying? If there aren't enough people out there preaching the gospel of Jesus Christ, it's because we have not prayed for the Lord of the harvest to thrust them out into the harvest fields. It is my belief that the Holy Spirit is pleased to send forth laborers into His harvest fields in response to our prayer.

Let me remind you of some instances of the Holy Spirit working. In Acts 8:26-39 we find that the Ethiopian eunuch was reading from the prophecy of Isaiah, but he didn't know what he was reading. It was the Holy Spirit of God who sent Philip (Acts 8:29) to preach to the eunuch. The Holy Spirit not only sends—He also guides.

Also in Acts 10 is the story of Peter preaching to the Gentiles. At first Peter would have nothing to do with anything as unclean as a Gentile. But God sent him a vision from heaven in order to make him willing to go and visit the Gentile, Cornelius. And then we discover that when Peter was responsive to God, the Holy Spirit was involved in his ministry: "The Spirit said to him, 'Simon, three men are looking for you. So get up and go downstairs. Do not hesitate to go with them, for I have sent them' " (Acts 10:19-20). Here is the Holy Spirit at work in response to the prayer of Cornelius. We are to pray to the Lord of the harvest, and He'll thrust forth laborers into His harvest field.

In Acts 13:2 it says that as the apostles "were worshiping the Lord and fasting, the Holy Spirit said, 'Set apart for me Barnabas and Saul for the work to which I have called them.' " Notice that word, "fasting." When the people of God fast, they exhibit a determination to get next to God. Fasting purifies my spirit. Fasting prepares me to listen to God. And while they were worshiping God and fasting, the Holy Spirit spoke. They were praying, and the Holy Spirit was working. Notice also verses 3 and 4: "So after they had fasted and prayed, they placed their hands on them and sent them off. The two of them, sent on their way by the Holy Spirit, went down to Seleucia and sailed from there to Cyprus." The Bible first says the church sent them, but then it says the Holy Spirit sent them. He was the one behind their commissioning.

The Holy Spirit is the One who sends; the Holy Spirit is the One who guides; the Holy Spirit is the One who empowers. And all of that happens because of prayer. You see, when you pray and ask the Holy Spirit to do something, you're also praying that He'll work in the hearts of the people He wants to touch.

The Role of Prayer

What, then, should you do as a Christian when you pray for world evangelization?

PRAY FOR YOURSELF AND FOR YOUR FAMILY

I remember years ago being in a Baptist church as one of our missionaries spoke to us before returning to the field from which she never expected to come back to America again. When she spoke, she moved the hearts of the people. And the pastor got up and gave an invitation to the people. There were probably two hundred people there that night. He said, "How many of you parents would give your children for the mission field if God calls them?" Three people stood up. Only three parents out of two hundred were willing to give their children to God for the mission field. They appeared to be good people; they didn't drink, they didn't go to the movies, they didn't dance . . . but they wouldn't give their children to the mission field, either.

The first thing I want to pray is this: "Lord, here am I, send me." The second prayer I pray is this: "Lord, here are my children, send them if you can't send me." And the first thing that I need to do as a father is to pray that the Holy Spirit will save my children. Evangelizing the world begins with prayer, and prayer begins with the family.

PRAY FOR THE CHURCH

I was raised in a Presbyterian church in the United States of America. I am the only one from that church that I know of who went into the ministry. And I didn't go because I was encouraged to do so by my church. I felt called later while I was at Wheaton College and we had a revival. The Holy Spirit spoke to me, but I wasn't quite ready to listen to Him. I had been a Christian all my life, but I had never accepted the lordship of Jesus Christ.

After I graduated from college, I went to visit my uncle in Seattle, Washington. I was reading a book given to me by the girl who later married Billy Graham. It was Oswald Chambers's *My Utmost for His Highest.* That was the one book I never should have read! The Holy Spirit laid hold of my heart. For the first time in my life as a Christian I said, "God, I'll go where You want me to go, I'll be what You want me to be, I'll do what You want me to do."

You see, there was one thing I knew I didn't want to be: I didn't want to be a minister of the gospel. The best fights I ever saw, I saw in the church. But when the Holy Spirit touched my heart, it changed my whole manner of thinking about the church. Now I wouldn't exchange being a minister of the gospel for being President of the United States. I have a higher role to play than the President of the United States. I am an ambassador for Jesus Christ, the King of kings and Lord of lords. And I need to pray that the church will be right with God.

PRAY FOR THE NATIONS

Prayer is the greatest power in the world. Do you pray for the people of the Soviet Union? North Korea? I even have Castro from Cuba on my prayer list. I'm praying that God will overcome the communist powers so the gospel of Jesus Christ can get to the ends of the earth. And I'm expecting God to do this. Our God has infinite power. And we can tap into that power through prayer.

In this generation the world worships power. We have nuclear bombs that can destroy the whole world. But prayer is greater than nuclear power. Prayer is greater than all the armaments of all the armies of the world.

There is only one way in which the power of prayer differs from all the powers of the world: it is the only power that cannot be used for evil. Every other power of the world can be used for good or for evil. But the greatest of all powers—prayer—can only be used for good. And God has promised that by prayer you can release His power to fulfill the preaching of the gospel to the ends of the earth.

There is reason to be concerned about the threats of nuclear, chemical, and biological warfare. But our safety is not found in building more bombs. We need to vault into a much higher and more powerful level of defense. We need to pray that God will defeat the plans of those who would use nuclear bombs or chemicals that are destructive. Our God whose power is made available by prayer is able to restrain evil and prevent catastrophes from happening.

Psalm 115:3 says, "Our God is in heaven; he does whatever pleases him." What is God pleased to do? He is pleased to send you and me to the ends of the earth. He's promised to be with us wherever we go. He will not fail us. He has given to us the power of His Holy Spirit.

OUR UNIQUE ROLE

There is one thing that only man can do: only we can preach the gospel of Jesus Christ. Angels cannot preach the gospel. Nowhere has any angel ever preached the gospel of Jesus Christ, but you and I can preach that gospel. You and I can use that power to do the work of God for His glory. The youngest as well as the oldest Christian can do it. The richest man in the world has no more power in prayer than the poorest man in the world. The highest in society has no more power in prayer that the lowest. Women have as much power in prayer as men. God doesn't listen to one color man more than He listens to anyone else. It makes no difference what the color of your skin is—red, yellow, black, white—it's all the same to God. He looks at the heart, not the skin.

You can have a doctor's degree from the best university in the world, and it doesn't give you any more power in prayer than a man who doesn't even have a high school education. As a matter of fact, we may be hindered by what we have if it tempts us to rely on our own wisdom and abilities rather than on God's power through prayer.

EXAMPLES OF PRAYER AT WORK

Let me note a few illustrations of God working in prayer.

Samuel. You may remember a little boy named Samuel. His mother was Hannah. His father had two wives: Hannah and Peninnah. Peninnah had several children, but Hannah had no children, and she desperately wanted a baby. So she went to the house of God and began to pray. When Eli the priest saw her, she was moving her lips, but he couldn't hear any words and assumed that she was drunk. He said, "How long will you keep on getting drunk?" She said, "I'm a woman of a sorrowful heart." And as she prayed, she said "Lord, give me a baby, and if You'll give me a baby, I'll give it back to you." And when she told Eli, he said, "The Lord grant thee thy petition." God granted her that petition, and Samuel was born.

Hannah kept her promise, and as soon as he was weaned she gave Samuel back to the Lord to learn and serve under Eli. He became a great priest and prophet of God.

Daniel. When Daniel was in Babylonia during the Captivity, the Bible says of him, "Three times a day he got down on his knees and prayed, giving thanks to his God" (Dan. 6:10). Three times a day he prayed! He was delivered from the den of lions; God shut their mouths so they couldn't hurt him. He was a missionary to Babylonia. He was a missionary to the king; he told him the meaning of all the things he dreamed. He was a man of prayer.

Nehemiah. Nehemiah came back after the Captivity to the land of Judah, and he heard reports that the people were in great trouble: that the walls of Jerusalem were broken down and that the gates had been burned. In Nehemiah 1:4, Nehemiah said, "When I heard these things, I sat down and wept. For some days I mourned and fasted and prayed before the God of heaven." And as a result, revival came. His prayers were answered. The hand of God was upon him. The work of God was renewed.

Jonah. Jonah was a disobedient missionary. He was called by the Spirit of God. God said to Jonah, "Go to Nineveh, that great city, and cry against it; for their wickedness is come up before me" (Jonah 1:2). But Jonah ran in the opposite direction until God finally had to send a storm on the ocean and cause the ship to almost be wrecked. Then the sailors, realizing that Jonah had displeased God, threw Jonah overboard. He ended up in the belly of a great fish. But God still didn't get his attention. It took three days and three nights before God got Jonah's attention. Finally Jonah repented and we read: "Then Jonah prayed unto the Lord his God out of the fish's belly" (Jonah 2:1). And the Bible says, "The word of the Lord came unto Jonah the second time" (Jonah 3:1). That word was given to the same man—Jonah—and it sent him to the same place—Nineveh—for the same purpose—to preach repentance to the people. That time Jonah obeyed. And all Ninevah repented and put on sackcloth and ashes; and a great awakening took place. But it was imperative that Jonah repent first so that God could finally get him to go where He wanted him to go.

Paul and Silas. When these missionaries were in prison in Philippi they spent the night praying and singing songs of praise to God. At midnight there was a great earthquake. The doors of the prison were broken open, and the prisoners' bonds were set free. The keeper of the prison feared that he would die if the prisoners had escaped. But Paul and Silas reassured him that everyone was still there. And then they led the jailor and his family to Jesus Christ. So the gospel was spread, and souls were won as the power of God was manifested in signs and wonders. Later, Paul told the Philippians in his letter to them: "In everything by prayer and supplication with thanksgiving let your requests be made known unto God. And the peace of God, which passeth all understanding, shall keep your hearts and minds through Christ Jesus" (Phil. 4:6-7,

KJV*). Paul never would have said that unless he believed that God would hear their prayers, and that His power would be released, and signs and wonders would take place.

THE MULTIPLIER EFFECT

In Leviticus 26:8 the Bible says, "Five of you will chase a hundred, and a hundred of you will chase ten thousand, and your enemies will fall by the sword before you." That was God's promise to help Israel defeat their enemies. But notice the arithmetic. When five chased one hundred, the ratio was one to twenty. But when one hundred put one thousand to flight, the ratio was one to one hundred of the enemy.

I believe the same principle is true of prayer. When one man prays, you get what one man's prayers can do. When five join together, their effectiveness is multiplied. but when the whole church of Jesus Christ prays, you're going to get power upon power such as the world has never seen before in all of its existence.

If you want to see the gospel of Jesus Christ preached to the whole world, the most efficient method is not to become a Lone Ranger evangelist but to get the whole church to pray. When you've done that, pray some more, and keep on praying. For when the gospel is preached to the whole world, then shall the end come.

Even so, come quickly Lord Jesus.

*King James Version.

26

Developing Prayer Support
for Missions

Wesley L. Duewel

Dr. Wesley L. Duewel has been involved with OMS International since 1940, first as a missionary in India for twenty-five years, then as vice-president and later as president of the mission society. He is currently coordinating a ten-year evangelism and church-planting thrust for OMS called Decade of Harvest, which in the first five years has resulted in 295,000 decisions for Christ of which 135,000 have been baptized and integrated into local churches, 520 new churches, and 300,000 prayer warriors worldwide praying daily for this harvest. Duewel is also author of the best-selling book Touch the World Through Prayer *(Zondervan, 1986).*

Evangelical missionary work is not primarily a matter of sociology, psychology, or anthropology. All these areas, of course, have important implications for missions. But missionary work is primarily a spiritual ministry seeking spiritual results. That is especially true for evangelism and church planting. But it is also very true for all other missionary work, whatever the type of service—medicine, literacy, radio, development, education. The ultimate goal of every evangelical missionary is not merely professional excellence or meeting valid needs, but spiritual results.

Spiritual results are the work of the Holy Spirit, and the Holy Spirit is given for life and ministry in answer to prayer. Even if all missionary endeavors were to remain at the present level of numbers, equipment, and ministry, with multiplied prayer support no doubt the spiritual results would be greatly increased.

There is no simplistic formula assuring that a certain percentage of increase in prayer time will bring a guaranteed percentage of increase in results. We cannot earn God's blessing, God's guidance, or God's assistance. The theology of intercession is not a theology of works.

Yet the Bible is very clear on the relation of prayer to spiritual results. As co-heirs with Christ, we have this promise from the Father: "*Ask of me*, and I will make the nations your inheritance" (Ps. 2:8 emphasis added). Prayer is an essential ingredient in revival: "If my people, who are called by my name, will humble themselves and pray and seek my face and turn from their wicked ways, then will I hear from heaven and will forgive their sin and will heal their land" (2 Chron. 7:14). Our spiritual struggle in the Christian life and Christian ministry is "not against flesh and blood, but against the rulers, against the authorities, against the powers of this dark world and against the spiritual forces of evil in the heavenly realms" (Eph. 6:12); and the bottom line for victory over all these powers is to "pray in the Spirit on all occasions with all kinds of prayer and requests" (Eph. 6:18).

More than organization and structure, more than the philosophy of missions, more than schemes or strategies for evangelization, the priority concern for attaining God's objectives for our generation is mobilizing the prayers of the Church for the lost world.

Has any missionary organization done more than make token efforts to build prayer into all its annual plans, all its structures and strategies, and all its promotion and financing?

With this basic need in mind, I wish to set forth some prayer precepts for missionary organizations and prayer groups and partners, to suggest guidelines for developing a structure for raising prayer support, and finally, to offer a sample listing of methods which have been found to be effective in mobilizing prayer.

PRAYER PRECEPTS

FOR MISSIONARY ORGANIZATIONS

Prayer is the foundation for all mission efforts. The most important step that most missionary organizations could take to advance their work would be to mobilize a greatly increased volume of concerned and specific prayer. The missionary organization that does not mobilize a greatly increased volume of concerned and specific prayer. The missionary organization that does not mobilize adequate prayer for its personnel and their ministry sins against them and, to some extent, wastes their lives and ministry. To avoid spiritual naivete, we must build motivation for prayer and guidance of intercession into every aspect of our mission organizational structure, strategy, and service.

Prayer is the responsibility of all mission personnel. If prayer is truly priority number one, then not only will our evangelistic teams have nights of prayer, but so will our boards, our staff, our retreats, and our conferences. Board members, staff, or missionaries who are too busy to pray are busier than God wants them to be, too busy to accept Christian responsibility.

Every annual field plan should include an annual prayer plan. The missionary society budget must provide adequate support for mobilizing and focusing the prayer of the constituency. Special prayer calls and prayer provision should be a planned and scheduled part of every field strategy.

Prayer training is essential to candidate preparation. If prayer is basic to maximum personal anointing and blessing, then candidate committees will very carefully examine the prayer life of all candidates. Prayer seminars or schools of prayer should be as important in pre-field preparation as cross-cultural orientation or seminars for language acquistion skills.

Specific mission roadblocks need specific prayer. Since missionary work is especially opposed by Satan and his powers of darkness, there are some missionary situations and needs which will never be resolved or met apart from prayer mobilization specifically for the ministry, place, or situation.

Personalized prayer backing is more important and more urgent than financial support. It is usually easier to mobilize and raise financial support than to mobilize and focus prayer support. But other things being equal, the missionary or Christian worker covered and supported by the most vital prayer will experience the most blessing and fruitfulness.

When prayer is given its rightful priority, other needs will be met. The local church that regularly prays for your missionary organization, your specific ministry, or your personnel by name will tend to be more faithful in financial support than a non-praying church. The same is true of individuals: the person who regularly prays for you, your ministry, or your mission by name will usually support you as he is able.

Prayer letters should focus on prayer needs. Many missionary "prayer letters" are more news letters or family letters than prayer letters, indicating that the missionary does not understand the crucial role and great potential of prayer for their ministries. Unfortunately even missionaries on the field may be out of touch with the real prayer needs. Each missionary should be sufficiently close to the national church to know the constantly changing prayer needs and requests of the churches, for whom he or she is responsible to raise prayer.

A call for prayer must provide an opportunity for prayer. Just as it is improper to give an evangelistic message but provide no specific way to respond to the invitation, it is wrong to give a missionary message calling for more prayer involvement without providing for some specific form of prayer commitment. And just as we want to encourage a local church to pray beyond its own ministry and needs, a missionary organization should not call for prayer only for its own ministry and needs. If prayer is as essential to missions as we say it is, each missionary conference must provide adequate time to actually pray for missions—mission organizations and missionaries praying for each other.

FOR MISSION PRAYER GROUPS AND PARTNERS

Prayer vitality begins with the leaders. A church which has not been taught to pray will show little interest in prayer for missions. A church which has a dynamic prayer life for missions, however, probably has a pastor with a vital personal prayer life for missions. This is where enthusiasm for prayer must begin.

A vital prayer group is a powerful spiritual resource for the church. A missionary prayer group in a local church that really learns to prevail in prayer will gradually become a spiritual power resource for the whole life of the local church. (One practical problem: most prayer meetings for missions spend too small a portion of their time in actual intercession. Ways must be found so that prayer request information does not take more time than actual prayer for the request.)

"Retirement" can be productively invested in prayer. Perhaps the greatest wasted potential in the church today is the prayer time available to retirees. Few people enter retirement with a strong anticipation of a life of intercession; there are some, however, who look forward to retirement as their time to enter into a fuller intercessory ministry.

The key to prayer is love—love of Jesus and love for those for whom we pray. Perhaps the greatest thieves of time for intercession are the TV, newspaper, and radio. Most Christians find it easier to listen to a message on prayer, read or sing or talk about prayer, than to spend time in prayer. But we should be thrilled to talk to and spend time with those we love. The person who finds prayer time thrilling shows how much he or she loves Jesus. The person who loves to pray for missions proves his love for missions and for the souls of others.

We should encourage each other in a life of prayer. Probably one of the greatest regrets of Christians at the judgment seat of Christ will be the time comparatively wasted instead of being invested in intercession. "Each one should be careful how he builds. For . . . his work will be shown for what it is, because the Day will bring it to light. It will be revealed with fire, and the fire will test the quality of each man's work" (1 Cor. 3:10-15). We can do a Christian no greater favor than to help him establish a blessed and fruitful life of intercession for the church, evangelism, and missions.

GUIDELINES FOR RAISING PRAYER SUPPORT FOR MISSIONS

THE PRAYER COORDINATOR

If an organization purposes to really build prayer for missions into a priority place in its annual plans and ministries, someone must be designated as the Prayer Coordinator, with recognized responsibility. This must be a person with a known personal life of intercession. You cannot assign this job to someone who has only had casual or feeble intercessory ministry up to this time.

The Prayer Coordinator must be filled with the Spirit, able to effectively challenge others, and bring people to the point of prayer commitment.

Divine guidance will be constantly required in such matters as:

a. Which of the prayer and praise items supplied can be included in any given bulletin.

b. How to condense and word the items.
c. The day on which a specific person or request should be prayed for.
d. Any specific words of promise or challenge which may be included as brief nuggets.

GATHERING PRAYER ITEMS

Gathering praise and prayer items must be carefully organized to avoid common problems. The length of time it takes for a request on the field to reach the prayer partners committed to pray can be a crucial factor in effective prayer. Often national pastors and leaders are neglected and have far less prayer support than the missionaries do.

These and other problems can be avoided by the following:

1. Designate a person responsible to report for each field, section of field, or ministry to be covered with prayer. Unless it is a recognized priority, this assignment will tend to be crowded out by what are perceived to be more urgent duties.

2. The person designated to furnish the items should be someone who is constantly informed on up-to-date requests and answers to prayer. This requires minute knowledge of and close relation with the national church.

3. In order to cut down the amount of time required for each prayer item to reach the prayer partners, ask the persons to send their items directly to the Prayer Coordinator, rather than having it go through the hands of another person on the field.

4. Assign a specific date each month (or period) for prayer and praise items to be in the Prayer Coordinator's hand.

5. Computer use in telephone hookup can be a means of disseminating and receiving requests.

CIRCULATING PRAYER ITEMS

The cooperation of every department and person involved must be secured to cut down to the barest minimum the amount of time needed between placing the prayer or praise item into the mail on the field and the time it is actually in the hands of the prayer partners. Prayer requests lose their potential if they are out of date.

The Prayer Coordinator must make immediate reproduction and distribution of the prayer sheets a priority. It is essential to cut the red-tape, get the item out through editorial and printing departments and into the mail in the shortest possible time. Even so, two to three months often elapse from the time an item is dropped into the mail on the field and the time when the prayer bulletin reaches constituents in the farthest parts of the United States.

Some factors to keep in mind:

- Airmail from several nations averages from ten days to two weeks before it is in the hand of the addressee in the United States.
- A prayer bulletin mailed second-class in Indiana takes up to three weeks before it reaches the West Coast of the United States.
- Prayer information printed as a part of a magazine usually takes a longer time before it reaches the prayer partners than information sent as a separate prayer item in the mail.
- Prayer sheets sent by bundle to a local church are largely wasted unless there is a guaranteed method of distribution in the church. Thus, for example, you will need to identify and work through (a) a person in the local church who will take responsibility to hand the sheets to the various prayer partners. and (b) a person who will take responsibility to insert the prayer sheet in the weekly Sunday morning church bulletin.

A PRAYER EMERGENCY TELEPHONE SYSTEM

A special means of circulating emergency prayer needs must be found. Often this may involve a phone network.

1. Some mission boards have a phone number which prayer groups or local churches can call and receive a recorded weekly prayer and praise message, condensed to a one- or two-minute period of time.
2. Some local churches have their own emergency prayer network. Within an hour or two of the church coordinator receiving an emergency request, fifty to one hundred or more people will have been informed of the prayer need. Each person who is called has six or eight more people to inform, till all have been reached.

3. Mission organizations can use volunteers to build their own emergency prayer network coordinated through their regional representatives.

CAUTIONS TO OBSERVE

In everything, there are cautions to observe, and coordinating an extensive prayer effort is no exception.

1. Beware of being a prayer promoter who exhorts others to pray but personally has a weak prayer life.
2. Beware of asking for prayer commitments of blocks of time longer than people are willing to promise, or are able to use wisely.
3. Beware of promising follow-up material which you cannot provide on time.
4. Beware of prayer groups which spend most of the time talking, in Bible study, or with speakers. Make sure that a prayer group really *prays* and that a prayer meeting is a *prayer* meeting.

EFFECTIVE METHODS FOR MOBILIZING PRAYER

Each mission organization or church denomination and each local or regional Prayer Coordinator will discover and utilize methods that work best in their own situations. But here are several methods which have been effective in helping to mobilize prayer efforts, bringing prayer needs from the mission field and prayer partners together:

1. Brochure-type, up-to-date monthly prayer calendars (these prayer guides should be designed to fit in an average Bible or shirt pocket)
2. Annual prayer directories
3. Prayer reminder book and Bible markers
4. SOS prayer sheets or letters for urgent prayer needs; these are in two categories:
   a. Those for the local or regional Prayer Coordinator
   b. Those to be distributed to the personal list of a missionary
5. SOS prayer chains—usually by phone

6. Dial-A-Prayer request or prayer answer hotlines
7. Prayer Sundays
8. Special days of prayer or days of prayer and fasting
9. Monthly days of prayer or of prayer and fasting
10. An annual day of prayer or of prayer and fasting
11. A special week of prayer or of prayer and fasting
12. Small prayer groups. These are often best planned to meet frequently, briefly, and to make prayer the chief activity
13. Lists of people personally committed to prayer support
14. Lists of people personally committed to specific time allotments of prayer
15. Prayer reminder cards with photos of the missionary
16. Designating a missionary of the week (or month) in a local church
17. Including one missionary's need in each Sunday morning's pastoral prayer
18. Including one or more missionary prayer requests in each weekly church bulletin
19. Supplying each attending member of the church prayer meeting with a missionary prayer sheet for the week; dividing the people attending the service into small prayer groups so that during the prayer time available the number of people praying for each request is multiplied
20. Arranging for prayer partners:
    a. Paired prayer partners
    b. Telephone prayer partners
    c. Prayer partners for missionary organizations
    d. Prayer partners for special ministries
    e. Prayer partners for missionaries
    f. Prayer partners for national co-workers
21. Prayer maps
22. Prayer cassettes supplied monthly to prayer groups (besides listing praise and prayer items, cassettes can contain brief challenges to prayer or meditations suitable for use by a prayer group)

23. Annual prayer calendars with a person, place, or ministry printed on the calendar for each day of the year

24. Prayer tours to a field or ministry (with emphasis on both exposure to needs and what God is doing, and carefully scheduled prayer time related to each exposure)

25. A lay person taking the responsibility of forming and shepherding prayer groups in a given area (such a person can help schedule the groups to meet in non-conflicting times so that this volunteer prayer organizer can be present with each group each month)

26. An all-day or weekend school of prayer

27. A circulating library of books on prayer

This is God's harvest day. Harvest is God's priority for the church, and harvest intercession is God's priority for each believer. Each local congregation can be a center for effective harvest intercession.

In a day when earth's unsaved billions are more numerous than ever before, each mission organization must place an all-out emphasis upon multiplying harvest. The most certain and effective way to do this is through multiplied intercession. God is longing to be gracious. He wants His house to be full. Increased harvest is ours for the asking.

27

What God Is Doing Through Prayer Around the World

Evelyn Christenson

Evelyn Christenson is the author of What Happens When Women Pray, *and has conducted seminars all over the United States and in several countries on the subject of prayer. She is organizer and chairman of the board of United Prayer Ministries, a nonprofit corporation based in Minnesota. Evelyn has helped organize citywide prayer chains in many cities throughout the United States.*

I have been to many countries around the world and have experienced something very exciting. Revival is starting. We are not saying, "God, would you start. . . ." It has already started. In many, many places around the world, God is moving.

James wrote: "The effective, fervent prayer of a righteous man avails much" (James 5:16, NKJV*). I have already talked about being that righteous person with a cleansed life—coming with holy hands into the holy presence of the holy God. (See chap. 4, "Prayer and the Cleansed Life.") Now I would like to look at the power that will result from the cleansed life.

The International Prayer Assembly for World Evangelization met in Korea in 1984, and one of its primary goals was to see and experience the power in prayer that is in Korea. It is fantastic! The growth of Korean churches is phenomenal, and it's absolutely breathtaking to know that it has come about through prayer. After

* New King James Version.

a visit to Korea, Dr. Peter Wagner, a professor at Fuller Theological Seminary, wrote this: "I am convinced that Korea's greatest gift to contemporary Christianity is prayer. While church growth is complex, I cannot help but conclude that the chief principle of the explosive growth of the Korean churches is the power of God released through fervent, enthusiastic, extensive, and believing prayer."

In 1981, I was in England, and I found an expectancy and a desire for God to move in England like I have never seen before in my life. The women there were determined that their praying was going to save their country from disaster. We had prayer seminars and prayer groups formed all over England and they started to pray. Two years later I went back for "Mission: England": I did the first step and Billy Graham came a year later to do the last step. I was to gather the pray-ers together, teach them, and have them sign up for "triplets" (which I will explain shortly). Well, they started to pray. A year later I heard from Billy Graham's manager in England that Billy Graham was having the greatest results he's ever had in his whole ministry. In the first meetings in Bristol, 8 percent of those huge audiences accepted Jesus Christ for the first time. In Sunderland 15 percent of those audiences—huge audiences—accepted Jesus Christ. Half of those people had never gone to church.

When we started "Mission: England," I did not want to go back to America. I didn't want to miss the revival that I felt was coming to England. Billy Graham's manager said to me, "Evelyn, do you know why all this is happening?"

I said, "Yes sir, I think I know."

Billy's manager said, "It is because of all that prayer."

What he was saying is this: the women organized to pray for their country. Two years later they organized in a much deeper way and started "triplets." That meant that three Christians would each choose three people who didn't know Jesus—that gave them nine non-Christians altogether—and for more than a year, those three Christians got together once a week to pray by name for those who didn't know Jesus. They then brought those people for whom they had been praying to Billy Graham's crusade.

The "triplet movement" is tremendous; it works. The pray-ers are trained, then they are organized; they learn about the cleansed life, and then they pray. All around the world we have seen this working: prayer chains, prayer groups, 24-hour prayer clocks.

When we go overseas, I personally have thousands and thousands of people praying for these meetings. In Australia, never less than 25 percent of every audience has accepted Jesus Christ. In Adelaide, Australia five hundred out of one thousand accepted Jesus Christ. In Madras, India, in the big beautiful cathedral there, for the first time in the history of India, the elite ladies and the very poorest of ladies came together and held hands in little circles. All of the denominations of India were involved in prayer together under one roof, and the caste system broke down at that point, because of all the prayer.

In Belfast, the Catholics and the Protestants came together and they prayed together. Hundreds of them organized a network of prayer chains all over Northern Ireland and phenomenal things are happening in Ireland today. In Scotland, it is the same thing; the whole country is organized for prayer.

Yes, God is moving in answer to prayer. But the pray-ers are trained, they are committed to God, they have been willing to pay the price of a cleansed life and a disciplined life—spending hours and hours a week in prayer—and when they do, God moves.

A Nigerian lady came to me in London and said to me in an autograph line, "I have to tell you something very exciting! A whole group of us in Nigeria had one little book, *What Happens When Women Pray.* We started a prayer group, and not one of our husbands knew Jesus Christ. We prayed by name for our husbands; now, every husband knows Jesus Christ!"

A minute later in the autograph line, a lady from England came by and said, "We have started a prayer group, and not one of our husbands knows Jesus as Saviour and Lord." Then she asked me, "If we pray, will our husbands find Jesus?"

I smiled and said, "I think you are asking the wrong person that question." I called the woman from Nigeria back and asked her: "If these ladies pray for their husbands, will their husbands find Christ?"

The lady from Nigeria smiled a big smile and said: "When sisters pray, brothers get saved."

The effective, fervent prayer of a righteous person, does avail much. I want to share with you the testimonies of three women whom God is using in their own countries. But more than representing a country, each represents an area of the world. Julia Thomas, Women's Director of the Evangelical Fellowship International, is from India; Katie Williams began a radio prayer ministry in the United States; and Julia Swartzenbach left Switzerland to become a missionary in Africa. As these women share what God is doing, ask yourself: What ingredients has God used in that part of the world to pour out His Spirit? What has produced power? Why is God doing a work in these parts of the world?

JULIA THOMAS: INDIA

When the Lord first brought me to Korea a few years ago, I was a very disillusioned, disappointed Christian. But as I saw what the Spirit of God was doing in Korea, as I saw the women praying, I knew that God was still raising up His people everywhere to work out His purposes. So I returned challenged and it was then the call to full-time ministry came to me from the Lord.

India is very close to my heart because, unlike Korea, which has had only one hundred years of Christianity and already such a great percentage are Christians, we in India have had more than 1900 years of Christianity and yet we are only 2.7 percent Christian. The tragedy of India is that we are divided—divided not only politically but spiritually. It is very difficult for the Spirit of God to work.

And yet, in recent years, the Spirit of God has been raising up His own believing people to pray all over India. Pockets of people are forming cell groups to pray in different parts of the country. I feel we are on the brink of something. There is a restlessness throughout India, both in the church and outside—is God trying to prepare His people for something? We pray it is a movement of the Spirit sweeping through India, but perhaps it will come through persecution.

This verse in the Bible keeps ringing in my ears: "I looked for a man [or a woman] who would build up the wall and stand before me in the gap on behalf of the land so I would not have to destroy it, but I found none" (Ezek. 22:30). God created India in love and care; he created the Indian people in His image to demonstrate His life and His beauty. He does not want to destroy this land or these people; He is looking for people to stand in the gap before Him for the land and He finds none.

As I read this verse, I pray to the Lord, "Lord, I am nothing, I don't have anything, but teach me to stand in the gap before You for my land that You might not destroy it."

I have been very encouraged by women who have come to me and said that they are praying for my country—women from Indonesia, from the Philippines, from the States, from Korea. Evelyn Christenson came to us, sponsored by the EFI, to conduct prayer seminars among women in four cities in India. That was the first time in the history of the church in India that women met together on a large scale on an interdenominational level. We are so divided. We work in our denominations, we work in our groups, and we find it difficult to mix. But it was an exciting thing that once we came together and began to learn from and share with one another, the women discovered what a wonderful thing it was. Several came to me afterward and said, "We want to have this every year."

In India, women are very timid and backward. The woman is more of a chattel than a real person. Even though we have had a woman prime minister, we are not bold enough to come forward to do anything much. Women, therefore, do not get very involved in church affairs. However, women attending these prayer seminars realized that there is one thing that every woman can do—she can pray.

Forty women stayed behind and said they wanted to participate in ongoing prayer. I thank the Lord that in four cities prayer chains have been formed; today they are functioning and growing. We hope to encourage the formation of local prayer chains in other parts of India also.

Recently, the Lord led me also to call for a prayer retreat, where for three days we fasted and prayed and waited on the Lord. We have had prayer conferences where we have talked much about prayer, but during this conference we wanted to really pray.

Some of the women came to me at the beginning of that retreat, and said, "What is the program? When is our free time when we can see others and do other things?"

I said, "There is no program. We have come to pray, and as we pray let the Spirit of the Lord lead us as He places burdens upon our hearts."

That was a unique experience. There were only fifteen of us and the Lord knit us together in a tremendous way. He led us from session to session in prayer, sharing the Word, confessing, and praying for revival and the evangelization of India. At the last session we said we could not have drawn up a better program.

Out of that prayer retreat we have formed a national prayer chain, praying mainly for the evangelization of India and four burdens which the Lord laid upon us:

- To pray for our political leaders.
- To pray for the cults that are so abundant, that God would come against them.
- To pray that people will come to know that He alone is the living God, that He is not found in the temples or shrines or masks that we see every few feet.
- To pray for the church which is so disrupted with rivalry, factions, and divisions—that in His Spirit we may be united as one.

As I have been more involved in prayer, the Lord has taught me some things personally.

TO WAIT ON THE LORD

Feeling my inadequacy, knowing that I don't have much experience or training, I tended to look to people to give me programs and other activities. But the Lord stopped me and taught me to wait upon Him, to seek His face, and to know His will. This is how my ministry has been going—not taking programs and pushing them on the people, but waiting upon the Lord and letting Him lead me step by step. It has been a wonderful, wonderful experience.

TO BE A BROKEN VESSEL

If we as women want to be in the Lord's service in any way, we need to be broken vessels; we need to pay the price. There can be no blessing for others unless there is a bleeding within ourselves. If we want to demonstrate what God can do in the world, then in our secret room we need to allow the Lord to break us. I needed to allow the Lord to break me. Hard areas, barriers, and walls that I protect in my life, that come between God and me, have to come down. For example, I sometimes tend to fall upon my own strength to do things and then it becomes flesh effort. The Lord broke me in my health so that every time I am in weakness I may know His grace and know that it is sufficient for me. I have rejoiced that in my weakness, His strength has been made perfect.

TO UNDERSTAND FORGIVENESS

Through the prayer seminars we learn the dimension of forgiveness. I used to think, if *I* do something wrong to someone else, I need to go and ask forgiveness of that person. But then God taught me that that was not enough. I have had to learn that even if somebody has something against me and I don't have anything against him or her, I still need to go and be reconciled to that person; and that was hard. In my own life there was another person with whom I tried to be reconciled, but she was very angry with me. So I just said, well, that's that. But the Lord challenged me; it took me more that three weeks to get up courage to go back to that person but the Lord enabled me to do that and to have His feet and His forgiving Spirit in me.

TO BE AVAILABLE

The Lord taught me availability—not activity, but to be available for Him to lay His burdens upon us.

TO PRAY AUTHORITATIVELY

The Lord has been teaching me about authoritative prayer. In Matthew 18:18-20, Jesus says that if we bind anything on earth it will be bound. And so we come together in the name of the Lord to bind the powers of darkness and to loosen His truth to all.

God can use anyone, whoever hears, as long as we are open to God to start a movement of prayer in our country for His glory; for this is His will.

KATIE WILLIAMS: UNITED STATES

Several years ago—the story seems to be the same—Evelyn Christenson came to northeastern Ohio to put on a prayer seminar, and I believe that the radio ministry that I'm involved in is a direct result of Evelyn's visit. But I also believe, as I look back, that God used stepping stones to accomplish what has happened. I would like to share those stepping stones briefly to show that things don't just happen—BANG!—in a great, big way, but that it is gradual.

In 1969, as I was reading Scriptures relevant to being a new Christian, I was stopped by 2 Chronicles 7:14: "If my people, who are called by my name, will humble themselves and pray and seek my face and turn from their wicked ways, then will I hear from heaven and will forgive their sin and will heal their land." God indelibly impressed that verse of Scripture on me—that it was the answer for the United States of America.

From 1969 through 1971, my husband and I went to Campus Crusade for Christ and received leadership training. In 1972, a Billy Graham Crusade came to northern Ohio, and I was privileged to head up the women's prayer committee. We recruited seven thousand homes open for prayer. Billy Graham's Crusade was bathed in prayer, but I could figure no way to sustain that prayer power.

In 1976, Here's Life Cleveland came to town; again we were able to recruit willing women to pray, but the question was how to sustain a prayer movement. Evelyn Christenson came in 1981, and during the seminar she asked women if they wanted to become involved in a prayer chain. If so, they were to fill out a card with their name, address, telephone number, their church, and turn it in when they left. As Evelyn left for the plane—God bless her—she handed me the cards and said, "By the way, Katie, would you just handle it."

I took the cards home, dumped them on my table, and discovered that I had 614 women from 154 churches in seventy cities who wanted to be involved in a prayer chain. How do you communicate with that many people? We invited fourteen people to a leadership meeting and explored the idea of a metropolitan prayer chain. but first we decided that we should each go home and improve our own prayer lives; we would get a prayer partner if we didn't have one, and then get the permission and assistance of our own pastor to start a prayer ministry if we didn't have one in our own churches.

The next night, my husband and I attended a radio fellowship meeting. At that meeting a still, small voice said, "Katie, radio could be a means of communicating prayer requests with all those people in all those cities." A man got up right after the still, small voice and quoted 1 Corinthinans 16:9: "A great door for effective work has opened to me, and there are many who oppose me." I haven't seen many opponents, but a great door opened in northeastern Ohio.

I went home and immediately wrote a letter to the manager of the station, telling him of my burden to see a prayer ministry in our area. He wrote back and said he was interested, would I come in. I visualized a deep voiced announcer who would give our prayer requests, but maybe the Lord had a different idea, for the manager said, "Kate, I think you should do it." I was sixty years old and had no radio training, but I had learned that God is less interested in our *ability* than He is in our *availability.*

So on September 1, 1981, we began the prayer ministry. We are heard on radio eighteen times a week giving prayer requests of interest to the whole Body of Christ. One program is "Pause for Prayer," a two-minute program heard three times a day, fifteen times a week. Three times a week we also have a program, "Called to Prayer," which is an exhortation and teaching on prayer.

I see two purposes that have come out of the ministry: assisting the local church in setting up their own prayer ministry; and uniting the whole Body of Christ in prayer for prayer requests which are of interest to the whole body.

Finally, I want to share what has come out of the radio prayer ministry. First of all, Christians in northeastern Ohio are becoming more and more aware of prayer. We are uniting a community of believers across denominational lines, and are seeing greater participation of men both in prayer and in leadership. We are broadening our vision of the scope of our prayers; so often the prayer request in the average church prayer meeting is for the physical rather than for the spiritual; we are so busy giving requests that are self-centered, rather than listening to what God wants to say to us. And finally, we have developed quick access to the praying community, and I believe this is one of the most valuable things that has come out of it.

For instance, I read in the newspaper that a "swingers" convention, very sex-oriented, was to be scheduled in Akron, Ohio. We immediately put it on as a prayer request on the radio. All I can say is, the "swingers" weekend was cancelled; Christians stood up and were counted for morality in our community, and I believe it was a direct answer to prayer.

God has said, "Call to Me and I will answer you and show you great and unsearchable things you do not know" (Jer. 33:3). God can work through you if you are available.

JULIA SWARTZENBACH: AFRICA AND SWITZERLAND

I was saved in Switzerland in a camp; two years later the Lord called me to work for Him in Africa and I went in 1947. I wanted to bring people the Word of God and teach them to pray and to believe in Jesus. But the Lord had to deal with me first; I had to learn to repent. I was a missionary but I did not have a victory light.

Through the message of one African from Uganda, I received grace from the Lord to understand that, even as a Christian, I had to repent each time I did something wrong—not only before God but also to go and say, "Excuse me." This made a very big difference in my life. I had been hiding my sins before the Africans, but I could say, "Excuse me," too.

When I gave my life to God for Africa, it was all my life; I never thought He would direct me in another way. I was in Angola first, but after fourteen years, because of the war, I was not able to get a visa and couldn't return. When I couldn't go back, I had to learn to trust the Lord for what He wanted to do. I learned to lean on Jesus and just wait; I knew His ways were perfect. Now I thank God I couldn't go back and had to go another way, because God taught me many lessons. It took God many, many years to break my own will, until I could say, "I am fully satisfied with all the will of God." I was a girl with many problems, but when I have problems, I bring them to the Lord so that He can deal with them. I had much to learn.

A few days ago in my Bible reading, I came across this verse from David: "Who am I that you brought me there?" *There* means "to this country," but it also means this life of the grace of God. I, too, feel, "Who am I?"—this feeble soldier that the Lord is using.

For nearly twenty years I have been involved with young people through Bible groups in high schools and camps. I have seen miracles in the lives of Africans through prayer. We don't have Evelyn Christenson's organization; I read her book just a few years ago and it challenged me. But in our African camps, the leaders get up very early before the campers; we kneel down before the Lord and pray. And we have seen miracles, hundreds of young people who have come together and found the Lord. Muslims have come to the Lord, all in answer to prayer.

My work was to teach these young people to pray—not just to pray, but to open the Bible and find how to pray after God spoke to them. Now there are many young people who are working with the Lord. One young man who was studying in Romania brought another brother from Ivory Coast to the Lord. He was in a communist country, but he prayed for the student who was in the same home and God answered his prayer; this student was converted.

I remember a Muslim boy who was converted. His father was dead, and when he was converted, the neighbor said to the mother, "You must throw him away." So the mother did. The boy went to the missionary, thinking, "Maybe the missionary will take me into his home." But the missionary didn't; he said, "Now you have trusted God; go on trusting Him." Then what did God do? This boy prayed and after a few days the mother called him home; he brought the gospel of salvation to his mother and she was converted also.

When I was in Angola, many young people converted and a few of them are still doing the work of the Lord as pastors. In Angola today there is war; people are dying of hunger. But the Christian stands; the churches are full. Through prayer we are crying to God, and through prayer God is answering in His own way.

One pastor was put in prison, then moved from that prison to a bigger one. When a servant of God visited him—for one time he could visit him—the pastor said, "I received a word of God in prison. God has told me, 'Serve the Lord with joy.'" This is answer to prayer.

I am now back in Switzerland, my own country. There are German-speaking ladies who are gathering each week to pray together and I have been visiting some of them. My desire is now to create some Bible study and prayer groups in French-speaking Switzerland. There are other women who pray for children; they gather children once a week in their home, using something similar to the "triplet" system, not only their own children but the older children around the area where they are living. What do they do with the children? They open the Bible, read with them, and pray.

There is a lady in Switzerland who was reading in a newspaper that in a communist country, every child has a biography of Lenin. She said, "What are we doing as Christians so that every child will have a biography of Jesus Christ?" So she wrote a little booklet which is called *It's True and Everybody Should Know It.*

I, too, feel we must pray for the children, because half of the people in the world are children. The Communists are working with children because tomorrow those children are going to lead our countries. So let us pray for the children.

28

Prayer for World Evangelization

Akira Izuta

Akira Izuta is the pastor of the Nerima Baptist Church in Japan. He also serves as the executive director of Japan Protestant Council and the Japan Baptist Church Association. He is a professor at the Tokyo Christian College.

This is my first visit to Korea. Because of the history of Japan's unfortunate invasions, I felt guilty and did not want to visit Korea. I have not come as a soldier to fight, not as a businessman to make money, nor as a tourist for sight-seeing. Rather, I've come as a Christian to ask for your forgiveness in Christ and to share in prayer our burden for world evangelization.

GOD'S PLAN FOR WORLD EVANGELIZATION

We believe strongly that the Bible is the infallible Word of God and that the promises it contains will be realized in history without fail. Jesus Christ predicted, "This gospel of the kingdom will be preached in the whole world as a testimony to all nations" (Matt. 24:14). This promise has literally been fulfilled in human history; the gospel has been proclaimed throughout the world, even to the far eastern islands of Japan. The Protestant churches of Korea are now celebrating their centennial. World evangelization is the vision of our Lord Jesus Christ and the wonderful plan of God.

In order to realize this plan, the Lord Jesus Christ chose disciples, trained them, and commissioned them, "Go and make disciples of all nations, baptizing them in the name of the Father and of the Son and of the Holy Spirit, and teaching them to obey everything I have commanded you. And surely I am with you always, to the very end of the age" (Matt. 28:19-20). The Lord Jesus not only issued this command, He also gave a wonderful promise. "You will receive power when the Holy Spirit comes on you; and you will be my witnesses in Jerusalem, and in all Judea and Samaria, and to the ends of the earth" (Acts 1:8).

In this way we see that world evangelization is the vision of our Lord Jesus Christ, it is the plan of God, and it is implemented by the power of the Holy Spirit.

Our Role in Praying for World Evangelization

World evangelization begins with prayer and is accomplished through prayer. The disciples of Jesus, following His command to "not leave Jerusalem, but wait for the gift my Father promised" (Acts 1:4), waited and prayed earnestly in an upper room in Jerusalem. Not only the disciples, but also the women and Mary, the mother of Jesus, and His brothers prayed constantly with one mind (Acts 1:14).

Here we find that the prayers of the disciples resulted in the first Pentecost. The Holy Spirit came to them, and they were filled with the Spirit (Acts 2:1-4).

It is when we pray that we are filled with the Spirit. And it is when we are filled with the Spirit that evangelization can proceed with explosive power. When there is no prayer, the Spirit doesn't work. When the Spirit doesn't work, evangelization doesn't progress.

The Lord Jesus Christ has used many people who have been filled with the Holy Spirit. Paul was one of them. He said, "I have fully proclaimed the gospel of Christ. It has always been my ambition to preach the gospel where Christ was not known" (Rom. 15:19-20). But Paul wasn't satisfied simply with that, for he earnestly prayed that he might be able to preach the gospel in Rome, the center of the world (Rom. 1:9-15) and as far as Spain, the end of the known world at that time (Rom. 15:28).

Our Source of Power for World Evangelization

Many years have passed since that first Pentecost, and we have gathered together from all parts of the world as brothers and sisters in the Lord to this International Prayer Assembly in order to pray together with one mind for world evangelization.

- Without *sincere repentance* of sin we cannot expect to do world evangelization. Therefore, let us pray before the Lord in a spirit of repentance.
- Without *sincere unity* we cannot expect to do world evangelization. Therefore, let us pray with a spirit of unity.
- Without *sincere cooperation* we cannot do world evangelization. Therefore, let us surrender all and cooperate in doing world evangelization.

In the past the Lord Jesus has used those who have prayed and those who are filled with the Spirit for the purpose of world evangelization.

Let us pray together with great expectation.

29

Systematic Prayer for the Nations of the World

Dick Eastman

Dick Eastman is president and executive director of Change the World Ministries, sponsoring agency of several highly respected prayer mobilization and training seminars including the Change the World School of Prayer, and the World Intercessor's Institute.

Because *God alone* can break down the barriers which prohibit total evangelization of the world, and because *prayer alone* touches God and brings His power into situations involving world evangelization, it is imperative that Christians who care about a lost world learn to pray for its total evangelization on a daily, systematic (meaning well-ordered, planned, and regular) basis. But in order to develop a meaningful prayer strategy, we first need to understand what the Bible says about the nations.

"The Great Commission" (Matt. 28:19 and Mark 16:15), which we usually think of as a New Testament theme, can also be found in the Old Testament. Note, for example, how the psalmist prayed for the nations: "May God be gracious to us and bless us . . . that your ways may be known on earth, your salvation among all nations" (Ps. 67:1-2). Hezekiah's prayer for deliverance likewise carried a unique world focus: "Now, O Lord our God, deliver us from his hand, so that all kingdoms on earth may know that you alone, O Lord, are God" (2 Kings 19:19).

Based on those two significant passages, an intercessor ought to develop a plan of prayer that claims God's salvation will be revealed throughout every nation on earth.

A FOUR-FOLD PRAYER FOCUS

By looking at the end result of a fully evangelized world, as described in Revelation 5:8-10, we also discover an interesting four-fold focus for systematic prayer. Here is where the Bible tells us that Christ was "slain, and has redeemed us to God by [his] blood out of every kindred, and tongue, and people, and nation" (Rev. 5:9, KJV*).

Let us look more carefully at the meaning of each of the four classifications mentioned in this verse, and at how we might pray for the penetration of these areas with the gospel.

EVERY KINDRED

The term "kindred" in Scripture (from the Greed word *phulees*) is most frequently translated "tribe," as in "tribe of Reuben," or "tribe of Judah," etc. Because a tribe is not a full nation, we may conclude that this word is a reference to smaller groups within a nation, such as "cultural groups."

Culture means "the totality of socially transmitted behavior or patterns, arts, beliefs, institutions, and all other products of human work and thought characteristic of a community or population." Some ethnic groups within a nation have clearly defined patterns of behavior or beliefs that differ greatly from the general beliefs of the nation in which the group exists.

Because there are several worldwide ministries that specifically target "hidden people groups," the "kindred" objective provides us with the following prayer focus: *frontier evangelism*. We need to pray for all ministries laboring to evangelize hidden peoples.

EVERY TONGUE

The word "tongue" (from the Greek *glossa*) refers to the languages and dialects spoken throughout the world. According to Scripture, at the final judgment converts will come from all languages of the earth, a clear indication that the gospel will have been given to all these people. Thus, our prayers are important for this

---

* King James Version.

second focus: *translation evangelism,* which is accomplished by ministries working in Bible translation in order that every language group can be evangelized.

EVERY PEOPLE

The word "people" in the Greek (*laos*) appears 143 times in the New Testament and refers to "human beings." The emphasis is upon the individual. Whole nations are not evangelized until people are evangelized, one at a time. Especially important in evangelizing people of a given nation is to reach them with a message that they can comprehend in the context of their own culture. For this reason, our third prayer focus is: *national evangelism,* or evangelistic programs developed and presented by nationals who actually live in that nation.

EVERY NATION

Appearing 164 times in the New Testament, the word "nation" (from the Greek *ethnos*) is most commonly translated "Gentiles." It refers to the nations of the world other than Israel. Some mission leaders believe it is another reference to the multiplied thousands of hidden people groups. I believe it also refers to the total population of people living within geographic boundaries at any given time. One thing is for certain: Revelation 5:8-10 clearly indicates that redeemed mankind will emerge from all the nations, countries, and people groups of the earth. Thus, our final focus includes systematic evangelism. Systematic evangelism is attemped by ministries which seek to organize Christian nationals to systematically reach all the people of their nation with the gospel.

REMOVING ENEMY STRONGHOLDS

But what can be done to deal with the multiple barriers that limit evangelistic outreach? Throughout the world Satan raises up specific strongholds designed to hinder the work for world evangelism. Removing these barriers should be part of our systematic prayer program. And although Satan is at work in every nation on earth, his strongholds seem to hinder the spread of the gospel most in the repressed nations of the world, such as communist and Arab/ Moslem nations.

When praying for a nation, therefore, we should exercise our God-given spiritual authority and command those strongholds to fall. What strongholds should we pray against? Following are three specific strongholds Satan uses most to accomplish his purposes:

GOVERNMENT STRONGHOLDS

This stronghold concerns those laws of a nation that directly hinder and prohibit the spread of the gospel. Communist countries especially come under this category. Their fundamental ideology endorses atheism. In those countries there are often laws prohibiting evangelism of any kind. (Albania, for example, actually lists its state religion as atheism.) To develop a systematic prayer approach to remove government strongholds within a particular nation, we should pray for the *Satan-inspired laws* of that land to be cast down.

CULTURAL STRONGHOLDS

This stronghold concerns the lifestyle or patterns of behavior of people living in a particular nation. Those patterns of behavior, especially amongst certain ethnic groups, often hinder the spread of the gospel. In some cases cultural strongholds make evangelism as difficult as in a communist or Arab/Moslem nation. A strong spirit of nationalism in a country is one such example. Nationalism is defined as "a feeling of independence of one nation from another." This spirit causes one nation to claim to another, "We are better than you," or "We don't need your help," etc. To develop a systematic prayer approach to remove cultural strongholds within a particular nation, we should pray for *Satan-inspired attitudes* or cultural characteristics of that land to be cast down.

RELIGIOUS STRONGHOLDS

This stronghold concerns the beliefs of various non-Christian religious forces in a nation. For example, we see the great barrier that rises in the Arab/Moslem nations. In those nations millions are bound by the demonic forces of Islam's false religion. For all practical purposes those nations have been totally shut out from the gospel of Jesus Christ for almost twenty centuries. To develop a systematic prayer approach to remove religious strongholds, we should pray for *Satan-inspired beliefs* of a land to be cast down.

HOW TO PRAY AGAINST SATAN'S STRONGHOLDS

Exactly how do we pray against these various satanic strongholds? We must claim the power that is found in God's Word, just as He spoke to the prophet Isaiah: "See, I will make you into a threshing sledge, new and sharp, with many teeth. You will thresh the mountains and crush them, and reduce the hills to chaff" (Isa. 41:15).

When you come to that portion of your prayer when you pray for Arab/Moslem and communist nations, speak directly to those strongholds and command them to fall. Generally speaking, you'll pray against "government strongholds" when praying for communist nations; "religious strongholds" when praying for the Arab/Moslem nations; and against "cultural strongholds" when praying for any of the remaining nations, including the multitude of unreached people groups throughout the world.

When taking direct prayer authority against any of these strongholds, remember that you must do so in the name and power of our Lord Jesus Christ. Further, you must never hesitate to command a barrier directly in prayer, just as Jesus instructed when He spoke of "moving mountains" (see Mark 11:22-24).

The late Dr. Paul E. Billheimer, author of *Destined for the Throne*, provides this meaningful insight on prayer:

> Prayer is not begging God to do something which He is unwilling to do. It is not overcoming reluctance in God. It is enforcing Christ's victory over Satan. It is implementing upon earth heaven's decisions concerning the affairs of men. Calvary legally destroyed Satan, and cancelled all of his claims. God placed the enforcement of Calvary's victory in the hands of the Church (Matthew 18:18 and Luke 10:17-19). He has given to her "power of attorney." She is His "deputy." But this delegated authority is wholly inoperative apart from the prayers of a believing church. Therefore, prayer is where the action is. Any church without a well-organized and systematic prayer program is simply operating a religious treadmill.

30

Prayer and
the Battle for the World

Harold Lindsell

Dr. Harold Lindsell is editor-emeritus of Christianity
Today *and a former professor of church history and missions. He is as well the author of several publications.*

We are engaged in a great battle. We need to understand who
the enemy is and how he functions. Our warfare is essentially
spiritual and is waged against Satan himself. He is known as the
devil and the prince of this world.

It is warfare between good and evil, between right and wrong,
between truth and error, between Almighty God and Satan, the
archenemy. Satan has as his cosmic purpose the defeat of God on
the planet earth and the control of the whole cosmos. Satan will
never succeed, but he will keep trying until his day is done and the
war is over. The devil strikes at us, and by doing that he really is
striking against God.

The Helpers of Satan

In this warfare Satan has many helpers.

Satan has all the fallen angels working for him. These fallen
creatures have great power, and they can do all sorts of wicked
things. They cannot be saved, and in the end they will be cast into
the lake of fire. But they are fighting to prevent that from happening.

Every atheist, whether he realizes it or not, is on Satan's side.

This includes the Marxists who flaunt their atheism on every hand and seek to make all of their people atheists, too. They teach atheism in their schools and in their propaganda. They serve the cause of Satan diligently and with fervor—more fervor sometimes than many Christians exhibit in their service of the true and living God.

All those who attack the Bible serve Satan. They say it is only a human book. A Bible story book has been published in China. It was written by a true believer. But the state has added comments which are humanistic and anti-supernatural. Those comments say that the creation story and the account of the Flood come from Babylonian mythology. They say that the Bible is not accurate and that modern science disproves the Word of God. They claim that the Bible is full of myths and that the theory of evolutionary development is more accurate. Thus, many people are deceived, even Christians.

Humanists are Satan's helpers, too, even if they don't acknowledge his existence. They place man above God and look to man for the solution to all human problems. They think man can be made good by improving his environment and making it function correctly.

Those who are Hindus, Buddhists, Shintoists, Muslims, and all who are under bondage to false religions are unwitting helpers of Satan. Many of them are fine people. They are pleasant and sincere in what they believe. They reach out to convert people to their false faiths. We respect their right to their own views, but we must never suppose for one moment that they are not agents of evil. By believing and spreading a false faith, they promote a lie of Satan's that competes with the gospel. Most of those people do this without realizing what they are doing—without realizing it is a lie. Nevertheless, whoever is against the true God is an agent of evil, no matter how well educated, how pleasant, how kind and courteous, how smooth such a person may be.

In America we have multitudes who embrace false cults. Some may appear benign to the undiscriminating observer. But a few even worship the devil, offer blood sacrifices, and engage in weird religious exercises. Some oppose everything Christians hold dear. They are in bondage to the devil and are his helpers against God and the true faith.

Satan also has helpers who promote homosexuality, pornography, fornication, adultery, divorce, the breakup of the home, and even wife-swapping. Radio and television are powerful advocates of immorality and often make fun of those who believe and act according to biblical standards.

The Critical State of the World

The world situation looks grim today. Evidence abounds which tells us that the end of the age may be coming upon us shortly. What are the signs that support this possibility?

There are wars and rumors of wars. Look at Poland and Afghanistan. Look at Latin America, where there are many wars. Look at the struggles between North and South Korea. Look at Ethiopia. Look at Southeast Asia and places like Cambodia where several million people have been killed. Look at the genocide of infants by abortion. In America more than fifteen million abortions have been performed in the last ten years. This is murder by any biblical standard.

Communism has taken over large parts of the globe. That movement is reaching out to conquer the world. No nation is safe from its tentacles. There are agents of this atheistic movement in every nation. Wherever it has gone, millions of people have suffered and died. Freedom is extinguished. Religious freedom, which is the source of all of our freedoms, is always attacked by the Marxists and destroyed by them when it is possible for them to do so.

There is the constant threat of nuclear holocaust. The weapons of destruction are numerous and potent. It is theoretically possible for all human life on earth to be destroyed. We are now finding out that the laboratories of the Soviet Union are working day and night to develop forms of germ warfare that could have as severe effects on people as nuclear bombs. In the United States, The *Wall Street Journal* ran seven articles warning the world of that development. The threat of chemical disaster alone might enable the Marxists to conquer the world lest it be destroyed in large measure.

There have been many earthquakes, many pestilences, and there is mass starvation in some places around the world. Those are all signs of an apocalyptic age.

Worst of all is the spirit of hopelessness. Man is now beginning to see that there may be no solutions to the world's problem. Bad as this hopelessness may be, perhaps God will use it to bring many to their senses, and they will see that God alone can solve the dilemma.

CHRISTIAN HOPE IN A TIME OF DESPAIR

We are Christians, so we must ask the question: What is the Christian's response to the world situation? What ought we to do? Is there any possibility that we can have hope, and is it possible to restore hope around the world? Despite the grimness of the current situation there are some bright spots, and some good things are happening.

OUR GOD REIGNS

In spite of the grim outlook, God is still the king of Kings.

God is alive and well. He has not abdicated His throne, and He has not deserted the church or the world He created. He is very much involved in current hppenings.

God is sovereign. He has infinite power. Nothing is beyond His ability. He speaks, and it is done.

God is at the helm of history. He is directing its course and bringing it to a climax and a conclusion. He knows what He is doing, and He will accomplish His divine purpose. Nobody and nothing can stop Him from bringing in everlasting peace and the destruction of all evil.

God's people are on the winning side. We cannot lose. His victory over history is our victory, too. The saints of all ages will be part of that triumphant company of believers who will celebrate the victory of the Lamb of God. However dark the outlook and however strong the forces of evil appear to be, God will win. And we will win with Him.

BY GOD'S POWER, GOOD IS TRIUMPHING OVER EVIL

God is presently at work and great things are happening around the world in spite of all the evil. Victories of good over evil often happen in places and under circumstances we least expect. For instance. . . .

Latin America. There has been a great revival in Brazil. Tens of thousands of people have come to Jesus Christ. There are churches with many thousands of members. There is a spirit of life and confidence. God is meeting every need. Thousands of other people in Latin America have come to Jesus Christ. Evangelistic meetings draw huge crowds and many conversions result.

China. This country, closed to Western missionaries for more than twenty years, is a remarkable example. The church in China has not only suffered persecution but has experienced the most remarkable growth in two thousand years. The prayers of God's people are bringing forth fruit. In many unexpected places multitudes are being converted to the Christian faith. According to world church statistician David Barrett, quoted in the May 15, 1987, issue of *Christianity Today*, China now has a total of 81,600 Christian worship centers with 21.5 million baptized adult believers and a total Christian community of more than 52 million. We are seeing that God has been answering the prayers of those faithful missionaries who had to flee from China so long ago. Billy Graham's wife, Ruth, was born in China of missionary parents. She has been praying for China for years. She went back recently, and she met and talked with many believers who have remained strong in the faith despite the persecution and who witness when they can.

I read a report recently of what is happening among some poverty-stricken people in Henan province in a remote mountainous area of China. An evangelist who visited one place there said, "In the past few years the numbers of those becoming Christians is just like the bursting growth of bamboo after spring rain. We had no sooner arrived at our destination than hundreds began to gather. I said to one brother, 'You must have announced our coming. Look at how many gathered.' The brother replied, 'No one has told them about your coming. Indeed if we were to let just the believers know in a radius of 10 li (about 5 kms), no less than two thousand would come.' "

One saint of God reported that in one small group of one hundred households there are only three or four who have not believed in Jesus, and they are almost ready to believe. The people laughed when they were asked who led them to Jesus. They said, "Nobody told us. It was Jesus Himself who led us to believe. We were simply searching for Him."

China remains formally closed to outside missionaries. But closed or not, God is at work and the devil is being defeated. God even uses shut doors to win people to His Son. And the prayers of many have been answered in China.

Africa. Many people have come to Jesus Christ in Africa. Statistics indicate that if the number of conversions keeps growing at the same rate, all Africa will be Christian by the end of this century. Even among those nations which have been overtaken by atheistic Marxism, Christianity is alive and well, and souls are being saved. This is a bright spot in the missionary picture.

WE CHRISTIANS CAN CHANGE THE WORLD

How can we help in this battle? How can we get the gospel to the ends of the earth so that Jesus will come again? There is one thing we can do. And if we do this one thing, all other things will fall into place. If we do not do it, then many good things that should take place will not happen.

The one great thing all Christians can do is pray. This is the greatest of all weapons in the spiritual warfare in which we are engaged. It is an international weapon for people of every tribe and nation and tongue. It is the church's greatest resource. It is the most powerful weapon entrusted to the hands of the simplest believer. It can be used anywhere, anytime, anyplace. Those who pray constitute God's secret army. This army has no guns, no bombs, no tanks, no airplanes, no missiles. But it has more fire power than all the armies of the world put together.

The Bible says in James 5:16 that "The effective, fervent prayer of a righteous man avails much" (NKJV*). The world has yet to see what God can do when the people of God get on their knees in prayer.

A LITANY OF HISTORY-CHANGING ANSWERS TO PRAYER

There are many biblical examples of the results of prayer. Church history also includes many such testimonies. I want to review some of the ways God has answered the prayers of others. It may seem like a list with which you are fully familiar, but read through it carefully anyway—maybe even aloud—as a litany of

* *New King James Version.*

praise to God. For He has not changed. What He did for others, He can do for us. He can and will do still greater things, if His people lay hold of Him in prayer.

- Job prayed, and his friends for whom he prayed were helped, and even he found deliverance from his distress and was made well.

- Moses prayed, and God delivered Israel from slavery in Egypt.

- Hannah prayed, and God gave her a son who became a high priest in Israel.

- David prayed, and God delivered him from his enemies. He prayed, and God forgave his sins of adultery and murder.

- Samson prayed, and God gave him strength to slay a thousand Philistines with the jawbone of an ass.

- Elijah prayed, and God restored life to a dead young man.

- Elijah prayed, and there was no rain in Israel for more than three years.

- Elijah prayed when there had been no rain for more than three years, and the rains fell.

- Hezekiah prayed, and 185,000 Assyrian soldiers were slain by one angel of God in one night.

- Ezra prayed, and a great revival came to Judah and Jerusalem.

- Nehemiah prayed, and the king released him and sent him to Jerusalem to help in the rebuilding of the city and of the temple of God.

- Solomon prayed, and God gave him the gift of wisdom.

- Daniel prayed, and was set free from the lions' den where his life was at stake.

- Daniel prayed, and God gave him the interpretation of Nebuchadnezzar's dream.

- The early Christians prayed for ten days in an upper room, and then Pentecost came, and they were transformed and souls were saved.

- Stephen prayed as he was being stoned to death, and God lifted him in triumph into glory and into His presence for eternity.

- Paul and Silas prayed and were delivered from jail in Philippi by a great earthquake. Their chains fell off, and they were free.

- Peter was delivered from prison by an angel after the people of God prayed for his release.

- Paul prayed, and the father of Publius on the island of Malta was instantly healed.

- John Calvin prayed, and the Reformed church was founded and the city of Geneva was changed for good.

- Martin Luther prayed, and all Europe was transformed as well as the Scandinavian nations.

- John Knox prayed, and all Scotland came on its knees to Jesus Christ.

- Hudson Taylor prayed, and scores of missionaries went to China with the gospel. He opened a new era in Chinese history.

- William Carey prayed, and God sent him to India. He translated the Bible in whole or in parts into more than thirty different languages and dialects.

- Pastor Gossner in Germany laid hold of God in prayer, and his biographer wrote: "He prayed up the walls of a hospital and the hearts of nurses; he prayed mission stations into being and missionaries into faith; he prayed open the hearts of the rich and gold came in from the most distant lands."

- Adoniram Judson prayed and later wrote to this effect that, as a result of prayer, "I never was deeply interested in any project, I never prayed sincerely and earnestly for anything, but that it came at some time—no matter the distance, the day, or the shape (probably the last I should have devised)—but it came."

- David Livingstone who opened up Africa to the gospel died on his knees as he was praying for the people of that great continent.

- The Moravians prayed twenty-four hours a day for many years for the spread of the gospel. Their people reached the unreached and brought the gospel to places it had never gone—and they did it by prayer.

I can give a personal testimony that as a result of prayer more than six hundred of my former students have gone to the ends of the earth with the gospel. Some are in Hong Kong, Korea, Japan, Latin America, and Africa. One of those students was Bill Bright, the founder of Campus Crusade for Christ, which has more than fifteen thousand staff members around the world.

Letting God's Will Be Done

Prayer glorifies God. Prayer gets God's will done on earth as it is done in heaven. We should pray as though we could never work and then work as though we had never prayed. Prayer is based on *faith*. We must pray in faith, believing. Prayer and works through faith can do anything.

We need men and women, young and old, from all the nations of the earth to join together in a covenant of prayer that we will pray for worldwide revival and awakening. And that we will pray that the gospel will go to the ends of the earth in this generation.

Let me tell you a story. It is about two elderly women on a small island off the coast of Scotland. One was eighty-four years of age and the other eighty-two. One was blind and the other bent over with arthritis. A certain evangelist, Duncan Campbell, was asked to preach on that island. He refused because he had other engagements. A second letter written to Duncan Campbell brought the same answer. He could not come. One of the elderly ladies said: "That's what the *man* says—God has said otherwise. Write again. He will be here within a fortnight." And he was. Prayer did the job. Revival began, and souls were saved.

Will you covenant with me to pray? Will you be God's man or God's woman to bring revival quickening to believers and salvation to multitudes who do not know Christ in this generation?

It can begin only by prayer!